Indian Odyssey

Around the subcontinent by public transport

Christopher Portway

impact books

First published in Great Britain 1993 by
Impact Books, 112 Bolingbroke Grove, London SW11 1DA

ISBN 1 874687 14 5

Typeset by Roger King Graphic Studios, Poole, Dorset
Printed and bound by The Guernsey Press, Guernsey

Acknowledgements

Everywhere I went – on the railways and bus services, in railway stations and in towns and cities throughout Turkey, Iran, Iraq, Syria, Afghanistan, Sri Lanka, Bangladesh, Pakistan and, most of all, India, I was invariably and unstintingly given a helping hand and an abundance of goodwill.

Among those individuals and organisations, at home and abroad, who actively encouraged, advised, aided and abetted me on my Indian subcontinental travels were:

The directors of the Indian Government Tourist Office, London, at different times, together with their hard-working assistants, Mr Kandhalar and Mr Salwan, in particular, and also their staff.
Air India
Welcomgroup Hotels, and in particular, the Oberoi, Bombay, and the Windsor Manor, Bangalore, together with Maggi Nixon, Oberoi Sales Director, UK & Europe
Sir Richard Dobson
Mr Ashley Butterfield
Mr Dev, one-time superintendent, International Tourist Bureau, New Delhi Station
Dev and Toshi Gupta
The Rajasthan Tourist Development Corporation and The Palace on Wheels
Rohan Designs Ltd
Trade & Travel Publications (*South Asian Handbook*)
Longman Group UK Ltd (*An Insight and Guide to Pakistan*)
Lonely Planet Publications (*Travel Survival Kit India*)
Random House (Fodor's *India*)
Simon & Schuster Ltd (*The Footloose Guide to Southern India*)
Hilary Bradt & Bradt Publications (*India by Rail*)

Oxford Illustrated Press Ltd (*The Great Travelling Adventure*)
Thomas Cook Publishing (*Thomas Cook Overseas Timetable*)

and most of all, Indian Railways and its indefatigable UK
representative, Dr Swaminath Dandapani, 'Andy Pandy', to whom
this book is humbly dedicated.

Contents

Where lies the land to which the ship would go!
Far, far ahead, is all her seamen know.
And where the land she travels from?
Far, far behind is all that they can say.

Arthur Hugh Clough

Introduction

There must be a bit of the Marco Polo in me. Asia has long drawn my eyes and, occasionally, my feet. Without doubt, journeying was more fun in Marco's day: he lived in a leisurely age when he did not have to suffer the brainstorms of governments creating devious hindrances to travel across their territory. Give or take a few 20th-century refinements in the transport field, the complications of the long-distance overland journey may have lessened little since the 13th century.

Except where my own two feet have provided the motivation for crossing portions of the world, I have chosen the common train as the primary vehicle for my overland perambulations. I have a 'thing' about trains. Technically unequipped, I cannot class myself as a railway buff but I do appreciate the often neglected offerings of a train. To me, a railway carriage becomes a world in miniature: through the window unfolds its territory; within, all equal, are the people of that world, a fraternity of travellers either hating or loving the experience of moving, but bearing it together. By riding a railway, one can become part of that world, observing its myriad moods and faces. One may be alone on a train – but seldom lonely.

My first self-planned long journey – by train where a railway track existed – was between London and Delhi in the early '70s. Since then I have covered much of the globe in the same fashion. Some of my transport was of the super-luxury, tourist-pampering variety such as the Venice-Simplon Orient Express in Europe, the Palace on Wheels in India's Rajasthan and the delectable Blue Train in South Africa. Trains that were less opulent, but of considerable fame or infamy, have been the then USSR's Trans-Siberian Express, the one-time Trans-Canada's 'Canadian', the likes of Amtrak's 'Broadway' and 'Empire Builder' in the United

States, and the ponderous Amritsar and Bombay Mails to Calcutta. Others have offered absolutely no luxury or opulence whatsoever but have been the more memorable for their humility.

It was those lowly trains and my experiences of riding them then and since, in India and on the Indian subcontinent, that have provided me with the longest-lasting memories and set me to the task of not only recording some of them in greater detail but also of adding to them. Thus my journeys narrated in this book are actually composite ones, made over a period of time. Essentially, three journeys form the framework of the chronicle; one between Europe and Delhi made during 1973 – my first-ever visit to India; the second, between Delhi and the extreme south of the country, in 1987, by which time I had any number of intermediate visitations under my belt. My third trip was to the far eastern Indian provinces in late 1991. Here and there I divert from, or supplement, the chosen route to recollect upon a particular, relevant journey made over those two decades.

In 1973 it was still possible to make the overland pilgrimage to and from India via Iran, Afghanistan, Pakistan and also Iraq, Syria and Lebanon as I did. Today, much of the route in north-west Pakistan, Afghanistan and the non-subcontinental countries of Iran, Iraq and Lebanon are either impassable or impractical to travellers through politics and strife. Even India's Punjab has, as I write, become a 'no-go' area. And while a bus service of sorts does still run through the sensitive region of Baluchistan beyond Quetta to – but not over – the southern Iran border, that incredible railway line called the Nushki Extension, traversing the burning desert to Iran's Zahedan, is now closed, its few train services 'temporarily suspended' as Thomas Cook euphemistically puts it. Thus my journeying over these currently forbidden zones may offer some general interest as well as a portent of what lies in store for the traveller when this part of the world returns to its senses.

Parts 1 and 3 of this book – the way to and from India's capital – trace my progress while travelling 'bottom-class'. In spite of the obvious shortcomings, I promise that this really is the best vantage-point from which to observe and taste the lifestyle of the majority of the Indian people. And, as will be seen, the currently impassable routes through those Middle-Eastern states now in conflict was not a simple undertaking even in 1973 when the hate was but simmering.

Part 2 concerns rail travel between Delhi and both the extreme south and east of India, undertaken in reasonable comfort and a contention-free environment. My less traumatic progress here shows, I hope, what an incredible bargain it is to move around this vast country by train; living, eating and sleeping within the great institution of Indian railways. Many people baulk at the idea of riding Indian trains, their heads stuffed full of horrific tales of hardship and acute discomfort which – in spite of those I myself reveal – need not affect today's rail traveller in India. Even by travelling first class, or the superior air-conditioned class, the train remains the best vehicle from which to observe the real India.

Like the army, the post office, the administrative services and even the Constitution, the railways are a now-acknowledged and valued legacy of the British. Yet when they were first built there was no wild rush among Indians to invest money in the venture. The money, the skill and the knowledge came from Britain. The more cynical among us will claim that the railways were built for internal security reasons, to tighten the hold of the forces of law and order. There is some truth in this but by opening up the country a revolution was effected. Bombay and Calcutta, Delhi and Madras, were brought into physical contact with one another, a big change from the days when distances were so great as to rule out anything except occasional travel from one end of India to the other. Today the railways are indispensable: in economic and social life, there is nothing that could take their place. It is a fact that the complex web of tracks that form effectively the largest railway network in the world is the very lifeblood and heritage of the Indian nation, as well as, to a great extent, a way of life. This is reflected, to only a slightly lesser degree, in the other railway nations of the subcontinent. Jan Morris might write somewhat disparagingly of the days of the Raj:

'For the British, the railway stations of upcountry India were fulcrums of Anglo-Indian security. The Indian railways stimulated the Englishman's imagination, and gave him a Roman pride.'

However, looking at the railway dispassionately and without prejudices about the Empire, it has to be said that India would not be India without her trains. It is not so much these trains and their tracks that seize the mind, but the passengers with whom one shares the journey and their hundred destinations. Day by day, year by year, the railways carry an immense population of people moving across its magnificent network, all of them motivated by considerations of business, family, religious fervour or simple devotional obligation. Certainly the whole body of India lives on, or close to, the train. From the air-conditioned class to the now eclipsed third class, all human life is here.

Apart from my first incursion into India, I have invariably arrived by air, with Delhi as my entry point. From the cramped chaos of the old airport, conditions have improved to the extent that the same chaos is now spread over a wider, more pleasant venue that is the gleaming new Indira Gandhi International airport. In spite of the antiquated methods of immigration control and body searches that curl the lip of the more sophisticated traveller, I still salute the little khaki-clad policeman who once insisted that my passport photo did not resemble me at all. As it had been taken thirty years before, when I was beardless and unlined, he had a point and he stuck to it. I had the devil of a job to dissuade him from returning me from whence I had come but I admired him for his tenacity, a tenacity I like to think is equalled by my own.

My latest flight had been uneventful, inauspicious and boring; my arrival smoothed by an uncontroversial passport. This, I ruminated, was a lamentable way of traversing southern Asia and entering India to embark upon my continued saga of discovery. Emerging into the warm sunshine, my mind began recreating that earlier pilgrimage to this capital of the one-time Raj, bulls-eye of all that Empire red that emblazoned our school atlases, hub of the glory, grandeur, guile and grime of the unchanging East.

Editor's Note

Certain sections of the text that are reminiscences of previous journeys by the author are separated from the main narrative by asterisks at the beginning and end, thus:

* * *

PART 1 – INTO INDIA

Chapter One

I sat at a baize-covered table in the bar of a small hotel close to Istanbul's Sirkeci Station and played dominoes. I'd played dominoes only once before in my life and that was on the Trans-Siberian Express. Then my opponents had been Russians. Now they were Turks. Again, however, I was soundly thrashed but it was an excuse for a chat. Turks are the friendliest of people but not as voluble as some. To get them going you have to go through the preliminaries. We talked, mostly with our hands, of sealing wax and kings, and how the then-new Bosphorus bridge was affecting the ferry traffic and Istanbul in general. Very little was the consensus. Istanbul, we wisely decreed, would survive any number of bridges.

Truly, Istanbul remains the most surviving of cities. It is not a beautiful place, yet there can be few other such sites for a huge metropolis. As you sweep round the headland from the Sea of Marmara into the famous straits there, one after another the imperial mosques of Istanbul appear against the skyline; the Suleimaniye, the mosque of Bayazit, both on the third hill. The Fetiye upon the fourth hill, the Soltan Selim on the fifth and the Shehzade, perhaps loveliest of all; while low down by the Galata Bridge so that its dome and minarets rise out of the smoke of the town, sits the huge bulk of Yeni Cami. It is a sensational revelation, something akin to a great orchestra with a preponderance of percussion, its kettle drums poised to play a titanic overture.

In this moment Istanbul is alone and tremendous. No water city in the world can compare to it; no other city of the Orient can clothe its hills with such man-made magnificence. It makes the ideal gateway into Asia; an enthralling terminus from which to catch a train to the subcontinent of India.

A money belt and a toilet roll. These are the prerequisites of such a journey. Take anything else you like but remember you're going to carry it. With a passport full of visas, a buff form to prove I'd had my jabs and a copy of the *Thomas Cook Overseas Timetable*, I was on my way.

My journey to Pakistan and India I shall narrate but briefly since those two great countries form the core of my story. However, the way there via the stepping stones of the ground route is surely of more impact than that of the swift sanitised flight of an airliner.

Trabzon, the ancient and more romantically-named Trebizond, I had designated my first objective – which was unfortunate for it was not on the railway. But Samsun, 250 miles to the west, stood on a branch line from Sivas, so thither I progressed on an aptly-named stopping train.

Samsun has one of the few harbours on the Turkish Black Sea coast and this has led invaders into its streets all down the centuries. Milesians were here. Alexander the Great named it Amisus. The citizens set fire to it rather than surrender to Lucullus during the war between Rome and Mithridates. The great names of the Arabs, the Seljuks, the Mongols and the Ottomans all passed this way. And the Genoese burnt it again when Ottoman Turks invaded for the second time. Today, modern Samsun has little surviving from her turbulent past so, catching a local bus, I transferred my allegiance from the railway to the road.

East of Samsun, along the quiet, neglected coast, is tobacco country, a prolific land backed by sombre mountains gaining in stature with every mile. A sunrise of burnished gold injected magic into each small, scruffy town; a sort of poor man's Riviera that had missed out in the march of progress. Hovels on stilts, clustered together in dense squalor, stood side by side with prosperous villas in a higgledy-piggledy confusion of status.

Tiny rolling breakers tip-toed into the bay of Unye and anonymous townships announced themselves with white walls and pointing minarets all around the shore. We passed sandy beaches, purple rocks, willow windbreaks and apple orchards set to burst into flame. The towns flaunted names like Persembe,

Ordu, Kesop, Gorele and Akcaabat – but all looked the same.

At Ordu we made a halt strategically close to the public toilets in the centre of the small port. It was bitterly cold that early morning as we queued at the convenience and I pitied the little man who waited, even at that hour, to collect the tolls. 'A Little One: 15 Kurus, A Big One: 25 Kurus' read the notice on the wall of the smelly establishment and because I was English and could therefore afford it, he requested 25 Kurus even for a little one.

Persembe means Thursday and I remembered Carsamba, beyond Samsun, meaning Wednesday. I tried to elicit from my neighbour whether there were any more days of the week along this coast but instead I got sidetracked into a history lesson on Giresun, once the Roman Cerasus, though its castle walls are Byzantine. From the small port through which we rolled, the first cherries were brought into Europe by Lucullus who, in 69 BC, seemed addicted to this corner of the world.

Trabzon had been the capital of an empire and, as such, is suitably endowed with the trappings of greatness. A certain Alesius Comnenus, aged 22 years, was the moving spirit behind this accomplishment and it was he who expanded the magnificence of the city where the trade routes of the Orient came down to meet the maritime merchants of the West. Defying the Seljuks and the Ottomans, it managed to retain its independence for 250 years until Mehmet II captured it in the course of his campaign along the Black Sea coast. Since then Trabzon has declined in greatness to become the delightful backwater with a silted up port that it is today.

Once the city was renowned not only for the magnificence of its buildings, its court and its elaborate ceremonial but also as a hotbed of intrigue and immorality. Even as the coach drew into the main square, Trabzon was living up to its record by introducing us to a double murder as if for our benefit. The removal of two dead students, who had knifed each other to death, was a fine Saturday morning spectacle for a crowd marking time until the afternoon football match.

The natural beauty of the place is enhanced by two ravines which sweep down from the mountains. Upon these slopes the old houses, minarets and voluptuous orchard gardens are laid out. Here and there, the old city wall breaks to the surface, fortifying a precipice or defying the sea. Inside the broken ring, there is an abundance of waterless fountains, neglected tombs and shrines, once graceful, now crumbling with age.

My hotel there was named, incongruously, the Kent. Its rooms were communal and, at 12 lira, then about 35p, hardly exorbitant. The manager kept appearing at my bedroom door to plead for a photograph of himself atop the flat roof of the hotel; to get him off my neck I went through the motions with my camera, for which service I was offered one of his assortment of daughters for the night.

The road south out of Trabzon followed a beautiful valley, with a river and pebbled meadows to keep it company. As we climbed, so hazelnut groves took over from the fields of maize, tobacco and rice. Conifers began to adorn the hilltops. In the villages the men were sitting out on chairs enjoying the sunshine.

Tile-makers, their kilns built into the side of cliffs, were languidly plying their trade higher up in the valley. The road twisted and turned until it settled down to a long steep grind right to the cleavage known as the Zigana Pass. Here, at an altitude of more than 6,000 feet, the forests and pastures were left behind, abruptly cut off by an unseen boundary line of temperature. In spite of the sun, compressed snow lay two feet deep but the road was clear. Level with other peaks, the view of Anatolia was an astounding one of mountains reaching to infinity. Snow flecked the crests and the half-hidden troughs between them were dark with anger.

Zigana town is but a row of two-storeyed *lokantas* buttressed by the snow but beyond lay Gumushane through which Xenophon and his 10,000 Greeks had passed on their amazing march from Mesopotamia, across the desert and the Pontine Mountains to Trebizond and the sea. In the great silence of high altitude, the footsteps of the endless file of wounded and hungry men still echo down the corridors of time.

The pass of Zigana Gecidi is one of the most remarkable in all Turkey. It is a rift between two worlds. Behind is the lush, damp green of the coast. In front lies the yellow dust of the dry Asiatic plains. In top gear, the bus lunged exhilaratingly down the other side.

Bayburt is a strange town. A huge fortress crested its hill overhanging the market square. Built by the Seljuks in the 13th century, its many towers and crenellations stood squarely, hardly worn down by time as if ready for use in a future age. We lunched in a crowded help-yourself restaurant, my companions seeing to it that I didn't stint myself from the great communal cauldrons of vegetables and stew. The town commanded the great caravan road between the passes of Zigana and Kop and, to this day, remains a military base.

The Kop Pass is the way to Erzurum. We were to have our money's-worth of passes that day. The Kop is 8,100 feet above sea level, higher than the Zigana, and we attacked it in a series of loops, bend and spirals. Around the skyline were horizons of mountains stretching into Armenia, Persia and to the valleys of the Tigris and the Euphrates. Nature here is as violent as its scenery, and storms can burst without warning. The locals have installed a bell – a relic from an Armenian church – which tolls a warning whenever the wind shows signs of blowing into a gale.

We had a tea break at Askale. The arrival of an Englishman in the small town was viewed with amazement and I became the subject of intense curiosity by onlookers who had nothing to do but await the arrival of the buses. All men, of course; the women were away earning the daily bread. Cheerfully aggressive children kept up a litany that was to follow me across Asia. 'Engleez? Allemagne? What ees your name?' were the stock questions and whatever fool answer I was goaded into giving it was always 'Good, very good', and a repeat of the question until a local adult felt it to be his responsibility to chase the little blighters away.

A railway track caught my eye but this was not the line to Iran. It was in fact the branch to Erzurum and Kars and onwards into Georgia. Once a week you could, if you desired, pick up a train here and go to Moscow.

Erzurum. The usual reception committee fell over themselves to fix me with a hotel, all but tearing me apart to get my person into half a dozen establishments. I came to rest finally on the fourth floor of the Hotel Tahran, the tariff in my room announcing that it was one with 'three wet beds' and that the 'shover' was 2 lire 50 extra.

In all honesty, I could not raise great inspiration from Erzurum.

Once known as Theodosiopolis, and as Arzum ar Rum – Country of the Romans – by the Arabs, it was a remarkable place to put it kindly. The old walls and the citadel had disappeared. Inside the ramparts, the town lay cramped with narrow, crooked streets, badly drained and dirty, the houses built of wood or grey volcanic stone with flat roofs. The most impressive building seemed to be the Cifte minaret Medrese. The great stone structure, brandishing its pair of minarets, stood in aloof silence, the more impressive for the ragged surroundings.

Dirty snow and ice lay slowly turning to mud in the streets. On the outskirts, the houses were built of no more than baked clay but still appeared more venerable than those of stone. There was an atmosphere of cheerful poverty about the place which disturbed me; this and the bitter cold and my lack of winter clothing. For warmth and companionship I joined the congregation of men assembled in a smoke-filled tea room whereupon a great hush descended. Then a chair was found for me and out came the dominoes. I had been accepted into the community of Erzurum.

Next morning, refreshed from immersion in both 'shover' and one of my 'three wet beds', I left on a midday train for Cetinkaya which lay on the line I had left at Sivas. Lake Van was to be my farewell to Turkey, a sombre farewell too, for Van is a deep sheet of water containing sulphur springs and very few fish. Its mysterious tide has never been satisfactorily explained and the landscape around it is a wilderness of volcanic rock and buried battlefields. To the north lies Mount Ararat or, to be more accurate, both Great and Little Ararat. They are an odd pair these two, rising straight out of a barren plain. Great Ararat is an extinct volcano, bare beyond its lower girth of pastures. It rises a full 17,000 feet and spurs of the mountain thrust out into Russia and Iran.

'In the six hundredth year of Noah's life, in the second month, the seventeenth day of the month, the same day were all the fountains of the great deep broken up and the windows of heaven were opened,' reports Genesis, describing the Deluge. 'And God remembered Noah ... and the waters assuaged ... And it came to pass in the six hundredth and first year, in the first month, the first day of the month, the waters were dried up from off the earth; and Noah removed the covering of the ark, and looked, and behold, the face of the earth was dry'. The survivors had landed on the top of Great Ararat.

It was raining again that day as my train approached the Iranian border.

Innumerable miles along the base of brown hills brought us to Tabriz. I had been recommended the Hotel Meshed close to the centre and to this I was borne in a wildly-driven taxi. It was little more than a cellar holding eight beds plus space for a member of staff on the floor. Two strange, dark-skinned individuals were already asleep in one bed – the one that turned out to be mine – but were chased away. I was dismayed to note that the couple had not been the only occupants of the bedding since its washing day and I was glad of my sleeping bag that night. Though I was to sink still lower in accommodation status, this was the one hotel on the journey where I actually saw a flea.

There are three edifices to see in Tabriz. Jehan Shah built the Blue Mosque, described once as the *chef d'oeuvre* of all oriental architecture, and although wars and earthquakes have destroyed most of it, what remains offers some of the finest tile work in Iran. Also in ruins is the Arg, or Ali Shah citadel. It is a colossal pile of buff-coloured brick, only a shadow of its former self when it was dressed in marble and gold. The height of the roof made a convenient platform from which adulteresses and other sinners could be pushed to their deaths. The third worthwhile structure in Tabriz is the railway station. Here, surely, is the city's pride and joy. It stood a mile or two out of town, a fine example of modern architecture and a monument to a concept of railway grandeur that never quite came off. For the serving of two trains a day – three including the thrice- weekly Turkey to Iran service – it is a piece of wild extravagance. When I entered the grandiose main hall, my footsteps echoing through the huge concourse, it was completely empty save for the man behind the information counter who waited in his box like a policeman at a road junction. Self-consciously I advanced into the great arena to submit my myrrh, frankincense and a question about train services.

Though her track mileage may be less, Iran is streets ahead of Turkey in railway conception and the lack of international trains must be partly laid at the latter's door. Iran's line to the Turkish border, though single track, is an impressive feat of engineering. It was constructed while Turkey was arguing about which side of Lake Van to build her line, eventually choosing the easy but inefficient method of ferry across the not always placid waters. The Asiatic-European rail link depends for its future so much upon Turkey.

Washing facilities at the hotel were singularly lacking. A wash basin in the passage served our room's complement of eight – and the water was cold. The second morning, after jetting a youthful tarantula down the plughole, I was approached by a veiled lady on the scrounge for shampoo. With my eyes full of soap, I gave her a packet liberated from an earlier and better-equipped hotel, which aroused the good woman's motherly instincts to the extent of her volunteering to scrub my back.

One cannot visit this city without seeing a carpet, and the bazaar – however weary you are of bazaars – is the place to see them. All Persian carpets are, of course, beautiful to behold but those of Azerbaijan – of which Tabriz is capital – are special. The Persian carpet has spanned the centuries, and in the villages rug-making is, like nearly everything else, woman's work. In Tabriz, the fervour of selling them is alarmingly aggressive.

This aggression is not only confined to carpet-selling either. Walking the streets, I soon became aware of a less than friendly edge to the constant staring of the locals. Belligerent children added the hint of a sneer to their monotonous attentions, while adults too were noticeably less inclined to smile as easily as did the Turks. I felt it was time to move on.

With such a station, the train was the only vehicle on which to leave Tabriz, and from the palatial edifice I succeeded in obtaining a third class ticket and seat reservation on the through 'express' from Istanbul to Teheran. My train was diesel-powered, full and late. The general idea had been to leave at 8.00 a.m. and arrive at Teheran by nightfall but I was in a part of the world where timetables bear little relation to the actual services run.

My compartment was occupied by an assortment of Persians, an Australian, a roll of carpeting and two live turkeys. The turkeys roosted on my seat but were persuaded to perch aloft on the luggage rack. Tabriz faded from view.

The line ran parallel to the snowy rampart of the Elburz

Mountains, over a desolation of stones and sand. Behind those ramparts lay the Caspian Sea. For much of the way, the black ribbon of the road huddled close to the railway as if holding hands in a land of no flowers and no birds. Between lonely villages, a few nomads camped in black tents, their retinue of ragged children, sullen and unsmiling, adding to the dourness of the landscape.

Modern Teheran is the creation of the late Reza Shah. Not until the second half of the 18th century did the village that had occupied the site since the 9th century expand into a town. In 1785, Agha Mohammed Khan, founder of the Qajar dynasty, ordained it the seat of government and the future of Teheran was assured. It was, however, Reza Shah who turned it into the pseudo-European city it then become. 'An opera house, a stock exchange and no camels', he ordained, basing his ideas on Ankara which was about the only other capital he had seen. But the opera house, faultily conceived by an Iranian architect, could not be completed and the stock exchange never got further than the drawing board. The camels, however, vanished. Reza Shah also cleared much that Agha built, including the walls and twelve gates erected chiefly with money sent from Europe for the Persian Relief Fund.

I emerged into the railway station and found my way to the Hotel Amir Kabir in the street of that name. By Asian standards, it was clean and comfortable. The drum-like building had bedrooms and patios on two levels and bore a close resemblance to certain prisons I could name, but had hot showers on the occasions the water was on, and a restaurant serving English delicacies such as eggs and chips which, after a diet of kebab, can be quite a treat.

Guide books describe Teheran as a jumble of old and new but nearly all the jumble I found to be new. I discovered the main square – Maidan-e-sepah – to be a museum piece of architectural disasters but not old enough to count as historic; the police headquarters, in Achaemenid style, a joke. Wide, tree-lined avenues, bisected by their *jubes* – or open drains – forced their way through a range of art nouveau structures hideous to behold. Yet occasionally, one is brought up short by something truly beautiful, like the grey and white marble National Bank in the

Avenue Ferdaysi or, on the antique level, the eight-minareted Sepahsalar mosque near the House of Parliament.

Back at the railway station, the acquisition of a ticket and the compulsory seat reservation was a chore that occupied me for most of the morning. I commenced operations by nailing the top man, the chief of the reservations department, who sent me to a lesser mortal who, in turn, directed me to an outside kiosk. The occupant of the kiosk was kind enough to escort me personally to an *inside* kiosk, from which I was deflected to an office on the platform where I had first applied. Negotiating a storm of form-filling and rubber-stamping, I was handed a sheet of paper but as everything written on it was in Farsi I then had to transfer to the information office to find out what it said. The station was crowded with holiday-weekend travellers, and there were a number of relief trains in operation to bolster Teheran's muster of seven services a day – which meant that the trains running in no way represented any on which I was booked. This notwithstanding, I was finally found a seat in a compartment of the Meshed train unclaimed by other contenders.

There were two trains daily between the capital and Meshed. I had chosen the night service and it was dark when we slid out of the station. As if activated by a time-switch, my companions ceased their chatter and composed themselves for sleep. I envy the Asian's ability to squat for long hours at a stretch apparently comfortable and entirely relaxed. But squatting wasn't the only posture adopted that night. The corridor became alive with men emerging from compartments to stretch out on the floor, wrapped in that garment so practical for train travel, the *chapan*.

The women, left with the exclusive use of the hard seats, proceeded to draw their *chadors* tighter around their bodies and, giving me pointed looks, stretched themselves out on them. I know when I'm not wanted so joined the men in the corridor. And there's another thing; it was a hard floor, yet everyone except me fell instantly into vocal sleep, jostling, kicking and murmuring as their dreams took control. With a pair of dirty bare feet in my face and excruciating kicks to my shin at regular intervals, I won't pretend it was one of my better nights. At 4.30 in the morning, just as fatigue had driven me into a doze, a cry shivered down the train and a freezing dawn showed red in the sky. In a moment the corridor was empty and the platform a carpet of prostrate figures. It was the hour for morning devotions.

As we moved ever-further east, I discerned a change in the countryside. The earth remained parched but cracked here and there with small plots, fresh and green, offering startling contrast to the harsh, grey-brown desert. The mud villages were better designed; some were even attractive, with domed roofs and miniature 'gothic' windows. Buffaloes worked in the tiny patches of cultivation and I watched an eagle soaring lazily overhead, ignoring the frantic mobbing of smaller birds. Back in the compartment, everyone became abruptly garrulous and friendly, my neighbour sharing his breakfast with me. The others, in a mixture of English and German, wanted to know the size of my family, and my disclosure of only one brother, plus a son and daughter, produced only sympathy and disappointment. A multiple family people are the Persians.

The line to Meshed is of comparatively recent origin and further proof of the railway consciousness of Iran. The 576 miles of track from Teheran eastwards is a line to nowhere. Nishapur is the largest habitation *en route* and Meshed itself is hardly a metropolis. There is little point in extending the tracks another 124 miles to the Afghan border since not only is there a lack of traffic but also no Afghan railway to which they can be connected.

A few miles to the east of Nishapur is the modern abomination that is the tomb of Omar Khayyam, the astronomer-poet of Persia, revered by Persians young and old. The district is dotted with tombs of well-known Persian personalities: Gadam Gar, Farid-ud-Din Attar and Sangbast amongst them; an exclusive neighbourhood.

More mountains, many of these hiding deposits of turquoise (Madan and its famous mines are just down the road), and Meshed was upon us. Its railway station, of similar architectural grandeur to that of Tabriz, had severe competition this time from equally fine edifices in this capital of Khurasan and former capital of Persia.

Meshed is the holiest city in Iran. The Tomb of the Imam Reza is the equivalent of Mecca for the Shi'ites and to go with such distinction are buildings of sublime magnificence. The place owes its foundation to the burial there of Harun-er-Rashid, of Arabian

Nights' fame. Its glory, however, stems from the bones of Reza, the eighth Imam, who died after eating a bunch of poisoned grapes a few years later and was buried in the same tomb.

The Persians are individualists to an extreme, and some people believe that the real purpose in founding the Shi'ite sect was to make themselves less dependent on the Arabs. This was in the days when fanatical hordes from the Arabian desert had conquered Persia in the name of the new prophet. The hapless Persians were forced to acknowledge Allah as the one and only God. As far as the successors of the Prophet were concerned, they stubbornly refused to toe the line with the other Muslims, who supported one of the fathers-in-law of the deceased. Instead, they elected one of the Prophet's sons-in-law, Ali, and his descendants as their temporal leaders. This led to bloody wars in which the Shi'ites invariably came out as losers. One after the other of Ali's descendants, who all went by the title of Imam, were murdered by the Muslims, all that is except for the one called Shia who, the Shi'ites believe, will one day rise again and convert the whole world to the true faith. The assassins of Alamut, the Shi'ite rebellion in Khurasan: different periods but all part of the age-old resistance to what was considered the imposition of alien beliefs.

The agglomeration of buildings known as the 'Shrine' consists of three large courts, two esplanades, the tomb-chamber crowned by its superb golden dome, the Goughar Shad Mosque, and a number of subsidiary mosques and *madresehs*, the whole encircled by a broad circular avenue cut ruthlessly through the old streets. The golden dome is shaped like a helmet upon which the sun draws flashes of fire hardly dimmed by the multitude of birds clustered thickly upon it. A pair of minarets, plated with gold, rise nearby and the dome of the Gaughar Shad Mosque is blue; a blue that changes its shade with the weather and the time of day.

I found all the entrances, except to the museum, forbidden to Christians; the two main buildings are inaccessible to infidels. Even to stand in the opening of an alleyway, delaying there for an instant to glimpse the forbidden wonder of the interior of the inner court, invited angry mutterings. Through ignorance of the rules, coupled with an unquenchable curiosity, I succeeded in evading the sentinels on one such alleyway and gained the inner courtyard. Its gold-encrusted cloisters were wondrous to behold and I had strolled about a quarter of the way around the central fountain before I was grabbed from behind, frogmarched to the nearest exit and expelled with considerable force. A few years earlier – or later – I could well have had my throat cut.

Wandering around the circular street of the old city I would have given much to possess the knowledge to place a man by the twist of his turban, for here were gathered pilgrims from all parts of the country and the world. And in Meshed, unlike Teheran, native dress was the rule rather than the exception. Passing through the crowded streets were *mullahs*, models of dignity with walking sticks and hennaed beards, hook-nosed Afghans, fierce-eyed Baluchis, and Mongols with high cheekbones and black skull caps. By the side of the central *jube* was an open-air market where the pilgrims loitered over their endlessly protracted bargaining or underwent the swift disfigurement of a religious head-shave. Diseased beggars were not to be ignored either in this city of prosperity and poverty which rightly lauded its modern hospital as an example to all Iran. They came, blind with scrofulous heads and severed limbs, singing of their misfortune. And this being Meshed, where pilgrims have not only to be good but to be seen to be good, the beggars were onto a profitable thing.

Yet it was the many women in purdah that created the deepest impression. As they walked, each a gliding tent-like figure, they were entirely concealed beneath their long, all-enveloping *chadors*. At one time, the *chador* was strictly prohibited in Iran, The Reza Shah ordered the arrest of all women who wore veils in public. He was indirectly supported by the Koran which does not command women to wear the veil. The order was resisted by the *mullahs* but the Shah was not impressed. Finally, after repeated orders to desist, the *mullahs* assembled in a courtyard adjacent to the golden Shrine to demonstrate their unanimous condemnation of the new law. The Shah replied through the machine guns of his soldiers and the courtyard ran with blood. From that day on, the veil was no longer seen elsewhere in Iran until it reappeared with a vengeance under the Ayatollah Khomeini.

My hotel was no less odd than the others. It was situated in a poor suburb a mile out of town next to a butcher's shop around which hung repulsive lumps of raw meat. The hotel owner had a sense of humour. 'If you're lost, follow the flies,' he advised and, do you know, he was right. I shared a room with three holy men who spoke not a word even among themselves.

While in the city I took this last opportunity to sample a Persian bath. The variation to a Turkish one is slight but involves a degree more privacy. From out of the steam emerged Hassan, a young doctor of chemistry, who invited me to his home for tea. The house, deep in a spider's web of backyards, was of whitewashed mud brick. It had its own garden enclosed by a high brick wall and was populated by an assortment of relatives. I was led into an upstairs room so cool that it required an oil stove and was bidden to seat myself on the carpet. Without the few cushions scattered about the room, it would have been completely bare, yet that rich carpet, together with others used as wall-coverings, made the chamber snug and home-like. I began to understand the real *raison d'être* of the Persian carpet. In Britain, it is looked upon as an expensive luxury; in Iran it is a basic necessity. Even the lowliest hovel has one or more for use as a bed, chair or room partition. With great deliberation Hassan brought in a bulbous silver samovar and fussed over the preparation of tea.

Later, Hassan insisted on taking me to the zoo, the most shockingly run-down display of half-starved wild animals it has ever been my misfortune to see. We dined together in an intriguing cellar restaurant I would never have found on my own and, having missed the last bus, caught a taxi back to the hotel. The taxi had two drivers; neither had heard of the hotel and both were drunk. They had the radio on full blast and zig-zagged along the streets taking the road islands on the wrong side until we all lost the way. Street by street, in a frenzy of singing, oriental chanting and waving arms, we arrived at the butcher's shop by the simple process of elimination of all Meshed's numerous butcher's shops. I'd tried to explain about the flies but the explanation had foundered in a haze of incomprehension and alcohol fumes. There are two things to avoid in Meshed: the zoo and the taxis.

The choice of route eastwards out of the city is limited. It's road or nothing. The road runs straight across a broad plain with blue, snow-capped mountains barring the horizon. By the roadside were yellow irises, scarlet tulips and a dead camel. At Fariman, two plaster lions guard the approaches to a model rural community that never was. Reza Shah planned and ordered it, his mind full of

Western innovations. Then he died, and that which was already built decayed or was looted by a deserting population. The lions, not being of combustible material, remained guarding the lost dream of Reza Shah's Utopian paradise.

Taibar is not the border but it is the border town. If you were very lucky and knew the dodges, you could reach Herat from Meshed the same day. The secret was to reach the Afghan bus that leaves from a different terminus at the same time that the Meshed bus is scheduled to arrive in the dirty little square. The Afghan bus was full of people not in the know and therefore stranded. Assuredly, the Afghan driver and his mate were getting a cut from the Taibar hotel people for every traveller left there overnight. I would not recommend the hotel to my worst enemy. It was composed of shacks around a central courtyard knee-deep in mud. Most of the shacks were without beds, although some had ledges optimistically titled 'thrones of sleep'. If the beds, thrones or floor have to be used, it should be as a last resort.

The Afghan bus, like the hotel, was original to say the least. Tall and ungainly, made almost entirely of wood, with orange crates filling the gaps where seats should have been, the outside painted with lurid pictures of unveiled, cherubic-looking women, camels and aeroplanes, and every inch packed, including the roof, with humanity. To my surprise, the thing moved and it moved fast. In it and on it, we rattled about a dozen miles on an exceedingly minor road. Bits fell off the chassis but nobody minded. Halfway down a dead-straight stretch of road a sign announced 'Afghanistan' but it was another five miles to the border control at Eslam Qaleh.

The frontier village of Eslam Qaleh was giving itself a face-lift when my Emmet-inspired vehicle drew up at the barrier. Solidly built hutments set in mud-walled compounds were being systematically replaced by featureless concrete hutments – on account, no doubt, of concrete being a symbol of progress. With the previous buildings made uninhabitable prior to demolition and the new ones incomplete, the formalities of crossing a border so necessary in the 20th century had to be undertaken out of doors with a keen wind slicing across the barren wastes. Inoculation certificates, travel documents and entry forms blew in all directions, chased by their owners to the childish glee of the officials for whom the occasion made a break in the dull routine.

Behind the new concrete facade, the few mud houses clustered together in the waterlogged, malarial plain; an infinity with no living creature except tortoises and ants. Down the road, behind a second barrier guarded by an unshaven soldier was another bus, whose driver beckoned us over.

We crowded onto the new vehicle – an improvement on the old – and in the aisle, passengers perched upon oil drums and crates.

The road was American and tarmacked, except in the dips where flood water had washed away the surface. Beside it ran the old road, sand-blown, ill-defined, but still holding its own. A new signpost indicated, in English, a dam – a German dam I was told – and I began to see Afghanistan as a hotch-potch of other nations' projects. We stopped at another border control, a tiny oasis of shrubs and trees, and it was here I discovered the real, systematic immigration check was to be made. The other casual affair was just to impress the Iranians.

Rumour had the encampment by the throat. Cholera at Kandahar, it said, you can't go on. You'll have to be detained in quarantine. You'll have to return to Iran. The place was in confusion and everyone was dashing about looking worried. I knocked at a door to see if I could elicit some information. A small boy of no more than twelve shouted something that sounded extremely discourteous; I retaliated. This went on until he slammed the door but my foot was in it. Reinforcements came to support the opposition; a wild-eyed bearded personage who turned out to be the chief customs officer. He was also the boy's father and made plain his objection to my swearing at his son. 'Get out of my office,' he roared, picking up a thick stick. I retired hastily and a minute later he beckoned me back. 'Welcome to Afghanistan,' he announced sweetly. 'I am pleased to see you.' He studied my passport, asked for details of my camera and then added with bland innocence, 'You have brought a nice present, yes?' I expected a return to savagery with my negative reply but not a bit of it. He bowed graciously and turned to the next client. I departed, sticking my tongue out at the obnoxious child.

The blast of a horn drew us back to the bus. The cholera epidemic had been resolved or ignored. We moved off along a dead-straight road that served as an unofficial racetrack judging by our vehicle's violent acceleration. The verges were littered with wrecks and toppled 50 m.p.h. restriction signs. The scream of the engine was supplemented by a haze of exhaust, inside the bus as well as without, to add to the sweet-smelling hashish smoke arising from the cigarettes of the Afghan passengers.

Controls at intervals along the road were ignored by our demon driver while picturesque old men in white turbans with long rambling beards leapt out of the way to stand shaking their fists amidst poisoned clouds of dust. A convoy of animals escaped annihilation by inches and a broken-down bus – occupants hunched dejectedly behind it – was ignored. Those of us who were non-smokers chewed betel nuts and spat green saliva onto the floor.

Mile after mile we drove across that lifeless plain. Broken towers of mud sprouting vertical wooden blades were a recurring feature and I would never have guessed they were windmills. Inside the bus, heads craned and fingers pointed and gradually I perceived the source of the interest. Four tall chimneys. But a factory with no town? Possible, but it seemed a little odd. Nearer, and odder still: chimneys with no factory. I should have known, of course. Herat.

The road made a detour of the city and brought us in from the east through cool avenues of pine and a scattering of villas. From a low rise, the whole oasis came into view, dark green against a desert horizon, with its four faint-pencilled minarets clustered together in the sun.

Old Persian Hairova, renamed Alexandria-in-Asia, lies in a lowland where the trade routes were bound to cross – a situation made for constant destruction and resurrection. Conqueror after conqueror, from the time of Alexander the Great, has taken it, destroyed it and then rebuilt it. In 1040, the Seljuks defeated the Ghaznovids and destroyed the fortress. They, in turn, were conquered by the Ghorids, who lost control to the Khwarizm Empire ruling from Merv. The Mongols bombarded Herat in 1221 and again in 1222, following which a Kurd dynasty administered it until Tamerlane came along to destroy the place again. Under his descendants, Herat reached its climax of wealth and splendour and became the richest and most civilised city in Asia.

Early in the 14th century, the Uzbeks, marching down from the north, captured the city, and for 200 years they and the Safavids of Persia struggled for supremacy. When, in 1747, Afghanistan came to be governed by its own people, the struggle continued in a wider field. With North-West India and Persia on the stage and England and Russia watching warily from the wings, the Afghans strove to possess what was theirs. In 1837, Lord Palmerston's protest broke the Persian siege and, twenty years later, when Herat had finally been captured, the British rescued it in a three-month campaign.

Thus the pre-20th-century vicissitudes of this small and epic town. Of all Afghan cities, Herat most reflects the history of Afghanistan. Crossroads of Asia, its history matches the savagery of the land. Cradled in the High Pamirs and Himalayas, whose peaks rise above 25,000 feet, bisected by the great Hindu Kush ranges, the melting snows roar down through tremendous gorges to water lofty valleys of luscious fruit and golden corn. Bypassing waterless deserts, the angry streams join themselves to the Oxus in the north and the Indus in the south.

What was then Soviet Russia lies across the River Oxus. A part of the Little Pamir is Afghan, but the boundary passes over a series of crags and untraversable mountain ridges to loose itself on the Chinese frontier in the snowfields of Sarikol. To the south lies the North-West Frontier Province of Pakistan attainable only via the Khyber and the Khojak passes. Westwards, the mountains and deserts of Iran merge into the rocky spurs and the Great Helman Desert. Afghanistan's position in the heart of Asia made it a natural east-west passage for thousands of years. It was first used for those strange migrations of peoples at the dawn of mankind, Then came the conquerors and traders. Every invasion of India passed through Afghanistan. King Darius of Persia was followed by Alexander the Great from Greece. Ghengis Khan came from the plains of Asia destroying all in his path. Babur destroyed, conquered and rebuilt it on his way to take India and become founder of the Great Mogul Empire in the 17th century. From then until the end of the Anglo-Afghan wars, Afghanistan knew no peace. And the pattern continues.

Marco Polo and the great traders of the world travelled this way. The trade routes from China and the Far East passed through to Egypt to cross the other great caravan highway from India northwards through Persia and Turkey to Europe. It was only in the 16th century, when the ships of the desert were replaced by the ships of the sea, that Afghanistan lost its importance as a great trading centre. This tremendous age-old history of a country that knew a civilisation co-existent with that of Babylon and the early Egyptians, has produced a legacy of cities and the ruins of cities, many still to be excavated, which are far older than the antiquities of Greece and Rome. Balkh was long believed to be the oldest city in the world, older even than Merv, and now they are finding others older still. Savagery by man and savagery by nature, continuing to this day, combine to make the Afghan nation the most enthralling on earth.

Nothing can save Herat from being the only western approach to Kabul and India south of the Hindu Kush but there are parts of the old town that the West has not yet ruined. Here, the Orient reigns triumphant. Even the few cars matched, in appearance, a past decade. Two wide streets bisected the bazaar and at their junction, under a tin mushroom, stood a Ruritanian policeman who, with operatic gestures and shrill blasts on a whistle, urged forward disdainful camels, children on donkeys and fast-trotting *gaudis*, who ignored him anyway.

Eager to see more, I hurried off the sweaty bus, fought my way through a commercial-minded crowd and dumped my bag at an establishment calling itself the Bahzad Hotel, which stood strategically at the crossroads. The hotel passed all expectations. My room and bed were clean and the dining room produced substantial and inexpensive meals at any time of the day.

At the top of the one-storied street stood Gaughar Shad's tomb. Here was another creation of that great woman of Herat renaissance whose Meshed dome had excited my eyes earlier. Her buildings and those of Baigara, clustered at this end of town, were levelled upon the advice of a British military advisor in 1866 to make a field of fire against a Russian attack that never came. Only the minarets remain, four gnarled fingers bending slightly with age, their pale turquoise and white mosaic peeling like rotten skin. Back in the city centre, the great citadel still rose to dominate the landscape of downtown Herat as it has done for centuries. Also, a newer building, the large mosque of Masjed-i-Jami, rebuilt and restored to a degree of nonentity. The streets and alleyways of old Herat retained their ancient flavour and in one cool, dark, mud-walled home, I was treated to a musical interlude played on a dutard, a type of banjo. The instrument, played so skilfully by a serious old man, produced strange music that alone could pull away the curtains of time from this city of enchantment.

A characteristic feature of the sparse traffic was the *gaudi* I mentioned earlier, a jingling little dogcart that plies for hire. Each was replete with ribbons and bells, as was the horse. They were the fastest vehicles in Herat, and next day, I took one into the hills beyond the Musalla minarets. I was dropped near Jami's tomb, the grave of a 15th-century poet unadorned save for a pistachio tree which had sprung from the tomb itself. Nearby was a newly-built mosque, outside which two ranks of holy men were carrying out their devotions by numbers. There was no nonsense about entering mosques or watching the devout at their prayers in Herat.

One of my objectives was to take a closer look at those windmills I had seen from the bus for they were a speciality of the district. The heat of summer here is aggravated by hot winds with a velocity which reaches 110 m.p.h. and blows continuously from June to September. Every village possessed one or more such windmills, and the design of their mud cylinders with wooden paddles has remained unchanged since the 7th century. In the first village, I collected a retinue of children and inquisitive adults who, as if I was the Pied Piper, followed me in a swelling cavalcade to the next. I was allowed to pass through the main thoroughfares of these communities of dried mud, yet each time I attempted to explore intriguing side turnings, I was courteously but firmly deflected.

However, in one village I was invited to tea in the main street; a hundred souls watched as I consumed it, sucking the hot liquid through the little sweets that served as sugar. I was shown the interior of the village shop, a cool and pleasant place in spite of its unpretentious igloo-like exterior. Making small talk to a hundred people – none of whom speak a Western language – is a daunting business and an observation I made about the heat of the day resulted in my being supplied with a horse. On this, surrounded by my troops, I progressed to a further village where the intricacies of its windmill were explained to me in a babel of tongues. Old men in robes and the Afghan headgear of a skull cap, around which a length of material is wound, held me by the hand; young men in baggy pantaloons, some with discarded American airforce jackets bleached by the sun, asked innumerable questions, and a rabble of young boys and girls in colourful rags endlessly repeated 'Hello, goodbye.' Even women, hidden beneath their silken armour, overcame their reticence to the extent of teetering at the edges of the crowd to stare at me. Later in the evening, weary beyond measure, I returned to Herat incognito in the back of a gravel cart.

The road to Kandahar is Russian-built and is 354 miles long. The bus I caught was exuberantly Afghan. We were a full load as usual, the men spitting constantly and expertly into little round tins placed in the aisle. The pale gold of the desert changed to chocolate and as the sun rose higher in the sky, the foothills grew into a great army of brown tents arranged in serried rows. The hills swelled to mountains stretching out to the horizon, till the snow began to cap their tops and they were lost in cloud and distance.

Kandhar. We arrived an hour before nightfall which allowed me a glimpse of the Chihil Zina, a monument carved into a cliff approached by a stone stairway. No tomb or shrine this, just a permanent memo ordered by Babur listing his domains. The centre of the town is the Shahidam Chawk, or Martyr's Square, with two brace of cannon guarding a traffic island. It was also the bus terminus and I allowed the touts to fight over whose roof would grace my head.

The result was the Marjor Hotel, which was even worse than it looked. Situated at first floor level, it was approached from a secret doorway in a restaurant and a flight of pitch-black, near-vertical stairs with a Z-bend halfway up. I became stuck fast with my bag on the bend but there were plenty of diners available to heave me free. I shared a room with an American youth, a ginger-haired Canadian girl, an Indian snake-charmer (in a state of desolation because someone had nicked his bag of cobras) and a Peruvian hippy. The toilet was outside on a flat roof and, if you *had* to use it, there was a two-to-one chance of overbalancing and falling into either the restaurant or the street.

This second city of Afghanistan is virtually a modern one. The ruins of old Kandahar, some four miles to the west, have the usual stormy history but have ceased to breathe. Architecturally speaking, there is no need to linger in either.

Not that this was the reason I left so early the next morning. The chief contributing factor was the Kandahar chorus. This started before dawn with a cacophonous symphony of barking by the canine population of the city, and this was taken up by the baying of a score of commission men in the pay of the bus companies. 'Kabul, Kabul, Kabul, Kabul, Kabuuul,' they shouted and the raucous high note at the end set the dogs off again. As if this wasn't enough, everything started trekking out of town: caravans of laden donkeys and camels, flocks of sheep, herds of goats, cows and buffalo – all with their attendant sound effects. I breakfasted on fried eggs, took tea with a trio of locals noisily slurping yoghurt through their fingers and dutifully caught a Kabul-bound bus.

We drove east out of Kandahar along a route jostled by mountains. It took us to Ghazni, another once-upon-a-time capital. It sat tightly about an almost imperceptible watershed surrounding a fort perched on a rock that was still a military barracks. Two carved minarets, older but only a little less graceful than the famous minaret of Djem, embellished the town. They were modelled, I read somewhere, on the Kutb Minar of Delhi and with Ghazni, we are within the sphere of Indian history. Her great gate, in a wall no longer standing, was supposed to be impregnable but Colonel Dennie of the 13th Light Infantry proved it wasn't. So Ghazni became a British battle honour and part of our history too.

Babur questions the charms of Ghazni in his memoirs. 'It is', he writes, 'but a poor mean place, and I have always wondered how its princes, who possessed also Hindustan and Khorasan, could have chosen such a wretched country for the seat of government'. I could see what he meant.

Our route passed by a brown mountain crowned by brown fortifications. Everything in Afghanistan is brown. Brown towns, brown walls, brown camels on brown plains. Yet brown is an indeterminate colour with a thousand shades. And, of course, there are other colours in the capital although brown predominates.

Kabul. A little more than a decade ago, there was not a modern building in the city. Adventurous modernity now pushed out among booths and shanties that have come down from the Greek ages to form an untidy sprawling town struggling for form at the base of the two hills. Box-like houses of mud and mud-brick climbed steeply beneath the precipitous skyline with here and there a concrete structure, a livid scar of white against the eternal brown. Many of the new buildings and public monuments were hideously avant-garde but their incongruity was so extreme that the total effect was comic rather than offensive. The streets had been paved by the Russians and looked it. Some of their own Siberian streets bear a marked resemblance. Thoroughfares pushed outwards with an eye to future development but Kabul remains, at heart, an overgrown village. Country people crowded the bazaars, pushing by with turbans askew wound round gold-embroidered skull-caps – the bright spot in their costume where everything else was the colour of dust. Their cotton trousers, unchanged from Sassanian or Parthian times, flopped loose under a shirt drooping to the knees; worn above this, a shorter western jacket – often a remnant of some foreign military uniform – took away any stray look of splendour that might have afflicted this ancient place. Afghan fashions for men look superbly dignified even when in tatters. Some of it is the Afghans themselves. They impressed me as a people with clear-cut personalities, in contrast to the rather characterless Persians. In stature they are taller than the Turks and Persians and are very handsome indeed.

Towering over the city, the modern mediocrity of the Inter-Continental Hotel should have been the site of the Royal Palace, itself hardly an architectural inspiration but at least more worthy of prominence. Instead, it sulked in the town within its high walls and behind a great square forecourt. Close by was the new Pushtunistan Square, full of men on bicycles, men on donkeys, men on foot, men in charge of herds of buffalo, men in cars, men in lorries and buses, and every man wearing a turban and long *chapan* that defied modernity. Camels and goats passed daintily by, taking their place in the traffic without noise and fuss.

Even the few semi-modern streets of what the guide book enthusiastically called the fashionable shopping district collapsed into a pot-pourri of rurality. Kabul gathers all the Afghan races: neat-featured, bearded Pathans, flat-faced Hazaras, long Tajik profiles, Indo-Iranians and the pagan hillmen of Nuristan with uncombed hair and darting eyes. Beggars made their rounds chanting their tales of woe, their brown faces and brown rags as colourless as the mud hovels from whence they came. Women, impeded by children, flitted about with surreptitious glances from under the silk grill that hid their faces.

Strolling through the bazaar, I was conscious of the fact that Alexander's soldiers must have witnessed scenes nearly identical to those that surrounded me – bakers cooking flat bread on leather cushions, the dough damped down with filthy water; camels walking in circles churning *mast* (yoghurt) in smelly little backyards; butchers skinning and disembowelling a sheep, throwing the scraps to the yellow, crop-eared dogs; tanners curing hides; potters skilfully firing pitchers of exquisite beauty and tailors cutting out the long fleece-padded coats which, when thrown over the shoulders of an Afghan, make him look like a fairy-tale king. Each trader smiled at me and went on working. There is a certain aloofness of the Afghan in contrast to the Persian, and one remembers that even though Afghanistan never attained the heights of civilisation reached by Persia, neither has she descended to Persia's depths.

On the west slope of Sherdarwaza Hill above the old city was Babur's Garden, surrounding the grave of the great Afghan ruler. With his conquest of India and founding of the Mogul Empire, he had half of Asia from which to choose his last resting place. But he loved Kabul, thought of it as the most beautiful place in the world, and asked that his body should be interred overlooking the valley and its ring of mountains.

Kabul has witnessed the passing of many great empires during its long history. According to legend, the city was founded by Adam's two sons, Cain and Abel – in Persian, Cabil and Habil – whose names were combined into Kabul. And you can't reach back much earlier than that. Once known as Kubha in 3000 BC, it was part of the Achaemenid Empire under Darius, and later the Seleveid, Mauryan, Bactrian and Kushan Empires in rapid succession. Alexander the Great, of course, passed by to crush the kingdom of Persia, and his feat makes Hannibal's crossing of the Alps look like a Sunday school outing. The passes of Afghanistan are twice the height of the Alpine passes and Alexander made his crossing in winter.

In 656 AD Kabul was captured by the Arabs after a siege

lasting a year. In those days, it was ringed by the great walls, portions of which can be seen today climbing almost vertically up the encircling hills. The city must have been a formidable obstacle and its resistance gave rise to many sagas in early literature. With the Arabs came Islam, which swiftly replaced the then corrupt and bankrupt Buddhism, its spiritual content lost in a flood of commercial materialism introduced by traders.

Six hundred years later it was the turn of Genghis Khan, that most horrific and dreaded of names. He left nothing alive wherever he went: men, women and children, animals – all were slaughtered, and city after city received the full treatment. Eventually it was Kabul's turn.

So Kabul passed through the turmoil of a further quartet of regimes: Seljuks, Ghorids, Mongols and, finally, Timurids. Only when the revered Babur disappeared from the Afghan scene did a period of civil war develop between fiercely independent tribesmen to delay national independence for another 400 years. And when at last, in 1747, the modern state of Afghanistan was founded, Britain, alas, was its chief scourge. Kabul was in a constant state of strife over the quartering of a British garrison – part of our defences of the North-West Frontier – which erupted into the Anglo-Afghan wars.

My hotel near the square was, for once, faintly dignified, within and without. My first day, I wandered round the active streets getting bearings, observing and listening. In the square, I joined a crowd watching a wrestling match but not for long. I was promptly challenged to a contest by a veritable King-Kong, the local champion and, I'm ashamed to say, I fled. In the livestock market, I watched some unenthusiastic bargaining for camels and buffaloes. To liven things up, I tendered a 100 Afghani note (then about 65 pence) and nearly came away with a goat. At the Palace, I caused a furore attempting to photograph it and was chased by irate soldiery. I simply couldn't put a foot right. Earlier, I had made another gaffe by photographing an outdoor barber's shop not knowing it was forbidden to take pictures of men minus their headgear. Turbanless warriors in my vision-finder leapt out of their chairs and came at me with contorted, soap-lathered faces.

Istalif. You must see Istalif, I was told, so to Istalif I went. A series of packed local buses got me there and I was not dissuaded from taking to the roof. Under a warm sun, it was a pleasant ride lying out on the baggage with a number of Afghan companions, and I marvelled at the conductor who, with the vehicle pushing 50 m.p.h., periodically swung out of the rear of the bus and scrambled up the ironwork to collect his fares from those of us on the wildly-swaying roof.

Our road led upward out of the city through suburbs of dome-shaped houses. At the top of the Khair Khana Pass (Pass of Goodness) the snow-dappled Paghman mountains came into view extending as far as the eye could see. On the descent into the valley so loved by Babur, the Koh Daman or 'Skirts of the Hills' rolled out like a delicate green carpet northwards, its fingers creeping up into the tree-clad Paghman foothills.

The overgrown village that dominates this valley from its site on the Paghman foothills is Istalif, a word derived from the Greek *stafiloi* or vine. Looking across a smaller valley to the town on the opposite side is a sight to stir the heart. The houses of local mud burnt white by the sun, flat-roofed and, seemingly terraced, extend halfway up the pale mountainside along the feathery trees and above them. Close by, Babur's throne basks within an English garden.

Poets, too, have been inspired by Istalif for centuries. 'He who has not seen Istalif has seen nothing' they say. But, like Naples, it is a place to be viewed from a distance. I entered the small town between high walls which gave it the effect of a walled city, and followed men and donkeys into the bazaar where the narrow mud-paved streets were a confusion of the usual commercial-minded citizenry of all ages. Istalif, in fact, had become an overgrown bazaar with a whisper of Greek instead of Afghan in the faces of the merchants though the tattered military overcoats worn over the long shirt and white baggy trousers were hardly an Atheneum mode.

I partook of tea in a *chai-khana*, or tea-house, a dirty little place with straw-matting platforms on which one squats, shoeless. Greek eyes started at me with passive hostility, and curious children crept in to stand, staring soullessly, as I drank my tea. To stare is not classed as bad manners in this part of the world though it is small comfort to the European. With a kind of glee, I was informed that there were no more buses back to the main road, a state of affairs

that involved me in an involuntary six-mile walk. However, I had
a companion in the guise of a pleasant Afghan student able to
speak a smattering of English.

It was well into evening before the student and I were again
ensconced on the roof of a bus to Kabul – though I didn't much
like the look of the half-dozen tribesmen up there with us. My
companion, alas, was alighting at a village a few miles down the
road and though he invited me to his home, I reluctantly declined,
not wishing to miss any more buses to the capital. Alone once
more, I braced myself for the expected attentions of the villainous
company, and it was not long in coming. Hardly had the student
departed than I became the plaything of the ruffians. I suppose I
was asking for trouble wearing shorts and, with the chill of
nightfall, regretting it. But now my regret stemmed from an
entirely different reason as my new companions sidled up and
allowed their hands to caress my bare knees and thighs. Slowly I
backed away until the rail at the front of the bus terminated further
retreat. I yelled, idiotically, for the conductor, and that worthy,
bless him, appeared like a knight in shining armour from the top of
the ladder of his steel charger. I heaved a sigh of relief. Now I'll
get some peace, I thought, but not a bit of it. Without so much as a
'good evening' or 'what's your name?', he jumped into the melée,
his hand stroking my calves. It was now dark as well as cold and
the bus ran out of water. While its radiator was being replenished,
I attempted to escape, but was forcibly restrained by all and
sundry; the conductor intimating that since I had purchased a
ticket to Kabul, then to Kabul I would go. On the move again, I
funked a James Bond-type leap onto the top of a second bus which
drew level with ours, though this would probably have been but
akin to jumping from the frying pan in to the fire if I hadn't killed
myself *en route*. A second water-replenishment operation in a
village did nothing to relieve the situation, a dozen members of the
community being invited 'upstairs' to partake of a feel of the
virgin English thighs. Unaware of the drama taking place above
them, some of the more religious-minded passengers downstairs
took advantage of the enforced delay to practise their devotions at
the roadside – but I bet none of them prayed as hard as I did. With
my virginity more or less intact, we limped into Kabul.

If I had received no intelligence of the amorous habits of

Afghans, I *had* been warned of a more mundane trait practised by the less civic-minded citizens of Kabul. Not that it did any good. My pocket was picked all the same. Just for one moment I was off my guard but it was once too often. While in the silver bazaar next morning, I felt a nudge; then a second movement, and my hand flew to the buttoned pocket of my jacket. The first nudge had undone the button; the second had removed my wallet, all whilst my attention had been momentarily diverted by an individual attempting to sell me a bracelet. The 'finger man' or 'dip' I glimpsed as he disappeared into the crowd and my attempts to follow him were in vain.

The theft was more inconvenient than disastrous. My main resources and passport reposed securely about my waist but the wallet contained a considerable amount of mixed currency, my credit cards, driving licence, and most serious of all, my notebook of contact addresses. My insurance cover was dependent upon my reporting the loss to the authorities, so I bent my footsteps towards the main police station with the object of so doing and obtaining a certificate to prove it.

In a country like Afghanistan, however, such tasks are easier said than done. To save time, I stopped a cruising police car in which mercifully sat an officer of the law who could speak a little English. 'Go to police station number seven,' he advised upon learning the district in which the alleged crime had been committed. With no little difficulty, I located police station number seven, there to interrupt a major crime conference that appeared to be in progress in the vestibule. To another officer admitting a word or two of my language, I explained the facts of the case. 'I don't expect you to find my wallet or the thief,' I added, 'I don't even ask that you become involved. I just want a certificate from you to say I've reported the loss.'

'Write out a statement,' I was told, so, in an anteroom, I wrote one out which was duly inspected by the committee.

'A policeman will accompany you to the scene of the incident,' they said and I thought it simpler not to argue. The minion chosen for this task was thereupon ushered into my presence and together we traipsed around the town. He seemed to know where he was going. I didn't. After a while he asked a question. I didn't understand but I presumed it to be 'Where exactly did the incident occur?' and since by now I hadn't the faintest idea, I put on a sleuthful face, took him round the corner and said: 'Here.'

'It's not in number seven district,' he stated, or words to that effect, and I could see myself starting all over again.

'Oh, perhaps it wasn't here after all,' I exclaimed hastily, and on we went through the crowds and the heat of the morning. All the bazaars looked the same to me and I couldn't make my man understand the word 'silver', which was the particular brand of bazaar I had in mind. However, when I felt we were back in the vicinity of police station number seven, I said 'here' again and stuck firmly to the lie.

Back inside the police station, a new conference was convened. I was given a pot of tea, but from the way in which everyone was looking at me, it seemed they thought I was making the whole thing up. And then came the confirmation. 'What you say couldn't have happened,' I was informed, 'Not in broad daylight, not in Kabul.'

'But it *did*,' I almost shouted. 'All I want is your stamp on this statement to show I reported the theft.'

'We have no official stamps in this office,' they said.

'Where *are* there any?' I asked in desperation.

'At the office of the prime-minister,' came the reply and I thought they were joking. But they weren't and I was ushered out.

I couldn't make the taxi-driver understand my requested destination. How *do* you mime a prime-minister? I dashed into a nearby institutional building, which turned out to be a hospital, and came out with an American nurse. She got through to the driver and I was taken to an office block near the palace. I began my piece all over again before a clerk where it had to be repeated to his superior.

'Initially we shall require a certificate confirming your status from your embassy,' the man said, 'We can do nothing until we have that.'

So I caught another taxi, grated 'Britische Ambassade' and arrived at the Federal German Consulate. The Germans were helpful and re-directed the driver.

Our man in Kabul had his office out of town so that anti-British mobs in earlier days could dissipate their ardour in the long walk involved to sack the place; I found the distance only increased my own exasperation. The embassy building was encircled by well-watered lawns with herbaceous borders. The reception clerk said, 'Yes, we can give you a certificate. It will cost you £2.80 and we shall need sight of your passport.' Then I remembered. The hotel had my passport. 'Can you ...' I started. 'No,' said the man, catching the drift of my plea. 'We must have your passport.'

Another taxi ride through Kabul and, on the return, the driver lost himself. But I was becoming acquainted with the streets of Kabul so I showed him the way.

Thus I acquired my certificate of who I purported to be, and the clerk was kind enough to add a few extra stamps and blobs of sealing wax to the document for effect. But back at the prime-minister's office they were going to lunch. I grabbed the chief clerk as he attempted to dodge me and triumphantly waved the certificate in front of his face.

'We shall require a copy for our files,' he pointed out following a brief perusal. 'You can get a photostat made just down the road.'

This operation took two hours and four attempts at four different locations because my document was too big for most of Kabul's photocopiers. Again I returned.

Mellow from lunch, the man in the PM's office examined the two certificates and half-heartedly began making entries in a ledger. Inspiration smote him and he threw down his pen. 'Why, you've got your signed and stamped certificate. You don't need one from us!' he exclaimed, and nothing would induce him to endorse it further. I left the office fuming but marvelling at the Afghani penchant for passing the buck.

Walletless, but with every square inch of leg discreetly covered, I left Kabul atop the afternoon bus to Jalalabad. The breathtaking Kabul Gorge rose with dramatic suddenness from the flat plain. Here, the mountains ganged up to form an awe-inspiring barrier through which the road has to pirouette its way down thousands of feet to river level. Drilling into this enormous fissure, the Kabul river threshed its way in an angry plume of spray.

Emerging from the climax of the gorge, you wonder what hit you and discover it's the heat. Suddenly, India – or at least Pakistan – is near. Not only was it an abrupt change of temperature, but an abrupt change of terrain too. Here was a tropical land very different from what had been before. The lowering hills changed from brown granite to red clay. A fertile earth excited into growth an abundance of oranges and lemons to the rhythms of crickets under the oppressive air. Cultivated gardens of exaggerated blossoms surrounded the suburbs of another town.

Jalalabad. The easternmost city of Afghanistan which the garden-mad Babur had had a hand in developing.

My impression was of a main street and crossroads of iniquity. I was hardly off the bus before I became the target for hashish sellers, hideously-deformed beggars, children demanding 'baksheesh' and unveiled women touching my arm to make me look at their diseased babies.

All around were dingy stalls, sweetshops and chai-houses in which the male population lounged under the shade of gum trees. Loudspeakers pumped out an endless dirge, while garish advertisements leered down from decrepit buildings to give Jalalabad a bankrupted Las Vegas atmosphere. Only the scent from the exotic blooms could counteract that issuing from the filth lying immobile in the waterless *jubes*.

As far as I could gather, there was no hotel, even one unworthy of the description, in the place. There were, however, plenty of doss-houses. The Majestic was one such establishment, where, surrounded by dried mud and corrugated iron, guests could doss down in rows for a fee that was the equivalent of five pence a night.

My sleeping partners in its one room were bearded, leering Afghan tribesmen sporting colourful garments and powerful smells, who, with communal spirit, had pushed the bed frames together. We turned in with one accord, they going to bed in their baggy trousers, boots and assorted weaponry, which included daggers, swords, rifles and AK 47s. I found myself, abjectly weaponless, in the centre of a soon-snoring mob of six, my immediate neighbour waking only to curse every time I moved to scratch myself. All too soon, the call of nature had me further in distress, while under the grey light of an exceedingly slow dawn, I beheld a giant hairy-legged spider, relentlessly descending from the roof towards my face at the end of its elasticated thread. My arms were pinned to my sides; I dared not move a muscle and my legs, of necessity, were firmly crossed. Thus, I was reduced to blowing at the thing, so that it swung, pendulum-like, from side to side – a movement which slowed its descent. And if I could get the beast swaying hard enough, my reasoning gave hope of it dropping off on someone other than me.

Came the grand awakening and we cascaded from our cocoons of dirty blankets in a welter of grunts and burps. The spider fell to the floor and was unceremoniously ground underfoot. For my night's lodging in Jalalabad, the five pence charge was larceny.

Breakfast was mango juice; then I caught the bus for the Pakistan border. More hills, these dotted with fortresses, deformed the plain as if to remind all who passed this way that they were in territory where trigger-happy tribesmen had been busy for centuries. The heat was intense.

A threat of conflict was in the air; more so than elsewhere. But then Asia, and particularly Afghanistan, is no stranger to conflict. I was on the threshold of a new country but one with a somewhat similar history of occupation, strife and slaughter. Assuredly, until the Asian people are once more permitted to be themselves with their own human, cultural and political rights, there will always be blood on Asian streets.

Chapter Two

Probably it is only the British who, secretly or openly, become charged with emotion at the mere mention of the Khyber Pass. Its fame is based on history rather than scenery, and the comparatively recent and universally-known story of the Khyber is exclusively ours: the traveller from Britain finds this not particularly sensational defile between cliffs of shale and limestone uniquely significant with its sad little graveyards, memorials and regimental plaques. Yet it is a strange mixture of contradictions. No other pass in the world has such strategic importance though it was not so much used before modern times as has been generally supposed.

Though the armies of Alexander the Great, the Moghul emperors Babur and Humayan, and those of the Afghan Mahmud of Ghazni, as well as raiding marauders through the centuries have used the Khyber for conquest and pillage, the British came to know it as well as any. They first marched up its treacherous defiles in 1839, sending the smaller of two contingents to the First Afghan War this way (the larger army moving up the Bolan Pass). We lost hundreds of men in the process, the Afridis ambushing them through every yard of the route. Whatever subsequent treaties proclaimed, it was the Afridis, in reality, who controlled the Khyber. The British, at best, only held it for short periods and then only if the tribesmen so willed it. Even up to Partition the pass had to be regularly picketed with troops to ensure that caravans and convoys would get through safely.

There are two roads through the Khyber and there is a railway line. The track is worn, the locomotives using it antique and the rolling stock hardly more than wooden boxes on wheels. Yet the line is also a stupendous piece of engineering and all for one train a week.

From the Afghan border at Torkham I took a shared taxi the five miles to Pakistan's Lindikotal, sitting on a few square inches of tailboard and hanging on like grim death in a cloud of dust. Small, square forts bristled on every hill commanding a stretch of road to the next bend where another hilltop fort took over. The whole area is run by the Pushtu tribesmen, who live with old British Lee Enfield rifles slung on their shoulders. This is truly the land of the gun, where firearms are worn like scarves as a warning to the official Pakistan presence in their territory not to become too cocky. The Pushtu's other accomplishment is a curry that is virtually a test of manhood. If you can get it down, they seem to think maybe you're all right. Not as good as a Pushtu perhaps, but then who is? All the way to Lindikotal these tribal sentries hang about at every corner, friendly and happy to be photographed amongst crumbling concrete dragon's teeth and rusting barbed wire entanglements.

Lindikotal is a den of thieves if there ever was one. It is hard to imagine this was the chief trading outpost of all the heroin in the world. You can buy nearly everything at its down-at-heel bazaar and superficially exotic supermarket surrounded by squalor and filth. Many of the goods are smuggled and, for the inhabitants, smuggling is their stock in trade. It is the sort of place you don't want to prowl around at night for law and order is of a very basic kind. The Afridi clans occupy it and Pakistan has inherited from Britain the job of controlling them. There is a sort of 'understanding' between the two. Nobody's baby is Lindikotal and the Khyber.

I walked by the food stalls to a wasteland where garishly-painted buses and lorries were parked. Groups of men gave me curious glances and soon individuals were sidling up to me to whisper propositions in my ear. But I was not in the market for anything legal or illegal this day and politely rejected their advances.

Within the evil darkness of a tea house I quenched a raging thirst and ate the local speciality which was as foul as the tea. The stock joke of the place was to allow a new and unsuspecting arrival to fall into a hole in the middle of the floor. The hole was full of filthy water and swill and was the receptacle of the regular clients' spit. Its edges were of greasy mud. Into this went my sandalled foot, and a cackle of laughter echoed round the dirt-caked walls. Then it was my turn as, lo and behold, a forgetful Pushtu villager went in with both feet. But my laugh was a solo for Pushtu humour has its limits.

I had chanced upon the day of the once-a-week train for Peshawar but it was scheduled to leave while I was thrashing about in the tea house. Under a pitiless sun, I hurried along to the station a mile out of town and found the three-coach special still undeparted. The train is a special indeed, being run to and from Lindikotal at the weekend – and at no charge – simply as a gesture by the then Pakistan Western Railway to prove to the tribesmen that the line, in spite of them, is open for business.

The old coaches were a morass of humanity intent upon going along for the ride. There was not an inch of space available; not even in the cab of the steam locomotive, British Vulcan Foundry-made vintage 1923 – the year of my own birth. Two grinning Pakistanis had installed themselves on the right-hand buffer – one sat astride the other. So with room to spare I installed myself behind the lone rider and was accepted straightway into the fraternity of railway buffer-riders.

The 40-mile ride that followed was a high-spot of my many years of subsequent train travel. The descent of the Khyber is the steepest non-rack and pinion stretch of track in the world. It is made in the form of a letter Z, the train changing direction at each apex and, on the steepest sections, safety track is installed to divert runaway trains into the hills. Until I became accustomed to the motion I felt extremely insecure astride my metal perch. To maintain balance I gripped the greasy ironwork with my knees as one does when riding a horse bareback, my hands clamped to the buffer flanges like limpet mines. Over my shoulder, the great hissing, threatening boiler licked me with jets of steam while my imagination worked overtime painting mind-pictures of what the relentless wheels close to my dangling legs would do to me if I fell off. My partner behind me perceived my alarm and clutched me, partly on his own account but more, I think, on mine.

We travelled at no great pace through a series of short tunnels with empty forts giving the standard walnut topping to every hill. The only occupied one seemed to be the big headquarter fortress of Jamrud; still in use by the Khyber Rifles guarding the southern approaches to the pass.

The Khyber's narrowest defile was commanded by one of the oldest forts, Ali Masjid, built on a cliff so high that only one turret could be seen from below. Of all the places where fighting had occurred, this must have been the corridor where it was the fiercest, a supposition given credence by a jutting rock that is the showcase of names of regiments, British, Pathan and Indian, carved in stone where years and blood lay eaten by the sun. Each badge, including those of the Royal Sussex, the Essex, the Cheshires, the South Wales Borderers, the Gordon Highlanders and my own Dorsets is freshly painted giving them a gaudy, almost toy-like appearance that speaks, vividly, of an uncommon bond, a curious comradeship formed by antagonists that had endured even at a time when the concepts of Crown and Empire were unfashionable to say the least. But the perception of courage as the more durable quality shines from that showcase of bygone valour. It is now the Pakistanis who hold the pass, closing it as dusk as we British had taught them.

All around was an alien scenery, burnt brown and exuding that air of latent hostility; so different to the green meadows of Dorset, the soft undulations of the South Downs, the mudflats of Essex, the tranquil estuary of the Dee and even the grandeur of the Scottish Highlands. Here was magnificence for sure, but its constituents were made up of sharply formed crags varying in colour from deep red to sandy yellow punctuated by jagged points of rock, the razor edge of ridges and peaks that offered no symmetry or reason. There was no consistent lie of the land; it went every way at once.

The plain below the pass was suddenly upon us, the brown and barren hills abruptly deflated. Fortified villages and dwellings, their high mud walls blank apart from firing slits, remained in evidence, their unseen occupiers presumably still ready to repulse attack from wherever it may come. At one point, where the line doubled back on itself, I could see the Khyber looking impregnable to man and train; not a gap or defile showed.

Limping into the station of Peshawar Cantonment we came to a halt at a crowded platform where our driver presented me and my fellow buffer rider with a glass of oily sweet tea. Had he known I was there he would have invited me into the cab, he said, even if it had meant throwing out someone else to make room. I assured him I wouldn't have exchanged my seat for a suite on the Blue Train, or words to that effect. Without their necklaces of humanity I perceived the nature of the coaches we had been hauling; first, second, third and servants quarters read the legend on their sides. Shades of the British Raj. Peshawar station reflected the sharp class divisions too with its graded waiting rooms, restaurants and station exits, and the question came to me, as it must to all visitors to the subcontinent, why the less attractive attributes of former British occupation had not been swept away with home rule.

A *tonga*, or motor-scooter, took me into town. It buzzed me to the paint-starved portals of the Konran Hotel on the edge of the old city and conveniently close to the new. Its fly-blown rooms looked inwards over a dreary courtyard but at no more than 25 pence a night, one could not expect the Ritz.

A hundred things to see at once, a hundred faces to absorb in a single glance. The caravan trails through the mountains had always halted at Peshawar, so that bazaars had sprung up and flourished in this seething town. I roamed through the street of story-tellers, the street of partridge-sellers, the streets of coppersmiths, of cobblers, of gold and jewellery – all with the higgledy-piggledy jumble of lesser streets with crate-like buildings so close overhead that the sky appeared like a slot through which coins of sunshine dropped.

Peshawar's ancient function as a meeting place continues still; no longer for merchants from Kabul, Samarkand and Bokhara, and not only for tribesmen, but for foreigners as well. Hence the multitude of articles for sale. Strange objects in ivory, slippers embroidered with mirror fragments, hubble-bubble pipes of every contortion and jewellery ornamented with the frankly imitation to the 18-carat genuine. All is piled into stalls of baked mud, concrete, canvas and plywood supported by heavy skeins of telephone wires. The sounds, too, are different to those of a western city; the high-pitched buzzing of the *tongas*, the clicketty-click of sugar cane cutters and the ringing blows of the coppersmiths blending into a symphony of small scale industry and commercial enterprise. A smell of rich spicy food and blocked drains permeates everything.

The new town, or cantonment, announces itself with a sign reading 'The Mall'. The atmosphere here was of a class distinction you could cut with a knife. First-class citizens, it seemed, were welcome in the cantonment; second-class ones tolerated. There were plenty of third-class 'untouchables' about but most lay in the gutters and so could not, for one moment, be confused with the residents. Smart villas peered bashfully out from behind lush shrubberies and the road names were pure Bayswater.

Peshawar consists of three towns within a town: the new university district, the cantonment and the central bazaar. Of the walls and gates once enclosing the city, little remains. As in other garrison towns of Indian origin, the British lived and worked within the cantonment, out of sight and earshot of the bazaar. Here they planted trees and built the barracks, offices, churches and clubs they deemed a vital adjunct to the task of administration and the running of an acceptable social life.

Outside a community hall an elderly man was knocked off his bicycle by a fast-trotting horse buggy. Passers-by looked the other way so I picked the chap up, dusted him down and set him on his way. For this service he insisted on treating me to a curry lunch and unlimited mango juice. 'All Englishmen are gentlemen,' he proclaimed. 'It was a black day for India and Pakistan when they went away.'

I made an excursion by a rattlebones of a bus through tribal territory to Kolhat. The Pathan tribesmen are still fiercely independent. They have succeeded in evading the armies and the tax-collectors of every invader coming through the passes for the whole of history. Their life has been one of peasant farming spiced with violence and robbery. No ruler has ever incorporated them completely. With Partition and the end of British rule the bulls-eye had been removed from the current target. Thus the rifle is beginning to surrender to the pen and the trowel, but the fact that a gun will never entirely fade from the personal effects of a Pathan is given impetus by the village of Durat. Here the local industry is gun production. It is all done by hand in dingy backrooms; dozens of little men filing, scraping and polishing, shaping solid steel without a machine in sight.

Two hundred rupees would have bought me a double-barrelled Sten carbine with a prodigious rate of fire and every side-arm from tiny handbag automatics through walking stick rifles. Anything, in fact, from shotguns to perfect copies of Bren and Vickers machine guns – and all available off the shelf. Each new weapon had to be tested, which meant that, throughout the day, single shots or withering bursts of fire shattered the uneasy peace of Durat.

As I caught my bus back to Peshawar a deranged Pakistani was haranguing a crowd in the street. Drenched in sweat, his features inhuman, he shook with crazed emotion. The children watched, awed, adults stared but none laughed. The bus got me to Peshawar in time to witness another exhibition of what some would describe as madness. This was a penance parade through the streets of the old town. Foreigners are not encouraged to watch these religious-based goings-on in which adults and children lash and lacerate themselves in procession. It was a puzzling sight but I was not allowed to gaze upon it for long. I was chased away angrily by the crowd.

The train that carried me out of Peshawar was the morning express to Rawalpindi. It differed from my Khyber Mail in length, age and stature but not in capacity. Since I was making this journey on a shoestring I gritted my teeth and stuck to third class travel when there was something lower than second class. People at home said I'd never make it travelling third in Pakistan and India but I'm tougher than I look. I gave as good as I got and won myself a square inch or two of corridor. This train was diesel-powered, a more serious locomotive not tolerating a garland of humans around its belly, and the only exterior 'strap-hangers' were those clustered around the steps of each coach.

Through a landscape changing from melancholy Scottish valleys to the cactus-land of Arizona we sped, and within an hour I was endowing Rawalpindi with the status of paradise. At least it would be somewhere to relax on two buttocks instead of one. Along this way, chosen by both road and rail, men and animals had marched when the Moghul emperors came down from Kabul. The Sikhs and British struggled for supremacy along it and, at Partition, pathetic lines of refugees stumbled over it. The Grand Trunk Road as it is called, though it hardly gives that impression, was laid in the 16th century. Two thousand years before, Asoka had lined the route with trees and used it as a royal way.

But older, far older, is the great Indus River which we were to cross at Attock. It was old when Alexander's Greek cavalry watered on its banks, and only the Indus knows the fate of the ancient, forgotten townships hereabouts, townships peopled by citizens of a highly-developed culture long before the Roman legions marched out over Gaul or the armies of Xenophon ravaged the land. And in 1398, after a long age of darkness, Timur the Lame swept across the waters on his swift and terrible descent from Samarkand to Delhi. From the ice-bound Kailas peaks it tumbles out of a stony source like a Scottish trout stream and sweeps in a great curve from the bitter, rocky steppes of Tibet. Onward, gathering strength for the ordeal ahead, it traverses the upland of Baltistan, carves a passage through the Himalayan gorges and spills into the Attock district of the Punjab, where, above Akbar's fort, it is joined by the Kabul River in joyous embrace.

And there, out of the train window, I watched the encircling wall of the great fort emerge on a mound of rock. Below the abutments of its walls the Indus charged swiftly by on a narrowing course to disgorge into a quieter land where it could relax and flex its liquid muscles. Dramatically spanning the angry waters at this point was the Attock Bridge, a cage of heavy girders on stone piers a hundred feet above the river and guarded by soldiers as an important strategic installation. In the whole of a thousand miles or more to its mouth at Karachi less than half a score of bridges cross the Indus.

The fort looked magnificent, commanding the confluence as if its jutting spur had been specifically made for just such an establishment. The walls enclosed an immense area of ground and followed the rise and fall of the rough hillside. Towers and a series of arches continued the whole length, formed, like those in European castles, and used, according to romantic fiction, for pouring boiling oil onto besiegers. Four hundred years of fighting and bloodshed had soaked these walls since the Moghul Emperor Akbar built it to protect the plains of India from northern invaders. A century ago the Sikhs and the British were fighting for it and it still continues its function in the business of war.

The nicest thing about Rawalpindi for me was the English cup of tea and cake and the sit-down they afforded me in the station. With only a short time to spare I saw little of the town but I was to observe it again years later when I took the road north to Gilgit, Baltistan and the border with China – following the tortured meanderings of the great Indus – in 1983.

* * *

'The knot of mountains through which the borders of China, Russia, Afghanistan, India and Pakistan meet, covers an area the size of France. There the bones of the world's skeleton jut into the high deserts of Central Asia.'

This description of the Karakoram mountain territory, part of the titanic Himalayan chain, helped to stir my curiosity, and the fact that the notorious Karakoram Highway – a section of the historic Silk Road – led this way aroused my wanderlust to a degree where I would simply have to go and see.

It is only fairly recently – certainly long after my first arrival in Rawalpindi – that foreigners have been permitted to proceed beyond the town of Gilgit, the main Pakistan centre for the area. However, it is the road itself that provides the chief deterrent to proceeding even that far. 'The most dangerous road in the world' it is labelled and there are many good people living in the plains of the Punjab who, if they have urgent enough reasons to travel to Gilgit, will only contemplate doing so by air.

This notwithstanding, the Karakoram Highway is another miracle of engineering. It was Field Marshal Ayub Khan who conceived the project, considering a road that would link the remote northern areas to the rest of Pakistan vital to the nation's security. The route was to follow the Indus Gorge from near the Tarbela Dam, pass through Kohistan – where no road existed – struggle over the Babusar Pass to Gilgit, then follow the Hunza River to the Chinese border. But instead of using the historic Mintaka Pass – the old Silk Road caravan route – it was to forge a path through the 4,572-metre Khunjerab route to become the highest-altitude highway on earth.

China was a willing collaborator in the scheme, seeing more than 1,240 miles lopped off her existing land route from Sinkiang to the sea. There were, however, few takers when Pakistan put the Karakoram project out to tender. As my colleague and fellow-traveller, Christine Osborne, relates in her book *An Insight and Guide To Pakistan*:

'For a start, 22 million cubic metres of rock had to be shifted and every piece of machinery flown in by helicopter. For the workers, at one time an estimated 10,000 Chinese and 15,000 Pakistanis, the road had to be built while enduring some of the toughest climatic conditions in the world – summer temperatures which blistered their backs through their shirts, and winter temperatures of -20 degrees Centigrade.

Two United States engineering firms who flew up the Indus Gorge by helicopter declared the job was impossible. Ultimately it passed to the Chinese and the Pakistani army engineers of the elite Frontier Works Organisation. Fortunately, most were ignorant of the task ahead. Men were to be blown into gorges by 130 kilometres-an-hour winds, avalanches swept others into the Indus, a truck carrying 45 road workers plunged over a cliff, then a shifting glacier in the Hunza region buried the road, men and equipment under three million tonnes of rubble. Near Sazin, one engineer was killed when a stone, the size of a pullet's egg, fell 900 metres piercing his metal helmet and ending up in his gut.'

Initially, the KKH – as the road is known – runs through undulating countryside through Abbottabad to Mansera. Gradually it starts to climb, curling around the hills and passing through bazaar villages into the rugged splendour of Kohistran. From Besham onwards the road hugs the Indus and the scenery becomes increasingly barren and intimidating. The gorge narrows with sheer sides, the omnipresent rock poised to fall.

My vehicle was another of those gaudily-painted buses only a degree or two better than those on which I had traversed Afghanistan. The seats were padded with plastic which, in the increasing heat, ensures a fried backside, but at least I had a complete seat to myself over the 12-hour grind to Gilgit.

Much of the ribbon of pot-holed tarmac had been laid on ledges blasted and chiselled out of the cliffs, hanging precariously above the river. Local drivers are not known for their driving care but the chief danger was the ever-present risk of landslide, avalanche and that of being struck by boulders perched horrendously on steep slopes of scree overhanging the road. Such an occurrence would sweep a vehicle either into the turgid waters hundreds of feet below or, more likely and unpleasantly, onto the dragons-teeth rocks. Our bus, and others like it, drove with the usual abandon, dependant for safe transit upon the will of Allah and the decibels of their horns. We were held up a number of times by landslides and mud flashes but the Pakistani army had engineer units posted at all the known 'black spots' of the highway so our longest delay was of no more than a few hours' duration. The road had to be cleared by dynamite charges, the resulting explosions increasing the risk of further slides, a factor not lost upon my fellow travellers.

Gilgit spreads itself thinly about two rivers, the Hunza and the Gilgit, which meet nearby. Shaded by a double row of trees, the main street is lined with shops and one-storey government buildings with the bazaar the centre of activity – from which the aroma of smoke from unseasoned wood mixes with that of *kava*, a green tea flavoured with cardamon and almonds. It is not a particularly attractive little place, though better than some of the unsavoury townships I had seen earlier astride the KKH, and a visitor will soon become aware that the town wears an aura of British lineage. The heat of the day was searing; the cool breeze of altitude soon turned to gusts of hot air.

In the heyday of the Silk Road, Gilgit was an important staging post but with the decline of the Tibetan Empire it slipped into oblivion surrounded by hostile tribes. But the 19th-century British Raj brought a new *raison d'etre* and a new prosperity. In 1877 the British established an agency in Gilgit which subsequently became a full-blown garrison and the most isolated outpost of the British Empire. Occupied with suppressing the local tribesmen, watching for Russian incursions from their own expanding empire, and involved in devious political manipulations, the town's new occupiers brought prosperity back to Gilgit. Now, under Pakistani jurisdiction, trade is once again the order of the day. From the lively bazaars, heavily-laden trucks set out for China to deposit apricots, peanuts and almonds in return for rich cargoes of silk from Kashgar. Engaged in this healthy enterprise are a colourful mixture of peoples of many races – Pathans, Kirghiz, Chitralis, Kashgaris, Tshins, Hunzakuts and the pale-skinned Gilgitis themselves, reputed to be descended from the armies of Alexander the Great.

Beyond Gilgit the KKH battles its way northward through a storm of mountains, its tarmac surface interrupted for long stretches where landslides have swept away the original bed. Here and there, side roads, mere dust tracks signposted as 'jeepable road', lead into the granite fastness. It is these tracks that have to be taken to reach the unbelievable oases of Chalt, Nomal, Dianter, Nilt and, most astonishing of all, Hunza. With my heart in my mouth I was driven wildly over paths that, compared to the KKH, give to that road the semblance of a motorway. In this manner I came to Chalt and Nomal, stone villages wearing lush collars of apricot, apple, cherry and peach orchards, grapevines, stately poplar trees and carefully-tended meadows of yellow corn, bisected by irrigation canals fed by mountain torrents.

To reach the communities of Gujjar nomads who occupy the summer-only villages of the smaller valley it was necessary to travel on foot. The walking was hard over the savage terrain and the rarefied atmosphere sapped one's strength but the welcome received from the delightfully-unspoilt villagers was ample reward. At tiny Shanti, its hutments hardly distinguishable from the glacial refuse of stone, I was invited to attend a wedding party where the lengthy intoning of passages from the Koran was interwoven with dancing and the serving of choice portions of goat meat. Not a woman – including the bride – was in sight but surely no wedding reception could ever boast of such a stupendous venue as that of the snow-capped peaks and sparkling glaciers of the surrounding Karakorams. In place of the Wedding March there was the incessant rumble of snow avalanches.

The way out of the Naltar valley led over the 15,000-foot Dianter Pass, an exhausting climb that had me stumbling about dazedly in snow and ice at the summit. On the other side was the Dianter valley, a replica of the Naltar and a botanist's joy of exotic wild flowers. The gorge of the Dianter too had to be negotiated, the path overlooking a thousand-foot drop as it zig-zagged to the vivid green and yellow oasis.

Northward again, the Hunza river leading the KKH along its serpent's course, and I found myself in Valhalla. On one side of the river lay the territory of Naga, dotted with a few trees and the occasional cultivated plot but a pale shadow of the luxuriance that belongs to Hunza to the east. This one-time mini-kingdom is celebrated for its happy, healthy people who suffer little disease, particularly tuberculosis and rheumatism.

Experts differ about the causes of this phenomenon. Some see the Hunzakuts as a superior Aryan strain isolated from contact with the germ-laden outside world. Others point to their food, which has influenced 'natural' diets in the West. Whatever the reasons, it must be said that the Hunza people are of an intelligence and integrity far greater than other Karakoram denizens. It shows in their husbandry and thrift. Nothing is left to chance and each minute plot of land is carefully sprayed and seeded every year. The slightest wastage of land or time could be fatal in their eyes. When supplies are running low, the head of the family ordains that it is better to fast than dip into stocks reserved for planting. These facts I learnt over tea, apricots and cake from Qudratullah Beg, a former Hunza state minister of education who, with his charming family, has lived all his life in Karimabad, the capital.

Karimabad offers an awe-inspiring view of 25,550-foot Rakaposhi soaring skywards at the further end of the valley overlooked, at the opposite end, by Ultar Nala, both a ravine and a multiple peak. Directly beneath it stands the castle of Baltit, for six hundred years the home of the Mirs – or rulers – of Hunza. Slowly rotting on massive timber pillars, the castle with its wooden bay windows adds a touch of fairytale magic to the scene.

On the move again, motivated by the impatient demands of the KKH, I journeyed on to the small community of Passu and the great Batura Glacier. To the north of the Passu plain, a ridge comprising a score of pinnacles dominates the view. Behind them runs the Shimshal river, entering a valley that is the epitome of remote but inhabited areas in the Karakoram where the snow lasts all through the year on its northern slopes and avalanches thunder down its flanks well into spring.

A few dozen miles onward lay the Khunjerab Pass and China. I walked hesitantly across a military-constructed and guarded bridge, knowing I could go no further. Below the trestles, the sound of rocks thudding down with the torrent were drumbeats of menace; as I stood contemplating the end of the KKH, my frustration was lessened by the prospect of a return journey back along the most exciting major artery ever built by man.

* * *

* It is now possible to continue to China.

It is said that British army officers stationed in Rawalpindi found the city to be a particularly pleasant post. 'Pindi', as they called it, had a golf course and there was nearby fishing and hunting. When the temperature soared, they took themselves and their wives to one of the neighbouring hill stations.

Though the temperature soared on both my brief sojourns there, I never got to the hill stations. Instead I sweated it out in Pindi itself, inhaling exotic odours of Moghul spices mingled with incense in the packed narrow alleys of the Urdu Bazaar that branches off the Murree Road to Islamabad. Disdainful of their new and very un-Pakistanlike capital, the local citizenry describe it as but a 'suburb of Rawalpindi'.

Returning to the trains I was approached by two begging children, one blind. While I was searching for a coin a man came up and threw a bucket of water over them so that they shrank hurriedly away. I knew then that I had reached a land overstocked with humanity and, in consequence, contemptuous of human values.

The train to Lahore was not crowded by Pakistani standards and by dint of swift action I got myself a seat. It was a dawdling, unconcerned sort of train, determined not to exert itself under the hot afternoon sun when only mad dogs and Englishmen were afoot. The landscape was devoid of drama but not of interest. Vultures roosted atop the thick-stemmed People Trees which have a religious significance that escaped me. Buffalo tramped eternal circles to operate capstan pumps and, on the roads, repair gangs leaned on shovels to an even greater extent than they do in Britain. Painted buses and painted lorries overtook our train, ragged urchins played in muddy water holes and, as the afternoon wore on, the road repair gangs started working again, two men to a shovel.

It was late evening when the train reached the stud in the neckband of Pakistan which is Lahore. l alighted into a vast station – but then, of course, Pakistani stations have to be vast to accommodate all the service rooms and classes thereof. Those serving the bigger cities have two types of restaurant in addition to their grading; one serving local spicy vegetarian food and the other a cuisine of more Western preference.

Escaping from the hubbub of the station I was at once in a city of faintly decayed beauty. The pavements and street verges were crammed as I have never seen a city crammed before. It was a restless crowd come suddenly alive and charged with emotion and an awareness that a long, suffocating day had relented. Groups sat around the hookahs outside the cafés and youths strolled clasping each other's hands. Both beggars and children held out theirs for alms in an automatic reflex at the sight of a foreigner.

The Clifton Hotel was one of many similar concrete blocks near the station. It was a dormitory of no comfort or character but sufficed at 30 pence a night. I was up early next morning to escape the claustrophobic confines and see the city before it could sink into its midday lethargy.

The bazaars lay just outside the old walled city but the citadel itself is today enclosed in the modern town, its gates only ornaments engraved upon what remains of massive walls. The site had been occupied from early times and much of it stands high above the surrounding country, raised on the bones of a succession of former habitations. Hindu tradition traces the origin of Lahore to Loh, son of Rama, some time at the end of the first century AD. It then fell under the domination of the Ghazni Sultans and, later, the Moghul Empire under which the city reached its greatest magnificence. Invasion and conquest formed an unoriginal ingredient to its history from the time of Bahadur Shah I until 1800. The Sikhs ruled over Lahore from 1768 until, with the rest of the Punjab, it came under British domination.

To me the place seemed choked with Moghul history seasoned with a dash of Kipling – if that makes any sense. A turmoil of impressions stick in the mind: the Badshahi Masjid's lofty structure of red sandstone, the buildings of Ranjit Singh – the great Sikh, the Shalimar Gardens with their placid pools and inoperative fountains – a few quiet acres of trees under which chipmunks romped, Lahore Fort with its graceful pavilions and gardens neater than Shalimar – where I evoked the Kipling era through Zam-Zam, the famous gun he wrote about in *Kim*, a caged relic girded about with wild traffic. Modern Lahore's Mall runs brashly through the new city, a wide leafy artery proud to show off some very lovely examples of avant-garde architecture.

I lost myself in one of the bazaars, the Anarkal, which is named after a girl. She was so beautiful the Emperor Akbar took her into his harem and she danced for him weaving round the great soldier a web of infatuation. Prince Salim, the emperor's son, fell in love with her and one day Akbar intercepted a look that passed between them. In his jealousy, he had Anarkal buried alive. The prince became the Emperor Salim Jahangir, another emperor who loved to make gardens, and on the tomb he built for Anarkal he inscribed: 'If only I could see the face of my love again, then until the end of the world I would praise my creator'.

So went the legend but Salim was by no means the blue-eyed prince; nor was Akbar as savage as the tale describes. History turns Salim into the 'baddie,' crediting him with raising an army against his father, though upon arriving in Lahore at the head of his 40,000 horsemen he fell contrite at his parent's feet. After his father's death he resumed his more characteristic ways and changed his name to Jehangir, the 'ruler of the world'.

Legend or history, the facts remain. The tomb of the lovely Anarkal is a miserly affair, nothing approaching the magnificence of the one he built for his supposedly despised father.

In the Shalimar gardens I made the acquaintance of a student who invited me to his home, where in his upstairs bed-sit we cooled ourselves before his fan. We drank iced water which, at a Pakistan midday, is nectar – though you discover only later it's polluted.

He was plainly a student of history, and possibly of psychology as well. I asked him about the caste system in the Indian subcontinent, how it worked and how it stood today. He launched into a spate of explanation.

Around 2,000 BC there was a movement of Dravidian people of the south to the north. Later, tall, fair-skinned Aryans who roamed the Middle East came to India. Their hymns became the Vedas, in Sanskrit, from which it became clear that they introduced the original concept of caste. This system assigned social rank and honour according to skin colour, so that when the Aryans intermarried with the darker local people, the coloured offspring could be assigned a proper place in society. Other practices associated with Hinduism, as it developed later, were already in effect at the time, among them the sacredness of cattle and the cremation of the dead. Today, caste has sunk to class – which was imported by the British, to whom any shade of dark skin represented an inferior being. But, as with many things in Asia, the injustices are dying and the borderlines of status becoming less pronounced.

I was made aware that my historical knowledge of India was not what it should be. To me the basic reasons for Partition were never clearly defined. My student thereupon proceeded to fill in some of the gaps.

The Aryans together with the native inhabitants settled down to a thousand years of reasonably harmonious growth until, in AD 650, the Arabs arrived. The Muslims' method of asserting their influence was the direct one of ruthless conquest and, on the way, taking a great delight in huge barbecues of the sacred cattle. No attempt was made at conversion, and the breach between two religions ensured that Hinduism would survive, eventually causing a physical partition of the nation.

Some converts to Islam were realized, however, especially among the outcast Hindus, who had nothing to lose anyway. They didn't gain much either, because each of the successive invaders from Afghanistan or further north brought their own administrators. None of these Islamic invasions was ever permanent – even those of Timur and Babur, who had profound effects upon the land, the latter setting up the great Moghul dynasty.

All successive rulers continued with the policy of Hindu persecution until 1761 when the British, along with the Dutch and the Portuguese, began appearing on the trading scene. The British stayed. To them a native was a native, and as long as he could make good tea it didn't really matter whether he was Muslim or Hindu. There was no attempt to mediate in the religious quarrels and, though it must be admitted that we materially helped both sides, our attitude was that as long as they weren't Christians, one brand of heathen was as good or bad as another, so what the hell. And so Hindu and Islamic nationalism developed separately and came to a head in 1947 when the Union Jack came down and two new flags went up.

The hate between the two simmers, and it has been encouraged by the first war between them that cut Pakistan down to size and produced, from her former eastern territory, a third nation, Bangladesh. And this hate is amply demonstrated by the sparsity of border crossing points along the whole of the thousand and more miles of frontier between Pakistan and India.

To make even a move from Lahore towards the border you then needed a Road Permit. This was obtained from a building called the Secretariat, where you were granted an audience with a man who filled out the necessary forms. If he didn't like your face he could, and did, refuse to grant you anything. The permit was gratis but the time wasted in obtaining it was expensive. The border was open only on Wednesdays and Thursdays. Arrive on a Friday morning and you'd be in for a long wait.

It is no good being in a hurry at a place such as this. Amritsar was no more than thirty miles ahead but travellers of this road gave over a whole day to the whims of authority and set their patience-endurance thermostats accordingly. Even so, I found it hard to suppress a feeling of accomplishment as I stepped onto a change of road surface that was India.

Hardly had I been in India for ten minutes when two sights struck me with considerable impact. One was the sudden increase in the number and visibility of women, the second was the comparative nudity of the men. During the drawn-out trivialities of the Indian border negotiation I was entertained by an ancient Indian character straight out of the pages of *Tom Brown's Schooldays*. From his perch on a cycle rickshaw, surrounded by a grinning retinue of loin-clothed courtiers, the old man regaled me with idyllic memories of his days under the British Raj. He reeled off a string of names – Queen Victoria, the Prince of Wales, Earl Mountbatten – with whom he had chatted on some viceregal lawn. He was, he said, of princely blood himself and would I do him the honour of joining him for a *chota peg* at his residence? Then, in a lower voice, he made a most unviceregal suggestion, and I was to learn that, as well as being slightly potty, his favourite procurement point was the frontier post. As an introduction to India it was a bit of a let-down.

It was a road, not a railway, that led me to Amritsar and a communal taxi that carried me there. In disbelief I found myself sharing the vehicle with eleven others. The driver laughed. 'My record is nineteen,' he told me, 'but it's hard on the springs.' The thirty miles was hard on my rump too, for

I sat on the bonnet trying not to block the driver's view.

Amritsar. Stronghold of the Sikhs. After the flat, undistinguished terrain of this part of the Punjab the city of the Golden Temple is heady stuff. Amritsar means, literally, the Tank of Nectar and it once consisted of a forest lake surrounded by a collection of villages. The pool was enlarged and the villages merged into a single community. In the middle of the lake the Sikhs built the original Temple. This shrine to an alien religion was as a red rag to a bull as far as the Moghul rulers were concerned and they destroyed and desecrated it again and again. But the Sikhs never gave up, even in the face of blood-curdling torture and persecution.

The founder of Sikhism was Guru Nanak, born in 1469. He believed in a sternly monotheistic approach to religion and taught penance and pilgrimages. He declared that all men had a right to search for a knowledge of God, irrespective of caste.

A visit to the temple is an experience not to be missed. The fervent adoration by the thousands of ever-present pilgrims is unfettered by formality or pompous reverence. True, like the Sikhs themselves, a visitor has to don some form of headgear, but this is counteracted by a pleasant lack of commercialism not shared, alas, by the Muslims.

The lake, or pool as it is described, is surrounded by a pavement of white marble, and the temple itself is reached by a marble causeway. Its bronze plates, lavishly covered with pure gold, burn in the tropical sun and reflect, dazzlingly, in the static water. What Mecca is to the Muslim, Benares to the Hindu, the Golden Temple of Amritsar is to the Sikh. When I was there, the water of a section of the pool was being changed, which involved the construction of a temporary dam of sand bags and loose soil. The work was a labour of love being carried out by queues of pilgrims, each individual balancing a bowl of soil upon his head. I offered my services but was courteously refused through a reasoning far stronger than any trade union dictums.

The hot marble burnt the soles of my bare feet. Day in and day out, people stream to the gilded jewelbox sanctum where priests chant hymns and the devout prostrate themselves before the *Granth Sahib*, the Holy Book. The temple is thronged, worn by feet and alive with the energy of faith.

The buildings around the Sacred Pool shelter pilgrims who come to worship from distant places. One such establishment is the *Langar*. Essentially a man of God, Nanak was a friend of humanity as well: the institution of the 'Free Kitchen' bears testimony to this. None knew better than Nanak that religious instruction sounds hollow on an empty stomach. Cooked food is distributed twice a day to all comers, irrespective of caste, creed and nationality, and paid for from Temple funds. Of similar principle is the *Shri Guru Ram Das Nivas*, which is a free hostel for pilgrims maintained by the Temple authorities. Of barrack-like proportion it contains bedrooms of simple adequacy.

In Jallianwala Garden, near the temple, where old men doze, there are holes in the wall ringed in iron. These are bullet holes, the scars of 1919, of General Dyer's massacre of 400 passive devotees. Twenty years after Jallianwala the British left India and the Punjab was divided. 'Everything was divided in the initial divorce,' an elderly railway official in the garden told me. 'After the track, the engines and coaches; even the typewriters and the stationery in the railway offices. But it wasn't just a division of property,' he went on, 'it was a division of people. The massacres were horrible, unbelievable, unbelievable in their frenzy – far, far worse than anything in General Dyer's day.' There was sadness rather than anger in his eyes as he pointed to the holes – and he was not to know of the future 1984 conflict between the army and extremists when the Holy Temple's gilded dome itself would be similarly pockmarked.

The town of Amritsar is a bewildering maze of narrow, overpopulated streets but it made a deep impression not so much for the town itself as for its citizens. The Sikh is a full-blooded Indian who, by the law of his religion, is forbidden to cut his hair or beard. The hair is therefore twisted up and often elegantly concealed beneath a turban. His general appearance is well-groomed and martial, like some magnificent battle charger. He is proud and polite, often truculent but, above all, he is a man apart. Punjab women wear wide pyjama trousers, gripped at the ankles, called *salvar* and a gaily coloured shirt, or *kamiz*, tightened at the waist, split at the sides and almost reaching the knee. The colour of the women and the stature of the men, for me, make Amritsar.

I moved around by bicycle rickshaw, a two-passenger affair of one-Indian power. The number of cycles and cycle-rickshaws is astronomical, and what amazed me was the skill with which Indians contrived to pedal a cycle through densely-thronged streets with staggering loads attached to both rider and machine. A passenger is expected to alight and walk on an uphill gradient, a consideration I was pleased to proffer for, in a temperature well above 40 degrees, I felt for my drivers.

My hotel, near the station, was grand by name if not by nature, though again prudently inexpensive. Curry was fast becoming my staple diet partly because of its cheapness and variety but also on account of my theory that no germ could possibly survive among the chillies and peppery substances that made eating akin to swallowing fire.

My second night I succumbed to an attack of dysentery nonetheless, and spent the whole of it in a semi-coma squatting miserably over a hole in a corner of the hotel courtyard. There were moments of that night when I would have cheerfully died – and in this, two vultures seemed to be in complete accord. They came and perched on a wall opposite, ominously watching with beady eyes, and it was they, more than anything, that effected my recovery.

After Amritsar town the railway station was an oasis of calm and order, rudely shattered when a train came in. Ragged figures lay about the station approaches though, in this part of the world, a man or woman lying in a street or public place does not always indicate abysmal poverty, disease or death. People frequently sleep outside their houses or workplace and, for the poorer citizens, the street is as good a place to rest as any. But everything in India has to have its contradictions. One poor wretch I saw sprawled on a platform choked his life away before his body was removed, quite unconcernedly, by two railway policeman.

My train to Delhi was the Flying Mail. The largest railway system in Asia and one of the most heavily used in the world was assuredly the greatest bequest the British administration made to India. Handed over as a cluster of private companies in 1947, names that have a similar ring to our own companies in Britain of a generation ago became absorbed into a nationalised system. Names like 'Bombay, Baroda and Central India', 'Great Indian Peninsular Railway', 'Madras and South Mahratta', have, like our own, become regionally titled. My Flying Mail belonged to the Northern Railway. As with all trains in India, their heaviness and frequent stops preclude fast travel and this one was no exception. It was diesel-hauled, made reasonable time and from its windows I saw a little of the countryside of northern India – though, in bottom class, compressed for fourteen hours with thirty-six others in a compartment designed for eight, my chief concern revolved around simple survival amongst the sweaty, unclean gel of humanity. My closest neighbour – his perspiring body hard up against my own the whole time – was a vicious Sikh who kept mouthing threats every time I moved, attempting to change position. I'm quite certain that, had he been able to reach the weapon, he would have happily knifed me before journey's end.

Buffaloes wallowing in mud ponds and half-empty rivers, storks on rooftops, vultures awaiting a death that is ever a part of life in India, occasional long-ruined mosques providing a terrible monument to the berserk savagery of Partition and, on station platforms, the beggars. These were the sights that registered and proved to my eyes that we were not passing through a dull corner of Surrey. The beggars, to my surprise, were aggressive, demanding and very much a tolerated part of the scene. They travelled on the train itself, passing, in spite of the scrum, through the coaches announcing their infirmities and bad-luck stories in sing-song voices or distributing the facts in specially-prepared leaflets. A different set of beggars 'worked' each section of the route and their takings were universally good.

We were still on the *Serak-i-acam*, the Grand Trunk Route. The Moghuls loved beauty in spite of their ferociousness, and in the dry, heat-laden plains they must have thought often of their cool Asian gardens. Thus, at every stage of this leg of my journey, long-established walled plots of flowering shrubs, exotic trees and green-walled tanks buttressed by elephant ramps sprang up along the route. Many were overgrown, but they enriched a mediocre scenery.

The train drew into New Delhi Station after nightfall. Shakily I emerged into the city passing dutifully through the third class exit.

If nothing else, I felt a close affinity with the country I had come to see.

PART 2 – ROUND AND ABOUT INDIA

Chapter One

On my 1987 arrival in India, the affinity took a little longer to establish. It was hardly accelerated by the status of my first night's accommodation. The Maurya Sheraton is not exactly representative of the average Indian's pad.

There was a reason for my choosing such an exalted hotel; actually, two reasons. One was that I had been granted facilities to stay at any of the Welcomgroup Hotels' establishments along my Indian route, and who am I to spurn such a handsome invitation? Secondly, my observations of the Indian subcontinent were not necessarily confined only to the lower end of the human scale; I wanted to see how *everybody* lived.

I fear I have become somewhat blasé about Delhi. Whenever I go there for reason of onward transit elsewhere, it is presumed I want a stopover to 'do' the sights. As a result I have 'done' them so frequently and usually in a frame of mind impatient for the region of India I have come to see that I grudge the time wasted there. That's being rather unkind to Delhi for, assuredly, it's worth any number of stopovers.

In Agra Fort, there is a room with a view. In this room Shahjahan was imprisoned seven years before his death by Aurangzeb, his jealous eldest son. Aurangzeb was a fanatic and a callous swine into the bargain. The view from his father's cell was that of the Taj Mahal, the creation of the imprisoned man that was also tomb and monument to his adored wife. But cruel though he might have been, Aurangzeb had something of his father's architectural vision. It was he who brought Delhi to its period of greatest glory. The Red Fort, sublime wonder of the capital, was again the creation of Shahjahan, though a defensive barbican was added by Aurangzeb much to his father's chagrin. From his prison Shahjahan wrote to his son, 'You have made a bride of the palace and thrown a veil over her face.'

These two men, in bitter opposition, did more for Delhi prior to the 18th century than any others. Following Aurangzeb's own death, the city declined. It was sacked by Madir Shah and then by the Afghan, Ahmed Shah Durrani, who made off with the fabulous Peacock Throne. In 1803, Delhi fell into the hands of the British, and from 1911 until Indian independence in 1947, we managed to complete the dream capital of New Delhi just in time for it to be turned over to the new nation.

When Calcutta was a village of mudflats, and Madras was but a trading post, Delhi had already been a capital of an empire for five hundred years. For even longer, it had been a concentration of eight villages which form part of Delhi today; an urban sprawl welding them together. And that, perhaps, is its saving grace for the dividing line between the old and comparatively new is sharp. From New Delhi to Old Delhi, one can witness the transformation from cool, spacious avenues to a labyrinth of small streets studded with temples, mosques and bazaars. Much of the impressive New is the brainchild of Sir Edwin Lutyens, though his love of European Renaissance was diluted by an oriental style beloved of Lord Hardinge, the Viceroy at the time, and his pro-Indian school of thought.

One of my earlier sojourns in Delhi had been with a group of senior ex-soldiers and civil servants under the direction of a one-time brigadier. The British Raj had been the theme of the visit and, though empire-building might be frowned upon in this day and age, once upon a time Britain was rather good at it, our Indian adventure settling comfortably into the nation's heritage. Though an ex-soldier myself from a regiment that saw service under Clive, I nevertheless felt an interloper – but my distinguished companions were a tolerant bunch. A pre-dinner drink brought us together with a clutch of Indian Army generals, summoned by bush telegraph to the Imperial Hotel's faded glories to share in the ritual of sipping our duty-free 'chota-pegs' and wax eloquent upon the 'the old times'.

I was to learn that anyone around today who served in Delhi in the time of the Raj, will not, on the face of it, see great change, except that Old and New Delhi are now virtually one city. All the famous features, the Red Fort, the Jama Masjid, Chowringhee Bazaar, the Kulb Minar Tower, Lutyens' haughty state buildings and the president's Palace (once Viceroy House) remain and are well preserved; the residential area around the Delhi Gymkhana Club is as regal and well-kept as ever. The present President's bodyguard, which we were invited to view in their magnificent scarlet and blue uniform with silver laces, is indistinguishable from the former Viceroy's bodyguard.

Still on a military theme, I came across St James's Church. It was built by Colonel James Skinner, who raised the famed Skinner's Horse, the right of the line in the cavalry regiments of the old Indian Army. At a time when he lay near to death, he swore to build the church if he recovered, which he promptly did. For me, however, there was a personal connection with those stirring times for my 1960s Territorial Army company commander was, for a period, none other than the colonel himself, who had, in the meantime, retired with the rank of major-general.

My living standards and grades of accommodation in Delhi have been as varied as the reasons for my sojourns there. Once, the roof over – or under – my head had been the simple Hotel Madras in Connaught Circus, where twelve of us slept in a room containing but three beds. By cannibalising them, we made a communal shakedown on the floor where we slept quite comfortably. But a sweltering temperature of over 45 degrees drove me to the roof, where the ceiling of an Indian sky offered an illusion of alleviation. At other times, my pad has been on more exalted planes though the less memorable for it.

But whatever the quality of one's home from home, to gaze in wonder at Humayun's Tomb, built by a grieving widow for her defunct emperor husband, is a privilege undenied. The husband was one of the earlier Moghuls and his wife, Haji Begum, was to join him there. Another treat is to walk along the Rajpath through India Gate; a kind of Marble Arch and Menin Gate rolled into one. This broadest avenue of Delhi is an essay in imperialism with its solid, portentous Secretariat Buildings – an oriental Whitehall – and gigantic Presidential palace. Nothing is beautiful here, not even the formal gardens. Instead, everything is heavily impressive, far more so than the equivalent structures in London. I like best the

Red Fort, standard sandstone symbol of Moghul power and elegance, and Old Delhi with its twisting lanes, seething bazaars and cows that sit complacently in the street. There is something faintly Chinese about the place – had I been dropped from an aeroplane straight into the Chandni Chowk I would have surmised I was in Canton – that is the very essence of the unchanging East.

The sometimes forbidding aspect of New Delhi fails to deter the Indian worker from publicly airing his grievances there. Demonstrations are as numerous in the Indian capital as they are in our own. So far I have witnessed two. In one, I was very nearly caught in the crossfire. It was, I remember, off the homely-sounding Chelmsford Road that I saw the gathering of the mobs and heard the twittering of voices raised in anger. I went to investigate. There they were: rank upon rank of Hindus swelling into a great bubble of humanity threatening to burst and spill out upon a main artery of the city. Police were barring the road, and as I skipped lightheartedly across the open ground in front of the crowd, the riot squad arrived. They poured out from behind a row of houses, visors across their faces and *lathis* brandished in their hands. It was then that I realized I was dead-centre between the opposing forces. But there is the tenacity of the journalist in me and I held my ground, trying to focus my camera on the daunting sight of the advancing law. My camera was one of those that requires a certain amount of adjustment and manipulation, and all I could think about was when the first stones were going to fly? Finally, in desperation, I depressed the shutter and got the hell out it, not daring to run in case it should draw the stones.

An economic way of getting around Delhi is to use the city buses. They are invariably full, but there's always room (though you'd never believe it) and they are cheap. They are fast, too, and at every roundabout have you all in a heap. On one, I attempted to reach the suburb of Kailash but ended up on the wrong side of town. At Kailash was the home of a business acquaintance of a cousin of mine and I thought it would be nice to see how a well-to-do Indian family lived.

Defeated in the quest, I transferred my trust to a turbaned scooter-taxi driver. He was a wild, flamboyant sort of chap who straightaway took me under his wing. 'My name is Sinbad, what is yours?' he began with a familiar formula. 'I am a Sikh,' he added proudly in a manner that made it clear he considered himself superior to the common Hindu herd. Having cemented relations and exchanged our life stories, his machine gave up the ghost. I suppose I could have left him to it but desertion – leaving him to the unsympathetic Hindu masses – seemed a betrayal so, beneath a fireball of a sun, with bits of magneto all over the pavement, we effected repairs. The name of my cousin's friend was Gupta, which is the equivalent of Smith in Britain. Our enquiries in the Kailash district unearthed the fact that everyone was a Gupta of some description. By a process of elimination, we whittled them down.

Whisky sodas on the patio, instant hot baths, superbly cooked Indian delicacies and a chauffeur-driven car at my disposal; the Gupta family did me proud. This was living at the upper end of the social scale. But even this held a moment of crisis. I was invited for a drink by the late General Chandhuri, former Commander-in-Chief of the Indian Army at the exclusive Gymkhana Club. My trousers and shirts were creased beyond recognition as well as being none too clean, and where the devil was the tie I thought I'd packed? Aided and abetted by my hosts, I was made to resemble something akin to a British gentleman and duly reported to the holy of holies. I needn't have worried. The General wore an open neck shirt and well-worn slacks. 'Why on earth did you want to come here dressed like that just to have a jar with me?' he enquired incredulously.

My host was a delightful personality; a man of the world if ever there was one. His conversation was not restricted to military matters either for he had later become India's ambassador to Canada, a new horizon that had opened to him in his eventful life. As we conversed, he sipped a succession of Bloody Marys, while I, with my well-cultivated Indian thirst, stuck to Indian Kingfisher beer.

For a start, it was back to high living again on my latest arrival in the Indian capital, with the Maurya Sheraton – indisputably Delhi's top hotel – pampering me rotten. A car from the tourist office arrived next morning to deposit me at New Delhi Station, where my brief new honeymoon with the nobs of high society abruptly ended.

New Delhi Station was not what it was. Even over the last fifteen years I could discern a change. Once, such termini had been fulcrums of Anglo-Indian security with steam, piston grease, the stuffy smell of waiting-rooms, starched white dining-room napkins and smudgily-printed timetables as their basic ingredients. In Indian cities, the grandest and most ornate of all public buildings were usually the railway stations and offices; all domes, clocks, stained-glass windows and immense glass and girder roofs, beneath which the glistening tracks lay like symbols of order in chaos. But though most of these ingredients are still present, a new undefinable element has crept in. The divisions of class remain but it has become an all-Indian distinction and somehow, they can't quite carry it off; the edges are again ragged and blurred. All around lay the theatrical confusion of India: a frenzy of humanity in dhotis, in saris, in swathed torn rags, in turbans, loin-cloths, yellow priestly robes or ill-fitting awkwardly worn Western type suits. No longer was there a vestige of order amongst this confusion which the Empire had once tamed. In the waiting rooms and on the rambling platforms, entire families sat or reclined on piles of baggage tied up with string while an occasional beggar darted spider-like out of his web to seize upon a likely straggler. Into this welter of confusion, I was pitched headfirst and the transformation was momentarily painful. But for my journey southward I was not, through necessity and desire, aiming to travel bottom class so the pitching was not quite from one extreme to the other. And I was possessed of an Indian Railway travel document – an Indrail pass – that would ease my new journeying considerably. The Indrail pass, I should explain, is in effect a railway ticket obtainable for hard currency payment by anyone permanently residing outside India and it gives unlimited travel for varying periods on any train on Indian Railway's network. It is available in the three current classes of travel, namely air-conditioned, first/AC chair, and second, for a sum of money that, given the size of India and the mileage of its railway makes it the travel bargain of the century. I detest air-conditioning so had opted for the first-class grade of travel which permitted me, should I so wish, to sit but not sleep (in a sleeper coach) in air-conditioned class.

I had also taken the precaution of reserving in advance a berth on the midday-departing Kerala Express, in which I would be incarcerated for two nights and the best part of three days during its whistle-stop journey to India's far south. I had fallen foul of the ticket and berth reservation-acquiring hurdle at stations on previous occasions and, for those readers not in the know, an insight into this seemingly simple task would not come amiss at this point.

There is, of course, 'no problem'. Anyone can buy a journey ticket from the booking office right up to the moment of a train's departure. But without a reservation, a journey ticket is useless – Indian trains are, even today, invariably full, so tickets are issued for specific trains only (and the procedure for obtaining a refund should you chicken out is so daunting as to be unthinkable). Thus you move to the queue for a reservation ticket, only to discover that before you can get this you need a form. Nothing in India is obtainable without a form and these forms come not from the reservations office or the booking office but the enquiry office. So you are standing in your third queue before you've got anywhere. The form requires a host of personal details: age, sex, address and telephone number, class of travel, place of departure, destination, special requests, two signatures, and – a catch question unless you've done your homework beforehand and obtained the information from the railway timetable (if not, it means another excursion and re-queuing) – the *number* of the train. Back in the first queue, you eventually – for Indians are masters at queue jumping – find yourself before a harassed clerk who will scrutinise your form for omissions and turn to a pile of enormous dog-eared ledgers. Your train, he will probably tell you – if you can understand his Indian rapid-fire English, which you assuredly won't – is fully booked. Here, two alternatives are offered to you. You can be the umpteenth on a waiting list or you can travel at a later date. If you opt for postponement, you are still unable to take possession of the reservation ticket until you buy a journey ticket, which of course means another queue and the whole performance commences all over again. However, it has to be said that the waiting list is not as hopeless as it might appear since all trains seemingly hold a quota of seats reserved for waiting list passengers. And there are short cuts, of which that godsend, the Indrail pass, is one. It affords a degree of priority and cuts out reservation fees and express train supplements.

Just as surprising in view of the stupefying bureaucracy, is that when you later present yourself at what may be a different station hundreds of miles away, there on the platform notice board and on the coach door is your name, probably misspelt, but unmistakably yours. In some extraordinary way, the whole ungainly system works. Though I had made my reservation in faraway London, my name, even correctly spelt, was displayed on the door of my first-class coach of the Kerala Express for all to see. Amongst the confusion of New Delhi Station and the far greater ferment of Indian Railways carrying upwards of 17 million passengers every day, the trains depart and arrive more or less on time with an unfailing regularity. Monkeys change the signals, dissident students derail the engines, floods wash away the track, cows fall asleep on the line, yet somehow the trains keep running. It is nothing short of a miracle, and what's more, one with no government subsidy.

In this instance, the minor miracle of my current reservation might have been helped along a little by Mr Dharom Dev, the then supervisor of the International Tourist Bureau of the Northern Railway Region at New Delhi Station. A fount of knowledge of things railway was Mr Dev, a delightful personage of square, squat build, with a face somewhat akin to a benevolent Mussolini. His domain had something of the air of the outpatients' department of an NHS hospital, the 'patients' sitting in rows of chairs waiting to be called before various desks dealing with different ailments. Behind each desk sat white-coated men and women intermittently calling 'next', and was it imagination or did I catch a whiff of disinfectant? In Mr Dev's inner sanctum, I was plied with sweet, milky tea and an enthusiastic tirade covering every aspect of Indian Railways' operations. Now and again, I was asked a question but was never given the chance to answer it. I would, he announced, return to Delhi from Bombay at the end of my current travels on the prestigious, air-conditioned Rajdhani Express and, without pausing for my assent, put the machinery of my berth reservation into motion there and then. With tea running out of my ears, I was swept from the office and onto the departure platform of the Kerala Express, to be shown into my first-class compartment. I was to share it with one other – Devendra Gupta Arya, M.Sc. (Ag.), Hort., divisional manager of the National Seeds Corporation Ltd, who would be accompanying me over the first half of the route. I was also introduced to the train commander, who was bade to keep an eye on me throughout the journey. Assuredly, my descent from high-living was to be a most gentle process.

Introductions and farewells completed, the Kerala Express slid out of the station some seven minutes late, and I settled back to enjoy the passing scenery of India. My compartment was a single one, designed to contain four daytime travellers and transform into two bunks for night travel. The windows were barred but openable; the interior walls in need of a coat of paint. A battery of fans affixed to the ceiling maintained a cooling hurricane at the expense of a sullen roar soon to be drowned by that of the train's ebullient movement. India's capital dissolved into fragments of urban slum and was gone.

To reach the south and its destination, Trivandrum, 1,898 miles distant, the Kerala Express carves a great arc through Central India. The first 125 miles and two-and-a-half hours to Agra I had covered before.

In 1964, a new train appeared upon the tracks of the Central Railway, the first in India to aim at luxury and high speed. Headed by a distinctive black steam engine, the Taj Express had whisked me to Agra. Perhaps 'whisked' is not strictly true but it was then the fastest I had travelled on an Indian train. More noteworthy was the comfort. Though I was travelling only second class, I was struck all of a heap by air-conditioning and tea brought round by white-coated waiters. My fellow passengers were mostly families on a day's outing.

It was Akbar who made Agra great. Not much happened before the Moghuls came or, for that matter, afterwards. The short golden age, during which Agra alternated with Delhi as capital, came to an end with the reign of Shahjahan but it had an unforgettable climax in the Taj Mahal. The population today is 500,000 although it is still nothing more than an overgrown and ramshackle village. I had joined up with a young Englishman to share a cycle rickshaw and, together, we explored the district.

One of the two shrines of Agra is its fort. Here, in rusty-red sandstone, is the story of the Moghul Empire. Inside its forbidding walls are white marble palaces, mosques and courtyards, which took three reigns to build. I found it somewhat more decrepit than that of Lahore but the architecture exciting in its shapeliness. Enclosed lawns provided a haven of peace from the hard-selling touts outside.

From the ramparts, the view is of Agra's other shrine, the Taj Mahal itself. It is a rear view, not immediately recognisable, with the shallow Jumna River and wallowing buffaloes in the foreground. What can one say about this greatest example of architecture of all time that has not been said already in poetry and in prose? Many great creations such as the Parthenon of Athens have a fame that surpasses their beauty. But here in the Taj Mahal, you have perfection together with the greatest love story ever told.

Shahjahan's queen was the inspiration. She died giving him their fourteenth child and her passing broke Shahjahan's heart. His hair turned grey, he changed his royal robes for simple muslin and, as the huge procession of mourners brought the body back from Burhanpur, he vowed to build a memorial surpassing everything the world had ever seen in beauty. He imported skilled craftsmen from the furthest reaches of the known world: from Persia to Turkey, from France and Italy. He put an army of 20,000 labourers to work, and when he himself died, his body was laid beside his wife where it remains today, a smaller tomb squeezed in beside the other.

It is said that the Taj speaks a different language to the soul depending upon the time of day – or night – it is looked upon. I would add that what it has to say depends upon the circumstances of one's coming. To the rich industrialist, it is a shapely piece of real estate, to the prosperous American tourist, it is an impressive backdrop against which to photograph 'Junior' for the folks back home. But for the overlander, as I was then, poor in pocket but rich in experience, arriving scarred by the grime of travel, it is the supreme reward.

This time round, however, I obtained not so much as a glimpse of the Taj Mahal as my train halted at Agra station and impatiently moved off again bent upon shaking the dust of central India from its wheels. And dust there was in plenty. With the failure of the 1987 monsoon, the countryside was to exhibit a pitiful face; the face of a desert when no desert should have been. Unfolding before me were the carefully-divided plots of land where crops and serried rows of green pasture should have shown, all now turned into a bleached skeleton; an ocean of dead soil roasting beneath a burning sun. And the irony was that to the east and in Bangladesh, everything was being destroyed by water following an over-abundance of rain.

To raise our own spirits, my companion and I engrossed ourselves in animated discussion, the subjects ranging from world affairs and the lack of discipline prevalent in the world to, on a more personal level, a discourse on the fortunes of our respective families. He travelled about India a great deal, he told me, especially between his home at Vijayawada near the east coast and Delhi and, despising the airlines, he did it all by trains. He was a fervent disciple of the railways so I couldn't resist reminding him of their British ancestry. He needed no reminding. 'It's the best thing you ever did,' he remarked, as if I was personally responsible.

Sewing a subcontinent together, the Imperial Raj set themselves a herculean task. A daily average of something like 17 million passengers and 800,000 tons of freight pulled by 11,000 locomotives over more than 38,500 miles of track linking 7,072 stations, all this maintained by 1.6 million workers is an achievement of which one can be proud.

The first train ran in 1853 on one of three lines begun to connect Calcutta, Bombay and Madras. But the British surveyors had learnt railway construction on a much kinder topography, whereas in India they were confronted by a merciless landscape: rivers that ran seasonally from a trickle to a torrent requiring immense bridges, sheer outcrops demanding formidable gradients, and the vast distances eating into slender resources.

Because two gauges of track had existed in competition in Britain, a single gauge of five feet six inches was decreed for India. But in 1870, to save money, a one-metre gauge was added. Narrow gauges of two feet six inches followed. And to compound the confusion, even after India went metric in 1956, it continued to convert its one-metre gauge track to broad gauge. Thus, in effect, there are two rail systems within Indian Railways: those of broad and medium gauge. But they don't compete. Instead, the compilers of the railway timetable strive to integrate the systems into one gigantic complex.

The major portion of Indian Railways is broad gauge and we were riding it now. Because welded track is something India cannot yet afford, the riding is bumpy and noisy but the additional inches make for extra space in the coaches. Even the toilets – some including rudimentary showers – are more spacious than their European equivalents.

Such was the heat of the day my companion and I took frequent showers, but because the toilets were not equipped with fans it did little to help. Even before redressing – difficult enough in a wet, confined and swaying space – one was once more covered in a muck sweat. Both of us had divested ourselves of our 'city' clothes, he donning his *lunghi*, an enlarged dishcloth southern Indians utilise as a skirt, and I my shorts. The *lunghi* comes in useful too at nightfall, and the transition of the compartment to a sleeper, when it serves as a sheet. Me, I had my sleeping bag liner, which was even better. On ordinary express trains bedding is not supplied, nor is it needed.

By mid-afternoon, we had reached Gwalior, a name practically synonymous with its fort, one of the oldest in India, being mentioned in an inscription dated AD 525. The story of its founding is told in the legend of Suraj Sena, a local chief suffering from leprosy, who met a Hindu saint, Gwalipa, on a rocky hill. This worthy offered the stricken chief water from a pool and he was immediately cured. Gwalipa thereupon directed Sena to build a fort on the spot, and thus Gwalior came into being. The Rajput fort is an immense turreted structure sprouting from the solid rock, the road to it – once used by elephants bearing royalty – being today too steep for cars.

There are no dining cars as such on Indian Railways, meals for those who want them being ordered ahead and picked up at selected stations. Our hot lunch had been served soon after the departure from Delhi on a compartmentalised tray parcelled with heat-retaining foil and, because I was European, it was presumed I would want meat. But my curried chicken was, as I expected, stringy and tough, so thereafter I stuck to vegetarian dishes, which are invariably good as well as being incredibly cheap. Our dinner was collected during the station halt at Jhansi and consumed between there and Bhopal. My meals this day were noteworthy in that they provided my first experience of eating without the aid of cutlery or equivalent and a right mess I made of it. I watched my neighbour deftly lifting portions of vegetable and soaking up the gravy with his *chapati*, hardly getting his fingers damp. Me, I wallowed about up to my armpits in hot sauces, dropping handfuls of curry all over the floor and myself.

A late September night had fallen by the time we reached Bhopal. All I saw of it was the handsome station, and if that was anything to go by, it must be an equally pleasant city. I'm told it is. Capital of the state of Madhya Pradash, it possesses two lakes side by side, one decorated with a cluster of white palaces renowned for their gardens. The Afghan, Dost Mohammed Khan, built and extended the walls of the old fort high on the hill near the largest of the lakes, and behind it is reputedly the biggest mosque in India, the huge, still unfinished, Taj-ul-Masjid. But, alas, Bhopal's fame has become infamy in recent years through the Union Carbide factory gas disaster that killed thousands of the inhabitants. Stretching my legs on the platform, I sniffed suspiciously but the smells that arose were from sources distinctly Indian.

With Bhopal behind us, we arranged our seats for sleeping, my companion insisting I occupy the lower bunk, the more easily to see out of the window. It always takes me time to accustom myself to slumber in a new environment and this one was no exception; it was a noisy, interrupted night and Indian trains as well as Indian stations are the noisiest anywhere. During the daytime, I had noticed little men at wayside stations standing with unfailing regularity on the platform or by signal cabins, solemnly holding up tiny green flags as a sign to the driver that the way ahead was clear. With nightfall came a variation. Instead of little men with flags were little men with whistles, who blew them shrilly at every level crossing and always right outside my window. And why is it that an Indian train crossing long girder bridges over wide, wide rivers makes such an infernal racket, the echoes so much louder than anywhere else? Indian stations, too, are the most vocal of places, the braying of vendors promoting their wares never ceasing throughout the night.

The morning view from my open window was of the same hillocks bucking a parched countryside the previous dusk had hidden but these hillocks were decorated with a green carpeting crowned by a coxcomb of granite. The night had brought welcome relief from the heat and I had been glad to crawl inside my thin sleeping sack. By mutual consent we had switched off the fans. I refused breakfast, a raging thirst removing the slightest appetite – especially for curried vegetables at so early an hour. On the trains, tea or coffee is supplied in small thermos flasks holding about three cups and these I drank avidly.

We rumbled across a wide, sluggish, brown river on a newly-repaired girder bridge. Mr Arya imparted some grim details. 'Just three months ago a flood washed away a span together with three bogies (coaches) of a train passing over it. The death toll was 140.' I found it difficult to reconcile this fact with so peaceful a waterway wending its way through a bone-dry land.

The night had hidden Nagpur and the Vidarbha region, renowned for its oranges which were out of season anyway, but a new and welcome freshness I had first discerned earlier that morning, was infusing the terrain. The rebirth of life included rice paddies and date palms to add an oriental flavour to the countryside. At Warangai, in the early afternoon, my companion departed and I felt strangely lonely on an Indian train with a whole compartment to myself. 'There's nothing worth seeing at Warangai,' had vouchsafed Mr Devendra Gupta disdainfully, though an earlier visitor, Mr Marco Polo, left a glowing account of the wealth of this ancient capital of the Kakatiyas – an Andra Dynasty – and praise for its gossamer fabrics. The train stopped an inordinately long time outside the station, held up by signals, and everybody, as is the custom on Indian trains, used the occasion for a stroll on the trackside and social exchange.

I was not alone for long. At Vijayawada, a Hindu pilgrimage centre, I was joined by another sales executive, one Boby George Thaliath, whose visiting card showed him to be 'in' cables. He was returning to his company – The Premier Cable Co. Ltd of Cochin – following a trouble-shooting assignment in Vijayawada where he had had the unenviable task of apportioning the blame for the failure of one of his firm's products to take the strain. While we crossed the mighty Godavari River by way of the two-mile bridge – the second longest in the country – he was drawing technical pictures for me of the cable fracture while half my attention was fastened upon the dramatic river views outside.

Having skipped lunch as well as breakfast, I was prepared to enjoy a little nourishment at dinner, which came aboard at Gudur during the prolonged halt at its station. Much as I enjoy long-distance train rides, I was beginning to feel as a caged lion must do, particularly at stations, where edible and drinkable offerings were pushed to me through the window bars. The sight of a European was rarer in the south too, and I came in for much scrutiny.

I slept better the second night and awoke at Coimbatore, a town to which I would subsequently return. Heavy rain had turned the streets into mud but even at seven o'clock in the morning, the sun was fast drying it out. Just beyond Coimbatore the line passes the state border of Kerala and into a different land. The change is abrupt. Suddenly we were in an environment of exaggerated fertility, rich vegetation, lakes and rivers, rice paddies galore, an abundance of coconut palms and villages where the roofs of houses are intricately thatched with palm fronds to keep out rain. I watched the first of many rice paddies being 'ploughed' by buffaloes and bare-footed men wading calf-deep in liquid mud. I envied them.

My latest companion left at Ernakulam Junction, which is one of the components of the city and port of Cochin. We were now on the west coast, having cut across from the Bay of Bengal to the Arabian Sea. After the graphic report on the subject of the defective cable and the usual exchange of family figures, we had relapsed into a desultory silence occasionally broken with the entry into the compartment of the train commander for a chat. So far, he affirmed, it had been an uneventful trip. I asked him what sort of troubles he encountered on a route he rode once or more a week and was given a catalogue of riot, revolution, strike, murder and simple violence that made British Rail's football supporter 'Specials' sound very tame indeed. Then he too left to keep other trysts within his domain and I was alone again. This solitariness on an Indian train was an unnerving business; I felt cut off and segregated, a new experience in India, and I didn't like it. Only a coach away, the denizens of second-class were mellowed by the fraternity of the train and friendships forged through prolonged 'togetherness'. But there was no room on the wooden benches for me and my appearance among them provoked only silent stares. It takes time, as I well knew, to be 'accepted' in such circumstances, so I lurched back to my lonely exclusivity.

For the remainder of the journey the line runs close to the coast. Kerala was born of the sea, scalloped by the sea and gifted back by it to the sea-faring people of Kerala. Parusuram, reincarnated Preserver of the Hindu Trinity, curled his axe into the sea, and the land emerged, rich and dripping, to become Kerala, pressed against the western mountains of India by the heartbeat of the sea.

Fed by the rains, forty rivers rush down the mountains to the sea, carrying nourishing silt, spreading across burgeoning fields, swelling the backwaters fringed with green-fronded coconut palms. Every monsoon, the sea eats the shores of Kerala, the fishermen of Kerala cast their dawn nets on these silt-enriched waters, after which, when the monsoon winds abate, the farmers of Kerala retrieve a little more land for themselves.

To this rich slither of land came Dravidians from the Mediterranean and Aryans from the cold northern steppes. These were followed by the Greeks and the Romans searching for pepper and spices, and Jewish traders and Arabs in their dhows. Then came the Portuguese in the footsteps of Vasco de Gama, who landed in Kerala in 1498. The Dutch ousted the Portuguese in 1663 and left the crest of their East India company above an old door in Europe's first colony in Asia: Fort Cochin. The last to come to Kerala were the British, who subdued the myriad warring princes of Kerala before handing the land back to its people in 1947.

After Ernakulam, the Kerala Express sinks to the status of a stopping train, calling at every village halt. But the going was pleasant, with glimpses and smells of the sea to revive a flagging interest. Quilon is the last town of any size before Trivandrum; one of the oldest ports along the Malabar coast. Phoenicians, Romans, Greeks, Persians, Arabs all traded at Quilon, as did the Chinese, the most industrious of all the city's traders, who established trading posts here under the reign of Kubla Khan in the 13th century.

The British made their presence felt at Varkala, just 32 miles short of journey's end, where the British East India Company opened its first trading post on this coast. Red cliffs with mineral water springs spurting from their flanks loom over the beach.

We drew into Trivandrum, the state capital, mid-afternoon, some 25 minutes late. I bade farewell to the train commander and hurried along the platforms in search of that British-inspired institution – now uniquely Indian – the railway retiring room. I suppose the equivalent in Europe would be the youth hostel (they have these in India too) but retiring rooms – overnight accommodation within the station confines, run and subsidised by the railway – require no membership. They are available to all railway travellers and are to be found in the most modest of stations; a board on the platform indicates their situation and state of booking. The board at Trivandrum showed no vacancies so I ran to earth the station-master in his lair, showed him my Indrail pass and put my trust in the Indian penchant for finding accommodation where none is seemingly available. In this endeavour, I soon had all the staff of the busy office running about checking ledgers and clipboard lists, eventually finding myself the possessor of bed number eight in an eight-bed dormitory. The fee was about 75 pence payable in advance. Had I obtained a room to myself, the cost would have risen to about £1.50. In both cases, the charge entitles one to the use of a shower, washbasin, toilet and a baggage locker (for which you require your own padlock).

Though the other seven beds in the big airy room had been reserved, I was the first guest to arrive. I was brought fresh, clean sheets and pillowcase, and my bed was made up. One window of the room looked out over the station platforms; the other onto the station square of Trivandrum city. I took a shower, locked away my rucksack and went in search of the reservation office, intent upon the acquisition of the more immediate of my berth bookings covering the subsequent leg of my journey.

This task took two hours and the completion of three sets of forms, plus the re-completion of two of them for having entered a wrong train number. Not having any fixed plans, I was reluctant to abide by an itinerary but Indian railways don't cater for the long-distance passenger travelling on a whim. Hungry and, as usual, thirsty after the documentation, I took myself to the station vegetarian restaurant to partake of a highly nutritious and substantial vegetable curry together with two jugs of tea for the princely sum of 25 pence. All the while, waiters came round with extra helpings for which there was no charge and, such was my thirst – hardly helped by the spicy curry – I even succumbed to drinking the local water. The restaurant itself, like most of its fellows on Indian railway stations, was more utilitarian than elegant but tables were energetically washed down at frequent intervals while the floor was in a continuous state of maintenance.

When night fell, I took myself into the town to stretch under-exercised limbs. By the time I returned, the first of my fellow bed-mates had arrived in the dormitory and others trickled in during the course of the evening, some after I had gone to bed.

In spite of the balm of a stationary bed, the accompanying symphony of the night was no less daunting than it had been on the train. In addition to the shriek of diesel units and the rattle of trains from one window, there was a constant dirge from a religious tableau set in the station square. This latter scourge petered out in the small hours, not long before some of my companions with early trains to catch, began their ablutions to the accompaniment of the inevitable hawking and spitting.

Trivandrum is, for an Indian city, a sedate sort of place, pleasing to the eye with proud buildings as behoves a state capital. Its fruit stalls were hung with every conceivable exotic fruit, including red bananas, giving colour to a broad-avenued ambience of streets from a regal era when princely families held sway. Attempting to locate the post office, I was directed to the post and telegraph office in a different part of town, which gave me a longer walk than I had bargained for in the heat of mid-morning.

I left on the midday Kanya Kumari Express, originating from Bombay, and since it was but a three-hour journey to the southern extremity of India, no reservation proved necessary. On the platform I had fallen into conversation with an elderly Indian, so joined him in his second-class compartment.

Almost immediately we entered a new state – that of Tamil Nadu – and with it a strange contradiction. Though fervently nationalistic and given to violence in their quest for cessation and the founding of an independent Tamil nation, its people are seemingly still proud of their British colonial past.

The Sri Lanka crisis of recent years has given a new fillip to Tamil nationalism and many of the people are dead against the Sri Lankan government's opposition to Tamil independence on the island. My travelling companion was enthusiastic about the peace treaty signed that month between India and Sri Lanka. 'All will be well now,' he purred, not realising that, even as he spoke, the north of the island had erupted into open warfare with the arrival of the Indian peace-keeping force on the Jaffna peninsula.

Tamil Nadu, with its capital Madras, is now only one of four states that made up the Madras Presidency of British days. Its people, swarthy and dark, are quite different from those of the north and even those of the Deccan in the mid-west of the country. It has four languages, all contrasting sharply with the more universal Hindi. The Tamils strongly resisted attempts by the Indian government to introduce Hindi as the alternative language to English.

The railway line passes close to Kovalam, where palm-fringed beaches stretch for miles. The few foreign tourists who reach this far south usually end up here, and there are plenty of hotels to cater for them. But Kanya Kumari, an Indian resort, is the end of the line and, as befits the southern extremity of the Indian rail network, the most striking new building in the small town is the railway station.

We drew into it nearly three-quarters of an hour late, the last outposts of the hills that had run down the west coast disappearing into the sea in a line of jagged rocks. There were no vacancies in the retiring rooms, which plainly would have offered a much more restful sojourn than those at Trivandrum, so I went in search of a religious order I'd heard about that offered accommodation to visitors. But I became caught in a web of intrigue spun by lodgement touts who fought over my custom and ended up at a hovel of a hotel.

However, it was close to the sea and I was in dire need of a swim. My room was a cell with iron bars across the only window, but there was a shower in a cockroach-crawling outhouse so I was willing to suffer it for a night.

Kanya Kumari, or Cape Comerin, is the Land's End of India and purports to have multi-coloured sands which, according to Hindu legend, were formed when Parvati, daughter of the King of the Himalayas, jilted at the altar by Lord Shiva, angrily tossed the uneaten wedding feast into the waters, where it was transformed into the sands of brown, yellow, silver, orange, blue, purple and russet. But it wasn't until the mind-blowing sunset for which KK is

also famed that I could discern any varying colours to the beach.
The scruffy township is revered by Hindus for its Kanya Kumari
Shrine and by all Indians for the Vivekananda Memorial that
becomes an island at high tide, as well as the Gandhi Memorial
that marks the point where the great statesman's ashes were
scattered after his cremation.

To reach a secluded beach, I had to plough miles along the soft
sand beach, initially passing through a maze of rude hutments
belonging to the fishing community. My presence generated a
certain amount of passive hostility which became uglier when a
pack of children followed me to throw sand and not a few stones
at my person. With a confidence I didn't feel, I turned and swore
at them and, to my amazement, they retreated.

The sea was extremely rough, with huge rollers surging in
between the jagged teeth of the reef. Deep-sea bathing was plainly
out of the question here, the treacherous currents, rocks and rough
waters making it a dangerous place for mariners as well. But I
located a lagoon close to a small fishing harbour and happily
immersed myself in clear blue water for hours on end, revelling in
the sunset as dusk fell. The colour was spectacular, the glory of the
sun's last rays seeming to persist long after night had taken over.
The fisherfolk were, unlike the denizens of Kanya Kumari, the
friendliest of people, who quickly restored my confidence in Tamil
good nature. One young man joined me in the water to impart the
fact that if I had three legs, I could have planted one in each of the
three oceans that met at this spot: that of the Bay of Bengal, the
Indian Ocean and the Arabian Sea.

In the dark I had the devil of a job to relocate my lodging, but
following an excellent supper, two bottles of mango juice and
innumerable cups of tea in one of the many small restaurants in the
town centre, I repaired to my humble bed for the quietest night I'd
found since leaving Delhi.

Though I had gone as far south as I could go, I hadn't quite
finished with geographical extremities. Sri Lanka is not, as some
would believe, the tear below the peardrop of India or the dot
below the Indian exclamation mark. The island I intended to be
my southernmost destination lies off-centre, further east, the port
that serves it being, with its narrow peninsula, an extremity of its

own. Rameswaram is the name of that port and by road was a distance of some 230 miles from Kanya Kumari.

To go there by rail meant a journey of more than twice this mileage and a retracing of steps via Trivandrum, Ernakulam and Coimbatore. But since I wanted to see something of Cochin – of which Ernakulam forms part – the detour was not without benefit. I left before dawn the next day on the Bombay-bound Kanya Kumari Express and, by leaving so early, had the bonus of witnessing the Cape Comorin sunrise, which is as celebrated as its sunset. While gazing at it over a station cup of tea, the thought came to me that this must be the only place in the world where you can watch the sun rise and set over different oceans.

Two days later, having made a stopover at Cochin (about which more later), I was back at Coimbatore station. And, abracadabra, there on the platform of the metre-gauge line to Madurai and Rameswaram, was a notice informing all and sundry that 'Mr Christopher Puriwas, M.64' held a reserved berth in coach 182 of the Rameswaram Express/Passenger Train leaving at 22.30 that night for the 250-mile run to the port.

I went in search of berth number M64 but was unable to find it. 'Where is M64?' I enquired of an official and he looked bewildered. I took him to the noticeboard and pointed out my name. He smiled broadly. 'That's *you*,' he explained, 'it's your particulars. You are a male and you're sixty-four years of age aren't you?' Now I understood the reason for some of the daft questions required by the reservation forms; it is so that the conductor obtains a vague idea as to who his charges are.

My third mobile night was enlivened by the antics of a couple of cockroaches and a marauding spider cavorting around the compartment light fixture, their reflected shadows enlarged to sinister proportions appearing on the opposite wall. The human inmates of the four-berth compartment were far less entertaining, one of them smoking incessantly.

I first caught sight of the sea again out of the right-hand window and, as the land narrowed into the peninsula, it appeared on the left too. With ponderous deliberation, we crept over the old railway bridge to Pandrum in the shadow of the skeleton of the then incomplete Pandram dual-purpose bridge alongside, a morass of girders and crane jibs combining to form a one-and-a-quarter-mile-long structure that would give improved access to isolated Rameswaram.

So they *were* preparing for an expected increase of visitors to Sri Lanka as soon as that country's troubles are over, I surmised. I had heard talk of improved facilities, including better train services and connections for those wanting to visit the island. I turned to my companions. 'For the tourists?' I enquired, indicating the multi-million pound skeleton. They shook their heads. Didn't I know that Rameswaram island was a pilgrimage centre for all Hindus coming to pay tribute to Rama, the hero of the epic *Ramayana*, who came here in search of his wife Sita and to do penance for killing the ten-headed demon king of Lanka? To the Hindus, Rameswaram is as holy as Varanasi and so intimately linked with Rama that every grain of its sand is considered sacred. This notwithstanding, I didn't think such an expensive bridge could be just for the pilgrims' benefit.

Rameswaram station turned out to be another temple to the railway, displaying an exotic exterior completely out of tune with its surroundings as well as its interior. I headed towards the port.

The road led through a scruffy part of the town made up of bazaars backed by mud and wattle huts. I thought at first I'd taken a wrong turning but signs repeatedly proclaimed 'To the Port'. After a mile and a half, sweating under a furnace of a sun, I came to it – a tiny fishing harbour, nets spread like carpets over the small quay. Further along the shore to the west was a substantial building which looked as if it might have been the ferry terminal but no vessel that could conceivably have been a ferry was in evidence. I hardly expected it either for the connection had been suspended many months previously. In the other direction, the temple of Rameswaram reared, squat and tiered, from behind a row of palm trees.

I approached a knot of men repairing their nets, and asked about boats to Sri Lanka.

'The ferry doesn't run anymore,' I was told, the men looking at me as if I was an imbecile. They didn't actually say 'don't you know there's a war on?'

I persisted. 'Would anyone contemplate taking me across the strait to Talaimannar?' This was on the peninsula the other side and opposite this one. Geographically they were almost certainly the same but the sea had submerged the middle of it. Less than 20 miles of water – known as Adam's Bridge of the Palk Strait – separates India from Sri Lanka.

The faces of my audience registered amazement. Nobody, it seemed, had made such a request. I intimated I'd pay them well and displayed a fistful of rupee notes, but money was not the point. 'It's strictly forbidden by the military,' I was informed.

On the nearby beach upon which a number of fishing boats had been drawn up for repair, I tried again. A group of friendly Tamil fishermen had waved at me from the deck of one of the vessels, so I clambered up the scaffolding to join them. Again, I put my request. The smiles faded but they were not unsympathetic, while the money I once more displayed was plainly a temptation. A dark, tousle-haired youth explained the situation.

'Both the Indian and Sri Lankan authorities have naval patrols in the strait for the express purpose of stopping illegal entry to the island; otherwise many of us would be over there helping our brothers in revolt,' his voice rose on a note of challenge.

I nodded bleakly, not wanting to become involved in political argument, and descended to the sand. Continuing my way along the beach, all thought of reaching northern Sri Lanka draining from my mind, I perceived that I was being followed. Out of the sight of the boatyard, my 'tail' caught up with me and urgently tugged at my sleeve. Before me there lurked a small, furtive Tamil.

'I can take you to Sri Lanka,' he whispered eagerly. 'Come, I'll show you my boat.'

Dressed in a dirty, torn shirt above an equally ragged *lungi*, my new acquaintance dragged me back to a corner of the boatyard where a decrepit structure, partly collapsed and roofless, had the greatest difficulty straddling a narrow, turgid backwater thick with oil, scum, sewage and seaweed. Within the gloomy interior reposed a surprisingly serviceable-looking craft replete with a pair of oars as well as an outboard motor.

'Is this your boat?' I asked, not wanting to be party to theft as well as any other crimes accruing from entering illegally into another country.

The man nodded with enthusiastic vigour, taking my voiced suspicion as favourable reaction to his vessel.

'I own it with my brother. We take tourists for pleasure cruises,' he explained, 'but now there are no tourists.' His shrug was eloquent of his hopeless situation.

'If you took me across the strait, would you be able to bring me back?' Once on Sri Lankan territory, there would arise the problem of returning to India.

'Of course. No problem.'

'Even if it meant you having to wait for me for a day or so?'

'No problem for me,' repeated the youngster, 'Indian Tamils, Sri Lanka Tamils, they all look alike. No one would bother me and I know people there.'

'When would we go?' I asked, 'the time of day I mean?' The practicalities of the project were fast overcoming a growing awareness of what I might be letting myself in for.

'Early morning is best. Fishing boats go out, so ours would not be noticed.'

'How far is the Sri Lankan coast from here?'

'The nearest point is very few miles.'

'How many?' I was conscious of the Indian vagueness when it came to judging distances and time.

'Twenty or so. I have been there before with tourists. But of course, we can't land at Talaimannar so it would have to be a little way down the shore. It would only take about two hours using the motor.'

It all sounded so easy and rather fun. But my unease would not entirely abate. Once on the soil of Sri Lanka as an illegal immigrant in a hostile and war-torn environment, I would be fair game for anyone. And I was a sucker for getting myself into trouble. Suspicion became my next emotion.

'How do I know you'll wait for me there?' I didn't like displaying my distrust but the matter had to be brought out into the open.

'You needn't pay me until we're back here,' said the youth without the slightest sign of his being put out by my implied doubts of his honesty.

'How much will you want for the round trip?'

'The money you held in your hand when you were talking to my colleagues.'

I was nonplussed for a moment, uncertain as to how many

rupees this amounted to, but calculated it must have been something close to the equivalent of twenty pounds, a fortune to a poor Tamil fisherman. To keep things on a firm business footing, I told him it amounted to about 400 rupees.

'I know,' said my companion. Obviously, he was quicker on the uptake than I when it came to totting up rupees.

I wasn't prepared to haggle. My immediate future lay in his hands and I didn't want it to be too cheap.

'I'll have to spend the night somewhere,' I went on. If all went well, I'd be back on Indian soil within 24 hours; maybe even in time to catch the subsequent train out and with a brief excursion to northern Sri Lanka beneath my belt to complement my current journey.

'No problem,' came the standard retort, 'I can fix you up. Come.'

We emerged into the hot afternoon sun, blinking under its brilliance, and ran straight into the party of fishermen I had spoken to on the boat, together with a khaki-uniformed character with a rifle. It didn't take any great powers of perception on my part to recognize him as a military policeman with the rank of corporal.

There ensued a multiple torrent of Tamil dialogue, everyone talking at once, everyone gesticulating madly and, every so often, casting dark, reproachful looks at me. They were all young; about the same age as my fellow-conspirator, who was talking the loudest, his voice shrill with indignation. The corporal was only a year or two older but his seniority slowly began to calm the verbal tempest. He turned to me.

'What you were planning is dangerous, very dangerous, as these men told you. It is also forbidden and we have orders to stop such illegal contact with the other side.' He indicated with his head the unseen Sri Lankan coast out to sea. 'You were very wrong to encourage this man to take you across. He could be in just as much trouble as you.'

I took my dressing down stoically, forbearing to disclose the fact that it was the young Tamil and not me who had initiated the proposal. As long as matters remained at a low level of authority, I saw no reason to make excuses.

My erstwhile partner-in-crime gave me another of his eloquent shrugs, this one indicating the contempt for his companions and the demise of the project. I never was to learn the facts of our betrayal but presumed jealousy might have had something to do with it. Unable to raise adequate reason for stepping in and scotching their colleague's enterprise on their own, they had enlisted the help of the military. I wondered if envy was a normal Tamil trait.

Once more, I put any thought of venturing further south out of my head, chalking up to experience the hiatus I had caused. It wasn't as if I'd never been to Sri Lanka; in fact, I had visited the island earlier that very year. But I had been denied the town of Jaffna and the northern district so had felt cheated. Now I had been cheated again, though maybe to the benefit of my health. However, except for the north, I could rely upon my memory of what had gone before.

* * *

Chapter Two

We flew into Colombo's Katunayake airport. Our coach ride into Colombo city followed the state railway's coastal branch line that runs to Negombo and Puttalam, its single track engulfed by bloated vegetation of which banana predominated. Serrated coconut palm trunks rose askew from the morass of shrubbery like drunken telegraph poles. As the palm-fringed outer suburbs degenerated into grotty concrete inner suburbs we crossed the Kelani Ganga river on a rusty girder bridge.

'They filmed *The Bridge on the River Kwai* a few miles upstream from here,' announced our guide, and in an awed voice added, 'you know they actually did blow up a whole bridge just for the cameras.' A mental picture of Sir Alec Guinness striding across the span flickered through my head and faded into new images in which lamp standards in erect concrete framed unsavoury hovels.

The architect of the Lanka Oberoi must have imagined he was producing a cathedral rather than a hotel. The reception area did rather better, I thought, than the nave of St Peter's in Rome with gigantic murals and expensive tassled banners hanging from the high-altitude glass roof. Across the entry portals – one could hardly describe them as mere doors – a banner shrieked 'Welcome to the Viceroy Special Group' and I realized it referred to us. Two sultry ladies in figure-hugging saris smiled bewitchingly from behind their guest-relations desks and, trying to observe both at once, I collided with a pillar.

Our group was sixteen strong, as emphatically independent-minded bunch as ever I've seen with a single interest in common. Trains. The one exception turned out to be a northern English couple who seemingly had failed to read the tour brochure properly, and so were in for a surprise. The leader was one

Clifford Jones, managing director of a well-known Manchester travel agency, whose powerful frame, ready smile and disarming manner quickly defused any rebellious instincts amongst the rest of us. Not that there were any such instincts beyond ominous rumblings of dissent from the female portion of the northern couple, now made abruptly aware of what they had let themselves in for. Not only was she a self-proclaimed 'lady', she was a town councillor to boot, and the impending mode of transportation – by the lowly train over two whole weeks – was plainly an assault on her dignity. The prospect could only please everyone else; indeed it was the chief reason for coming, especially for the redoubtable Kenneth Westcott Jones, travel writer and rail buff extraordinary, who, in his forthright manner was to ensure I imbibed the full technicalities of the Sri Lanka railway network.

Quite simply, the group had assembled for the express purpose of participating in the inaugural commercial run of the Viceroy Special, a steam-hauled tourist train composed of observation coaches and a restaurant car designed to carry, in reasonable comfort, a limited number of visitors around the island within an aura of nostalgic evocation. The train had no pretensions to rival the costly richness of the Venice-Simplon Orient Express in Europe or Rajasthan's flamboyant Indian Palace on Wheels (of which more later); instead, it was a down-to-earth, essentially good-natured little vehicle puffing energetically through tea plantations and rice paddies.

Its birth – or more accurately, rebirth in a new form – can be laid squarely upon the ample shoulders of Clifford, whose enthusiasm for railways must be second only to that of Kenneth, an interest no doubt fostered by a father who was a top link driver for British Rail.

It was while on travel agency business in Colombo in 1985 that Cliff spotted the plume of white smoke that was to put the Viceroy Special on the rails. The smoke was ascending from the sidings of the Dematagoda Sheds in the city suburbs and, intrigued, he turned to his Sri Lankan associate to enquire as to what type of steam locomotives were in use by the railway.

'We have no steam traction in Sri Lanka,' he was told in the acidly disapproving manner of a government spokesman upholding his country's progressive inclinations.

'Well what's that smoke?' Cliff persisted, knowing full well what it was, and, receiving only a shrug in reply, led his hesitant escort to the source.

And lo and behold, there before them was an old British-built tank engine fussing around a yard chock-full of discarded rolling stock of historic proportions including an ancient specimen of locomotive quietly expiring, a banana tree sprouting from its stack. Nor was that all. Several disintegrating Garratts and a number of antique coaches swam into Cliff's astounded gaze.

There was no stopping him now. Interviews with the ministers of tourism and transport led to one with the Prime Minister herself, who was to instigate a thorough investigation into the potential of the rotting treasure that lay neglected in the sidings.

As I write, hostilities on the island have suspended operation of the Viceroy Special but three locomotives and several coaches were in use before the suspension order. These we were to inspect that first afternoon at the invitation of the railway authorities, the dedicated band of Sri Lankan Dematagoda workers being treated to the spectacle of a dozen ill-assorted Brits attired in unsuitable European summer raiment traipsing self-consciously through or over dirt and oil-encrusted inspection pits and duckboard gangways and peering uneasily into fireboxes and boilers. The expressions on our faces revealed, all too clearly, the degree of actual or simulated interest and knowledge; the tall, angular Brian from Sevenoaks led the slow procession, paying ponderous attention to the technical commentary, which he plainly understood. The elegant, well-groomed Fay from Cambridge, on the other hand, didn't know a piston from a fish plate but was much too polite and considerate to show it. The newly-weds (surely this wasn't their honeymoon?) from the Surrey stockbroker belt – Peter and Carol – flew the flag of a deep-seated knowledge of things mechanical, easily parrying Professor Ken's technical conundrums that he is wont to inflict upon anyone admitting to the remotest yen for a railway train. Even the diminutive spinster from the Midlands managed to put on a brave, if bewildered, face for an occasion the poor lady had never experienced in a lifetime of more conservative holidaying. Inconspicuous by their absence, the northern couple were presumably engaged in pursuits more in keeping with their status.

One item of machinery particularly intrigued me, not so much for its design or purpose but because one of its Ransome iron castings had, almost certainly, been made in the Essex iron foundry which had been my family business. And judging by the number of blow-holes that pitted its surface the casting could well have been both moulded and poured by myself!

That morning Ken and I, together with a slightly apprehensive Geoff Thomas from Harrow, had taken ourselves on a personal rail excursion on the southbound coastal line. The third class (on Sri Lanka trains this grade of compartment/coach has been retained) fare was but 4 pence for a 20 minute ride and I was surprised at the emptiness of the coaches after the frenetic cramming of those in India; there were no more than half a dozen people with us on the wooden frame seats lining the sides of the otherwise bared wagon. Yet the volume of traffic on this fairly minor line was considerable and gave ample evidence that the Sri Lanka State Railway was heavily worked in spite of the seeming underuse of its trains.

I cannot say I found Colombo an attractive city and in this view I seem to have an ally in the *Berlitz Guide to Sri Lanka*:

'Noisy, frenetic, a little crazy, home to 700,000 people representing every ethnic group in the country – Buddhist, Sinhalese, Hindu Tamil, Muslim Arab, Christian Burgher. They're all rushing around trying to cope with the demands of a modern metropolis, its traffic, communications and constant demolition and reconstruction.'

But nobody minds. Breakdowns, traffic jams and electrical failures are received with a shrug and a smile. Life goes on. To add to the problems was the terrorist threat posed by the revolt of Hindu Tamils, who had evolved the distressing habit of derailing trains with the aid of explosive charges.

Sri Lanka is not a new name for the island as most folk imagine. The Romans knew it as Taprobane, Arab traders called it Serendib, the Portuguese named it Ceilao while, backward in time, Stone Age civilisations bequeathed cave markings relating the legends of the ancient Hindu sagas telling of 'a Splendid Land, the Grey, Green and Glorious Lanka that is like the Garden of the Sky'. Roughly 270 miles long and 140 wide – about the size of Ireland – the pear-shaped country came to be known as Ceilao or Ceylon only in the 16th century.

The constant association with nearby India is inevitable but it would be wrong to think of the island as no more than an extension of its larger neighbour. In the process of wresting itself from India, Sri Lanka has developed a distinctive personality. Sinhala is a language unique to the island as is the Sinhalese culture. Buddhism flourishes too – having been supplanted by Hinduism in India. The very fact of the island's proximity to that country, however, results in constant conflict with the Tamils, a Hindu minority of Indian origin rebelling against discrimination by the dominant Sinhalese, a fact all too well-known today.

Over the centuries many who came to trade, stayed to settle, so that the blood of the Sinhala became inexorably mixed with that of Arabs, Chinese and Greeks within the tolerant embrace of Buddhism, Venetians, French, Spanish, Persians, not to mention Indians, all made their way to 'The Splendid Land' but real Colonial domination came only with the Portuguese in 1503. This gave way to the Dutch and finally, during the upheavals of the Napoleonic Wars, the British seized the colony, coveting the fine harbour at Trincomalee as well as the cinnamon trade.

During the British era, tea, rubber and coconut became the economic backbone of the renamed Ceylon and the island was a much-loved jewel in the Imperial Crown. It settled down to a peaceful existence under British rule with Ceylonese rubber a key contributor to Britain's 19th-century prosperity.

Colonisation in its evolution from the Portuguese via the Dutch to the British grew ever more efficient and enterprising, but no less inhuman. However, as in India, Sri Lanka reaped many benefits from her occupiers, not the least of which was a broad gauge railway system as good, on a smaller scale, as the one Britain bequeathed to India.

In 1948 the island became an independent member of the British Commonwealth and, in 1973, declared itself a republic, assuming the old-new name of Sri Lanka.

But, for me, the Sri Lanka Government Railway and the journey I was to make this time as a pampered tourist became the narrower vortex of a further quest for knowledge in yet another segment of the Indian subcontinent.

Our four-coach train made a handsome sight. It was headed by *Sir Thomas Maitland*, a 4-6-0 B1A class, side-tank and tender engine, number 251, built by Robert Stephenson & Hawthorne in 1926 – or so I was assured by Ken – and though I have seen many much larger and more dramatic-looking steam locomotives, this one wore a sprightly air, with couplets of national flags and the emblem 'Viceroy Special' emblazoned across her front. All four coaches were painted in the bright red livery of the former Ceylon Government Railway and, outlined in gold, the CGT crest prominently displayed. A larger engine – *Lord Mountbatten*, number 213 – would be taking over the train at Kandy and this was a unique B28 side-tanker, built by Vulcan foundry at Newton-le-Willows in 1916, which we had inspected at Dematagoda.

Of the two observation cars, the one at the rear of the train was the most popular by virtue of giving an unimpeded view of the track and scenery unwinding behind it. And with the petering out of the Colombo suburbs, there unwound a lushly voluptuous land indeed – from what one could see of it through gaps in the cottonwood smoke issuing from *Sir Thomas Maitland*. All life was on display in a countryside liberally sprinkled with villages, coconut groves, paddies and buffalo herds. The track, as in India, was used as a pedestrian – even bicycle – thoroughfare, with the locals stepping off the rails only long enough to let the train go by, there to wave enthusiastically at our receding rear.

At Polgahawela, the junction for the Kandy line, we took on water and I transferred to the locomotive, having been the first to apply to do so. The cab was singularly crowded, due to the presence there of the driver, a learner-driver, fireman and learner-fireman, and an inspector. With the reintroduction of a steam train on the system, the railway authorities were conscious of the need for younger driving staff and those experienced in steam operation, hence the swollen footplate population. Reflecting the Indian model, the small station bore the unmistakable stamp of a pre-Second World War country station in Britain with its pots of geraniums, class-graduated waiting rooms and the old-fashioned semaphore signalling.

It was good to be back on the footplate, imbibing smoke and soot. I've been lucky to have had more than my fair share of cab-riding, mostly in India and Pakistan, but also in Canada and even

Russia, Korea and China. In this instance, however, I was no more than a tourist to be indulged, not simply a tolerated 'refugee'.

Another watering operation was deemed necessary at Maho Junction, though an overflow of water flooded the tender to immerse my sandalled feet in liquid coal dust as soon as the hose had been inserted into the tank. There is a famed story of the stationmaster at Maho being unable to set the points because of the presence of a persistent and unsociable leopard which took up residence for some days close the operating lever, an event that brought the whole CGR system to a standstill. But no such incident enlivened our brief stopover here.

On a gradient beyond Maho, we ran out of puff. This caused a degree of consternation and a prolonged delay while we built up a new head of steam. Everyone – members of the group and the locals – gathered round to gawk and advise as the Viceroy blocked the tracks. The cause of the mishap was a ruptured airline and, with its repair, all eyes were on the steam pressure gauge as it steadily rose to the point where we could move off again.

By mid-afternoon we reached Anuradhapura, the holy city. This was as far north as we were permitted to go for it is well on the way to Jaffna and the Tamil-inspired turmoil of the region. Already the state had decreed that no trains were to operate after nightfall as a measure to reduce the risk of 'incident'. At Anuradhapura, however, were less disagreeable matters to claim our attention.

The *Mahavamsa*, Sri Lanka's Chronicle of Buddhism, records that Anuradhapura was founded in 380 BC by King Pandukabbaya, though it was not until after the conversion of King Devanampiya by Mahinda in 289 BC at Mihintale, seven miles east of Anuradhapura, that the capital also became a holy city. Whatever the historical details, nothing can detract from the remarkable quality of the excavated ruins visible today, the timeless palaces, royal gardens, ritual bathing ponds and huge domed shrines, dazzlingly whitewashed or covered over with grass and vegetation of centuries past.

The next objective was Habarana on the Trincomalee and Batticaloa line. This involved returning to Maho and progressing east on what was, originally, the BTLR (Batticaloa-Trincomalee Light Railway) but which, after 1955 when heavier track was laid in order to take the increased traffic, became the main line. At one wayside station we waited for an interminable period while the Hijra (Pilgrim's) Express between Colombo and Batticaloa lumbered by in a cloud of diesel smoke. According to the meticulous Ken, it was nineteen minutes behind schedule.

At Aukana there was a special halt for the purpose of observing the forty-foot high standing Buddha, sculptured during the reign of Dhatusena in the 5th century AD. Aukana means 'sun-eating' and dawn is the best time to see it – when the sun's first rays illuminate the huge, but finely-carved statue's features. Alas, it was midday and uncomfortably hot, while the ugly brick shelter, more recently constructed to protect the image, further detracted from the allure of the enormous figure.

Lunch was ready upon our return to the waiting train and there was a rush for the first sitting in the restaurant car. I was invariably beaten to it by the town councillor and her spouse who, if not approving of trains, appeared to thrive on train-served food. Another activity favoured by Madam Councillor that raised universal ire was her daily appearance dolled up to the nines in pink frilly creations and voluminous hats more suited to Ascot than Sri Lankan rail travel. In this regalia she was wont to sweep majestically along station platforms, making quite a hit with the astonished local populace. I once came across the offending headgear lying unattended in the observation car and had to fight a mounting temptation to plant it atop *Sir Thomas Maitland*'s smoke stack.

A short train ride out of Habarana the next day brought us to Polonnaruwa, once a capital of Sri Lanka. When Anuradhapura became over-exposed to attack from southern India, the decision was made to move, and although Polonnaruwa is now a thousand years old, it is still much younger than Anuradhapura and its relics in much better repair. The newer, but still venerable ruins, rescued from centuries of jungle overgrowth, bear eloquent witness to the struggles of empire-builders, and a walk along the crumbling, age-blackened structures of this medieval capital is a very different experience from that of Anuradhapura. Wandering its silent stones, even under squalls of rain, I discovered more contemplative backtracking into Sri Lankan history with no modern restorations to jar the mood.

Some twenty miles from Polonnaruwa is Sigiriya, the 'Lion Rock', undoubtedly the most spectacular monument in the country. The massive fortress perched atop a granite mountain was the work of King Kasyapa to defend himself against the wrath and army of his half-brother, Moggallana. But when the long-expected attack finally came eighteen years later, Kasyapa spiritedly but unwisely rode out with his own troops to meet it – only to become lost himself and expire in a bog.

So the 'Lion Rock' became a folly, a folly of immense proportions, rising sheer and mysterious from the surrounding jungle and ringed by a moat and a rampart. At one time, a gigantic brickwork lion sat at the summit and the final ascent to the top commenced with a stairway which led between the lion's paws and into its mouth. Today this once-sheltered stairway has totally disappeared apart from the first few steps, and to reach the top means clambering across a series of grooves cut into the rock face.

The road cocks a snook at the railway when it comes to a journey between Polonnaruwa and Kandy, yet another former Sri Lankan capital. By road, the journey takes two hours; by train, ten. Thus, with some reluctance, we took to an air-conditioned motor coach to continue through bucking hills, thickening forests, rubber plantations and the ubiquitous paddy fields. There were tea plantations too, and fluffy balls of kapok hanging from telephone wires, all of which indicated the extravagant abundance of the land. We rumbled on through the spice gardens of Matale and across the wide Mahaweli river on the Katugastota Bridge, delighting at the spectacle of working elephants bathing in river and pond with their keepers – mahouts – soaping the great beasts as if they were recalcitrant children. For the last miles we followed the spurned railway into the city.

When the British conquered Kandy, the hill capital of the last Sinhalese kings, they ended a monarchy that had ruled for more than 23 centuries. Kandy's citizens consider themselves apart from other Sinhalese; until the British came they had remained relatively unaffected by colonial influence, courageously resisting the armed might of the Portuguese, the Dutch and, for a time, the British, preserving the nation's identity while the rest of the country collaborated with the colonial invaders.

From the appropriately-named Hilltop Hotel, I set out to explore this historic stronghold set amongst quite astounding natural beauty. It is the Temple of the Tooth that takes pride of place in Kandy. Sri Lankans made pilgrimages to this precious repository by the untold thousand. They come to venerate the sacred tooth relic of the Buddha, knowing they will not see it but content to be in its presence.

I, too, made my way to the temple, crossed over the moat and entered to the sound of drums and wailing flutes. Humanity swirled around me as I joined the queue to process by the shrine. Everywhere were brown-skinned people, young and old with respectful, yet cheerful, faces; there were none of the hushed tones and morose expressions we Christians are wont to exhibit when visiting a European cathedral.

Hidden within the surprisingly unadorned shrine, sheltered by bullet-proof glass, reposes the tooth. It lies in a golden casket beneath seven other caskets, or so I was told. Guardian monks looked on impassively as worshippers offered flowers and money.

Kandy is the latest resting place of the tooth. Far older Sinhalese kingdoms have harboured it and the relic has been plundered many times over the ages. The temple itself is something of an anti-climax, an unspectacular, nondescript building, but the wailing flutes, clashing cymbals, slow-moving processions of white-clad pilgrims carrying pink lotus blossoms plus the ever-pervasive scent of joss sticks give the place an undeniable mysticism.

The town today preserves it distinctive architecture characterised by gently sloping tiled roofs. But, above all, Kandy is an atmosphere, a spirit set apart from the rest of the island. Situated at an altitude of a thousand feet, its temperate climate and astounding setting amongst hills, forest and the lake that is the centrepiece of the town, gives to it a highly individual personality. In a suburb, Peradeniya, are the most beautiful botanic gardens I have ever seen; 150 acres of parkland containing thousands of trees and plants of every hue, scent and type. The orchids alone are breathtaking.

Back aboard the Viceroy Special at Kandy's solid British-built station, the reunion between train staff and clients was as fervid as if we had been away a year rather than a couple of days. And the journey we were about to make was to constitute a highspot of the tour.

At Peradeniya, where Lord Mountbatten, as Commander-in-Chief of the Second World War's Far East forces, had his headquarters, I was to join his namesake locomotive for another spell on the footplate. This time I was in distinguished Sri Lanka Railway company since the cab contained Mr Fernando, the divisional inspector, and Mr Paramanathan, chief locomotive foreman, who between them, shouting above the noise, told me something about the rail history of the island.

The 'Ceylon Railway Company' was formed in 1845, but it was not until 1856 that a provisional agreement was signed by the government of Ceylon and the CRC to construct a railway between Colombo and Kandy for £800,000, though it subsequently became clear that the cost would well exceed twice this figure. After long and protracted argument, the government took over the assets and liabilities and began work on what was probably the first nationalised railway in the world – the CGR.

A royal prince from Belgium was invited to open the first section of track between Colombo and Ambepussa in 1864, and three years later the final link to Kandy was completed. A century on and the total mileage of the CGR was 914 miles, of which 90 miles was narrow gauge; the remainder broad gauge. Most of the CGR rail system is single line though operating a two-way timetable. Its block and tablet safety system, like that of the minor lines in India, ensures that no two trains can be on any one section of track at any one time, while the antiquated but well-tried semaphore signalling is perfectly adequate on a railway where no great feats of speed are intended or likely.

I must have a jinx on me for at Hatton we ran out of steam again and, this time, *Lord Mountbatten* virtually lost its fire as well. We were now well into the central highlands – 'hill-country' as my empire-building forbears used to call it; the sweet air had turned cool and grey-blue mist hung in the terraced mountains around us. Tea-pickers made blobs of colour among the grid-lines of the plantations on the emerald slopes while the views across the distant blue ranges were magnificent. While we waited for our locomotive to find its second wind, we climbed a viewpoint to gaze at the 8,000-feet-high Adam's Peak, a superbly shaped, violet-tipped mountain revered by pilgrims.

A blast of newly raised steam sent us scurrying back to our

train, I struggling for a toe-hold in the crowded cab. We rattled and swayed through the early evening with a golden sunset of epic proportions turning everyone an unnatural maroon. At Nanu Oya, at 6,000 feet, we reached the end of the line – a line that is the longest and steepest broad gauge climb in all Asia.

Once a narrow gauge spur line ran a further six miles northwards to Nuwara Eliya but today the road has taken over. For more than a century Nuwara Eliya served as an outpost of Empire, a home-from-home for British planters. They built houses with gable roofs and bow windows, set out yews, evergreens and hedges, and attended services in a proper Anglican church. In 1886, to make life complete, they founded a golf club, still very much in use today by Sri Lankans, who are not at all adverse to following some of our quainter customs.

We were delivered to the century-old Hill Club, a fragment of 'olde' England that could hardly have been maintained better in its British heyday than it is at present. A huge fireplace dominated one end of the spacious lounge with stags' heads glaring down from the walls. Immaculate in a uniform as white as the napery in the dining room, barefoot soldiers came forward to serve us.

In my bedroom, a hot-water bottle was ceremoniously laid to rest in my bed and a discreet notice informed male guests that the Club expected 'gentlemen to wear jacket and tie after sundown'. My heart missed a beat. The only gesture I had made to gracious living was to bring a safari suit needing neither shirt nor tie. But the good Ken came to the rescue with a selection of ties representing most of the railway companies of the world so, attired in the colours of the Deutsche Bundesbhan and an old-fashioned jacket and trousers several sizes too large, I descended to dinner.

The next two days were given over to exploring Nuwara Eliya and district. Somebody described the little town as the Chislehurst of Ceylon, and one can see why. It was the British who discovered the charms of this Sinhalese Shangri-La and turned it into a hill resort and although the faded Georgian and mock-Tudor houses must sadden any expatriate ghost still haunting Sri Lanka, the 'Englishness' of the atmosphere remains. The gardens have immaculate lawns, tinted with rose bushes and herbaceous borders surrounded by privet hedges; the moss-covered gravestones in the churchyard are worthy of Thomas Gray's Elegy. The post office boasts an indisputably English clock tower and there are familiar red pillar boxes about the town.

Out on the winding road leading into the hills, the tea plantations succeed one another, proclaiming the old estate names: 'Westward Ho!', 'Melford' and 'Storefield'. Tamil women worked among the bushes, picking the new leaves and tossing them over their shoulders into baskets on their backs. I took myself to a processing plant – most are open to visitors – and was shown around the tea-grading facilities. The flavour of the tea depends on altitude, soil and rainfall; the higher the altitude, the better the quality of the tea. The tender new shoots and buds are allowed to dry until brown and wrinkled. Then they are crushed and dried further to produce what we know as tea leaves. The residue is fit only for tea bags, I was told disdainfully.

Sri Lanka is the world's largest exporter of tea and it is tea that is the cornerstone of the Sri Lankan economy. Yet tea came only to the island as an emergency substitute for coffee when disease wiped out the original coffee plantations. The bushes last about ten years before they are exhausted and have to be replaced. Unfortunately – and it is the same in India – the Sri Lankans may grow very fine tea but they are not always adept at making a good pot of it. The British introduced them to taking milk with it, however, and this custom remains.

I left Nuwara Eliya with a pang of regret but the Horton Plains had left me in a more cheerful frame of mind. Here is the hiker's delight and my feet began itching. A cliff called World's End, one of the scenic wonders of the island, drops down 5,000 feet providing a prodigious panorama over the southern coastal lowlands.

It is but a full day's journey back to Colombo, much of it, again, a retracing of steps but in countryside like this, one could cross it a thousand times without boredom. At Peradeniya Junction, we joined the line from Kandy, and at Kadugannawa our train had descended to a little over 1,500 feet from the 6,000 at Nanu Oya. For *Lord Mountbatten*, it was virtually free-wheeling home.

* * *

Chapter Three

Back in Rameswaram, smarting a little from defeat, I went in search of mollification. The heat of the day and the effort of walking on the soft, hot – if sacred – sand made a cool swim in the sea a priority objective. But the beach was uninviting; the edge of the sea an elongated refuse dump.

In due course, I came to what appeared to be the local *plage*. Indians are not enthusiastic swimmers and those splashing about in the shallow water were mostly women. Discreetly, I took myself a short distance along a breakwater composed of massive concrete blocks to disrobe behind one of them. The sea was lukewarm and brown, but refreshing. And then I discovered that my breakwater was utilised for a double purpose; the second being that of a public toilet for men. Facing me, as I wallowed in the syrupy water, was a row of bare buttocks poised over the edge of the blocks.

In India one must forget about the invention of the lavatory and the bathroom. Travelling across the countryside at sunrise, one's gaze is focused upon crouching figures deep in the cornfields or scrub as the nation's bowels are evacuated. The women are out before dawn; the men follow an hour later, all making their contribution to the countryside that benefits accordingly. Washing is more of a communal affair; men, women and children all dunking themselves in river, lake, pond, stream or under a pump or culvert. Here in urban Rameswaram, the sea made a convenient though unrewarding depository for 'night soil' and I'd chosen the favoured spot for my dip.

Reclaiming my clothes and dignity, I made for the town bent upon exploring whatever charms it might hold. The temple is far and above the chief attraction. It is almost certainly the most beautiful in all India in terms of sculpture, and rises as a vast rectangle about 1,000 feet long and 650 feet wide. It dates back to the 17th century, although the process of construction took no less than three and a half centuries. Inside, the corridors surrounding the rectangle are unique. Through occasional apertures, the sunlight filters to flit over the carved pillars lining them and the effect is sensational.

The town itself is unremarkable in spite of historic chunks of masonry wedged between the concrete structures of the 20th century. I would have liked to visit Dhanushkodi, at the tip of the peninsula and the spot where the Bay of Bengal meets the Indian Ocean, but the rail link to it had been destroyed by a storm.

My train back to Coimbatore was classed as a passenger train as far as Madurai before rising to the status of express. Again the magic had worked and I had been allotted a berth. While recrossing the shallow waters of the peninsula to the mainland, I was joined in my compartment by a young man whose family occupied the neighbouring compartment. He obviously wanted to strike up a conversation with me but didn't know how. The subject of the weather is not considered an opening gambit for a conversation in India so I threw in a comment about the bridge to break the ice.

From then onwards, I was plied with conversation, an assortment of strange sweetmeats and choice items of food from the good family's packaged stock, the flow only terminating when they alighted, with fervent expressions of goodwill, at Manamadurai.

With nightfall I turned my seat into a bunk and was on the verge of sleep when we arrived at Madurai. Vaguely I heard the bustle of the station and the invasion of multiple bodies into my compartment. It gradually percolated through to me that something was wrong; the babble of indignant chatter mounting by the second. Then I was roughly shaken to find myself staring into the angry face of the coach conductor. 'Are you *ill* or something? What are you doing on that berth?' he mouthed in fury and a titter of mirth arose from the two children of the family gathered around me. I was justifiably annoyed myself. 'I was appointed to this berth by the appropriate authority,' I primly pointed out in acid tones.

The official launched into a tirade and, though in English, I understood not a word. Nor, it seemed, were my response and explanation having any greater impact on him – partly because he wasn't listening.

'You have no ticket and no berth reservation,' he screamed at me with abrupt clarity.

I brandished my Indrail pass beneath his nose and tried to lead him outside to show the approximation of my name on the coach reservation list. But he refused to be drawn and, instead, tried to bodily eject me from the train with the help of the new inmates of the compartment.

I fought back, grabbing my scattered belongings as I did so, but was overwhelmed by sheer weight of numbers. On the platform, I espied another official but he was being besieged, and by the time I had drawn his attention to my fate the train was sliding out of the station.

Hopping mad, I took my protestations to the stationmaster and his henchmen who, in their bell-trilling office, listened to my complaints with mounting dismay. 'Indeed, you had every right to be on that train,' I was told, 'and the berth reservation was yours too.' In fairness to Indian Railways, I have to report that the staff of the stationmaster's office gave of their all to rectify the error, arranging for a berth reservation on the next train 24 hours hence, there being but one a day to Coimbatore. I was offered Madras as an alternative destination but I had no wish to go to Madras, thank you, so I was found a bed in an allegedly fully-booked retiring room dormitory. At least I could be thankful for small mercies.

In fact, I could be thankful for a much bigger mercy too. My enforced sojourn at Madurai was going to allow me to see one of the most famous man-made landmarks in southern India – the Temple of Minakshi, the Fish-Eyed Goddess. Following a relatively noise-free night – or what was left of it – and a breakfast of rice and vegetable samosas, I set out in quest of her.

Madurai is a town of great antiquity. It was the capital of the Pandyan rulers and when you remember that the Ptolemys brought pearls and spices from southern India, you should not be surprised to hear that there was a Pandyan ambassador at the court of Augustus in Rome some years before the birth of Christ. The Pandyans were eventually defeated by a Muslim general commanding a Turkish army and they, in turn, were succeeded by the Nayaks, the governors appointed by the kings of Vijayanager, the best known of whom – Tirumala – built a great deal of the temple as it exists today.

The city is a thriving one; a curious mixture of old and new. There are air-conditioned hotels, modern textile mills and a medical school, but in the swarming streets around the temple the people and their way of life have changed little in the last couple of centuries. It is a great place for festivals. There are six major occasions observed by the Hindus, two more by the Christians and a further three by the Muslims. The great temple is a town in itself and encompasses a market place, living accommodation for its resident priests, elephant stables, dance halls, sacred trees, a sacred tank and, in the heart of the maze, the holy of holies – the shrine of the Fish-Eyed Goddess. One of the most remarkable things about it is the structure's sheer size; the outer walls enclose an area that would hold at least six football pitches.

The towers of the temple were in the process of being restored and bright fresh paint had replaced the gentle pastels and crumbling stones of weathered Hindu sculpture. The result to foreign eyes is startling. A hundred or two incarnations of deities out of the Hindu pantheon leering at you from one of the Meenakshi *Gopurams* are not a sight you'll forget in a hurry.

My enforced 24 hours in Madurai were definitely not wasted ones, and with the new dusk I returned to the station – the designated centre of all activities in any Indian town. I shared my curry supper with a sacred cow that ambled not only onto the platform but into the vegetarian restaurant with a nonchalance that surprised only me.

The barriers between human and non-human are completely different in India to those we draw in pet-loving, meat-eating Britain. Most conspicuously different in status is the cow, which freely wanders in the road, halting traffic, munching garbage from rubbish bins, strolling in public gardens, sampling flowers, going for solitary walks through the countryside: revered, eccentric, placid and ubiquitous.

After the cows comes a vast menagerie of monkeys, mice, rats, mongooses, goats, crocodiles, hens, piglets, horses and vultures, all mingling with the equally heterogenous human population in the most disarmingly informal way. The streets everywhere are shared between man and beast, and so, as it would appear, are many of the dwellings. The only elephant I saw on this trip was helping himself to bananas from a roadside store on the outskirts of Cochin.

I was escorted back onto the Ramaswaram Express by the stationmaster in person, who secured a promise from the coach conductor that I was to be given every consideration, so ensuring me a two-berth compartment to myself. When I awoke, we were already in Coimbatore, with dawn yet to break, so I occupied the remaining hour of darkness scrubbing the more visible portions of my anatomy beneath a platform tap. Ready for further battle, I took up a position as first in the queue at the reservations office, intent upon effecting a further batch of berth bookings.

With Coimbatore, I was back on the main line from the south. I had already stopped off at Ernakulam and seen something of Cochin which had impressed me not at all. My first mishap – for which Cochin can hardly be blamed – occurred when I left the train at Ernakulam to fall into the hands of a bright young man who told me most convincingly that he had friends in Sussex, my own county. He was good enough to find me a hotel and then invited me to share with him his motor scooter for a tour of the city. At the other end of town, I alighted to take a ferry to Bolgatty Island, intent upon a swim, and asked what I owed him for the ride.

'Nothing at all,' he replied blandly, 'but I want to massage your body. I'll come to your room this evening. Let's say about seven.' I'd begun to smell a rat when he'd taken upon himself to caress my chest at the hotel but at least he was honest and open about his intentions. He got five rupees for his trouble and was not the least put out by my rebuff.

Cochin is, strictly speaking, the name of a former princely state. It is used today to describe a prosperous modern port – the third largest in India – and it consists of three distinct components. On the inland side of the harbour is Ernakulam, the former state capital, now the business centre. To the west, on the strip of land facing the sea, is Mattancherri, which has at its northern end Fort Cochin. In between the two is Willingdon Island, an entirely artificial piece of land thrown up as a result the ambitious dredging operation that was undertaken to create the harbour.

The trouble with Cochin is that it doesn't quite seem to know where and what it is, a green and watery place though undoubtedly it has become, and as unlike the received idea of India as it is possible to be. As well as Willingdon, bits of the city appear on other islands, including Bolgatty, to whence an overloaded ferryboat took me. At its southern end I discovered the Bolgatty Palace Hotel, once a real palace, now an old-fashioned hotel of faded imperialistic glories offering rooms for just £3 a night; even the honeymoon suite was available for only £6. Off its private jetty, I managed a swim of sorts in murky water smelling strongly of oil emanating from the tankers in line astern off Willingdon Island. My immersion made a hit with the locals and Indian hotel residents who viewed my marine activities with tolerant incredulity. Not much refreshed, I returned to the mainland.

Strolling the streets behind the docks, I came upon old merchant houses, go-downs and courtyards, heaped with betel-nuts, ginger and peppercorns. The air was pungent with spices. It was all very Eastern, and it came to me that Cochin was fortunate in being able to pursue its lucrative trades in a setting of shady lagoons, wooded islands and canals winding past houses raised on stilts in picturesque abandon. To me, Cochin strongly resembled China's Wuxi in Kiangsu Province, another of those rare towns where the 20th century and ancient civilisations can get along very pleasantly.

Cochin's history goes back a long time too. It is the oldest European settlement in India, known even before the first Portuguese arrived at the end of the 15th century. But Portugal has left its stamp upon the city since the adventurer Cabral took a cargo of pepper home in 1500, from which time, having made their way round the Cape of Good Hope, his countrymen came quite frequently. Vasco de Gama, naturally, was here in 1502, and Albuquerque a year later. Francis Xavier arrived in 1530, before the Dutch took over to be, in turn, defeated by the British.

Back at my hotel confusion reigned. Someone (not me) had left my washbasin tap running and water was pouring down the stairs. And I had the only key to the room in my pocket. With this second crisis defeated, I went in search of supper, intent upon an early night, whereupon all the lights in the town went out and stayed out for half the night. This occurrence is a common one in Indian cities and resulted in little inconvenience for me beyond the fact that without the fan, my little bedroom transformed itself into a sauna.

In the morning, an excited knocking on the door could only have been my Sussex-linked gay friend so I pretended to be asleep and eventually the pounding subsided. An hour later, I crept down the still-damp stairs, paid my bill and escaped.

My train to Coimbatore was due at noon, the hottest time of day. At the station I watched a child pee on the platform edge and a prosperous-looking, sari-clad mother sweep the liquid onto the tracks with her bare feet removed from elegant sandals for the purpose. Indian railway stations are, as I have said, the most entertaining of institutions.

En route to Coimbatore, we were hit by a storm of unparalleled ferocity, a wall of water blotting out the view. And at Coimbatore it was raining again; the place must be the Manchester of India.

Under a canopy of waterlogged cloud, I went in search of transportation to Ootacamund, lovingly abbreviated to 'Ooty' by generations of British.

One of the world's famed railways runs up into the Nilgiris, or Blue Mountains, in which Ooty is situated. A narrow-gauge steam-hauled train winds its slow way around the outside of these mountains, where some gradients are so steep that a central rack rail is employed. But, alas, for the outward journey at least, the timings were all wrong so I would have to depend on getting to Ooty by bus. A motor rickshaw buzzed me through the already alive streets to the bus terminal.

As in Britain, the comprehensiveness of the bus routes and the quantity of buses using them is far denser than those of the railway. At the bus station I found vast numbers of battered vehicles preparing to depart for a score of locations including those many hundreds of miles away, such as Madras, Bangalore and Bombay. And the timetable on the wall indicated a profusion of services on each route. So far as I know, there is not state coach company on the lines of our National Express; instead there are private companies serving districts and long-distance routes to main cities where a service fulfils a need of that company's home base and a profit for its management.

A bus to Ooty, via Coonoor, left about every forty minutes

throughout the day; a 3½ hour journey for a one-way fare of about 45 pence. One was on the point of leaving when I arrived and I was lucky to get a seat by a window even though squeezed up against it by a press of three Indians on a bench seat designed for two.

Along the flat and congested road to Mettapulayam, the bus bowled along at a rate of knots that had me thanking my lucky stars I was not up front seeing where we were going. I am a compulsive back-seat driver and I'm sure the risks that driver took would have scared the living daylights out of me. But the size of the vehicle and the banshee howl of its horn cleared the way. And from Mettapulayam the contortions and gradients of the winding road, with hairpin bends sometimes requiring a 'double-take' to negotiate, reduced the speed to less alarming proportions.

Even without Ooty at the end of it, the drive alone would have been worth the journey. Much of the route follows the little railway, crossing and recrossing it as if the road and the rails were playing a game of leapfrog. The Nilgiris lack height and majesty but their crags, waterfalls and forest-clad slopes are wildly beautiful; something about them akin to parts of Britain's West Country – a resemblance which must have caught the imagination of the first Europeans to arrive there.

The old Madras Presidency had a punishing climate so it was only a matter of time before the British officials and planters in south India came to look upon Ootacamund as a summer resort with its green downs, gentle rains and civilised British-like temperature. It was created from nothing to be the hill-station of south India. Explored at the turn of the century, it was settled, largely by enterprising Scots, in the 1830s. Every single thing that now exists on this delectable mountaintop plateau was carried up by dogged idealists. The trees, plants, flowers, the buildings, the recreations and amusements – everything. From the dense forests the British carved out a little idyll and then filled it with ideas and material objects that had never been seen there. Today Ooty is two places: a typical Indian bazaar town overlooking several valleys, and a dying museum.

Government House is now used only for receptions and has been left very much as it was. Inside is like going back into bygone, stately days, with portraits of past governors and their ladies hanging on the walls. I strolled, not without a vestige of sadness, in the cemetery of St Stephen's, a Sussex-like church containing massive and ornate tombs whose inscriptions reveal at what an early age the Victorians succumbed to heat and disease. Here, with a vengeance, was a fragment of England in a 'foreign field', and today goats forage amongst its green and pleasant pastures. The doors of the decaying church, its porch musty with neglect, were firmly locked. I took tea with the manager of the haughty Savoy Hotel and made to depart this stronghold of ghosts, this hill-station fast reverting to no more than an Indian town on the top of a mountain.

Ooty railway station brought me up short. Here, too, hovered an aura of the British Empire. Quite a small station with but a few train services a day, the usual bustle was remarkable for its absence. I walked up the line to the engine sheds to photograph a covey of tank locomotives, filthy, ancient and reliable, some hissing gently, radiant with steam. And then it began to rain – a gentle Sussex shower – and, rather than walk damply back to the bus station, I consulted the platform departures board and discovered to my joy a convenient train to Coonoor through which town the bus had passed on the way up.

It was a remarkable ride. The ancient coaches, including an observation car, inched their way down the gradients with ponderous deliberation, stopping every now and again to pick up essential supplies and a leavening of passengers. The train – they call it the Nilgiris Express – was far from full; obviously the buses have stolen most of its clientele. At one point, the guard gestured wildly towards a bunch of eucalyptus trees but I missed the two wild elephants he had seen. All I saw were the monkeys which hang about the mountain road and railway line for food thrown to them from passing vehicles.

The first company to attempt a railway here went bankrupt, and the reason is not difficult to fathom. At its steepest, the gradient is one in twelve, and the line has some dizzying features. Emerging from a tunnel brings you straight onto a soaring bridge and, looking ahead, the tracks seem to disappear over the edge of the world. The line between Ooty and Coonoor, which is rack and pinion, is assuredly the most dramatic, taking one through some of the most hair-raising mountain scenery imaginable. The temperature and humidity increased with every yard of descent but Coonoor was still cool.

And here is another, if lesser, hill station in the Nilgiris standing at 5,600 feet above sea level, a thousand feet lower than Ooty. The town, again with English county overtones, is surrounded by tea plantations and its rolling slopes alternate with *sholas*, the wooded valleys containing real English gorse imported as seed from Britain.

The rain belt had not descended to Coonoor and it was a lovely afternoon, clean and bright; not a cloud save those clinging to the upper slopes of the hills behind me. To the south, the sky was the colour of a tropical sea – greeny blue, reflected in perfectly still pools and paddy fields on the plain below. There was a sweetness in the air and, for a number of miles, no people – just colour and empty space and darting birds.

From Coonoor's bus depot, close to the railway station, I picked up a bus bound for Coimbatore for the price of 30 pence and a ten-minute wait. At Mettupallayam was a return to India proper and the steamy heat of the plain.

My night train to Bangalore bore no name. In the pages of the timetable, it was listed as simply Express No. 25, originating from Trivandrum. On the Coimbatore station platform berth reservations board I had been rechristened 'Mr Chritipher Hopeway.' I had plenty of time before my departure to partake of a leisurely supper at the station vegetarian restaurant. The waiters were beginning to look upon me as a regular client and my favourite 24-pence curry was placed before me with a flourish.

My compartment was shared with an English-speaking family from Mysore City, who reminded me that we were entering a new state, that of Karnataka, formerly the state of Mysore. They were adamant in their insistence I should know this, as if the loss of Mysore's statehood rankled deeply. I responded by airing my regret at not being able to visit their fair city, which I knew to be one of palaces, gardens and oriental splendour. The family made perfect bedroom companions, being silent, non-smoking and unobtrusive after lights out. We arrived in Bangalore more or less on time at 5.30 in the morning.

It was a little early to emerge into a new city so I toyed with a coffee on the platform and watched the world go by. Never shall I cease to marvel at and applaud some of the aspects of the Indian way of life as well as its contradictions. People do exactly what they want to do, where they want to do it and with no sense of self-consciousness or embarrassment – whether it's scrubbing their teeth under a platform tap, peeing discreetly but unashamedly in a quiet corner, or lying prostrate on the ground in the shade when there's nothing else to do. In India, everything is all so naturally carried out where, in Britain, such actions would be looked on as eccentricity. Particularly through its railway stations, I'm coming to see India for what it is: a vast, chaotic family. Superficially, the furniture of that family may look dirty and unkempt. But there's always a little man somewhere brushing up the mess on the restaurant or waiting room floor, or a little woman clearing up the refuse on the track after a train has come and gone. And, as I have already remarked, Indians are forever washing under taps or in rivers and puddles whenever the opportunity occurs. The family is composed of a myriad of backgrounds, types, looks, creeds and colours, young and old, marked or unmarked, whole or deformed; yet nobody takes the slightest notice of anyone different to themselves except, here in the south, for the lone pale-faced European, the stranger in their world. 'Where are you from?' comes the question from every quarter. 'England,' I say enthusiastically (Britain is not universally understood), expecting it to be the one country that would produce reaction because of its past influence on their lives. But no, I remain a moon-man from outside the family.

Welcomgroup Hotels had a hotel in Bangalore, the Windsor Manor, which I decided would make worthwhile contrast to my current mode of retiring room dormitory, train berth and doss-house. I found a handsome palace of a building at the ritzy end of town with elegant, high-ceilinged, pillared rooms of impeccable taste. Yet the luxury was not ostentatious. After a memorable bath, I spent the morning sipping Pimms by the swimming-pool.

Bangalore is the capital of Karnataka. The name means 'baked beans' but don't ask me why – and, for an Indian city, it is a beautiful one. Quite modern – most of it was built in the 18th century – the town is spacious, well-planned and graced with parks and leafy suburbs of manicured lawns and ever-blooming flowers. In some ways, it put me in mind of an Indian version of

Tunbridge Wells; somewhat lacking in the exuberance of more down-to-earth Indian towns.

A guest at the hotel poolside was incredulous. 'You mean you've been travelling around southern India by *railway*! How did you do it? What was it like? It's something I never *thought* of doing.' Admittedly the guest was American so was more attuned to the airlines than other forms of transport, but Europeans too had displayed a kind of wonderment that I could even consider such an undertaking. Yet these same Europeans regularly catch trains back in their respective countries, so what's different about *Indian* trains? Of course, a lot of the inhibitions stem from preconceived ideas of Indian travel culled from film and out-of-date fact.

Having seen something of the city the previous afternoon, I was content to go straight to the station the next morning. My scooter driver asked for a quarter of what I had paid to reach the hotel, which meant I'd been previously overcharged by 300%. Taxi-drivers the world over live by their wits but those of India, having to negotiate cow, bicycle and traffic-snarled streets on the lowest of wages, I resent least of all.

My next train was another nameless unit but graded as Passenger/Mail which meant it was semi-fast – or semi-slow – depending on which way you look at it. From a north-easterly direction, it swung north-west towards Bombay. Though the Udyan Express was a more direct vehicle for a journey from Bangalore to Bombay, it terminates its run at Dadar, a Bombay suburb about eight miles short of the city centre. This itself mattered little since there is a good electric suburban service from Dadar into Bombay Central, but I wanted to go there by way of Goa, which necessitated a still further westerly route than that of the Udyan Express. My compartment was communal and the company rather more exalted than usual, its denizens all speaking good English. In the corner was a lady taking up a new executive post in Bombay while opposite her was the chairman of a substantial company and his painfully deferential assistant. The conversation turned boringly commercial so I took refuge in sleep.

Of all the slow trains of my current journey this was the slowest and we drew in to Vasco-de-Gama late the following afternoon. I could almost have walked there faster – and certainly more entertainingly. But with Vasco-de-Gama, I was deep inside

Goa, the thumbprint of former Portuguese territory in India.

The Goa line terminates on a headland protruding into the sea so I caught a bus to the capital, Panaji, around the wide estuary of the Zuari River. From there, a motor scooter delivered me to a hotel close to Fort Aguada Beach. And, of course, for most people beaches are what Goa is all about. On mine a whale had got itself stranded, to expire a week before I arrived; its corpse was now being methodically carved into sections for convenient handling and removal. The remains ponged vilely which allowed me most of this exotic strip of golden sand on the Malabar coast all to myself the following morning.

In Panaji I ran to earth a friend of mine, the diminutive one-time assistant director of the Indian Government Tourist Office in London, Mr Kandhalar, who took time off to race me enthusiastically around the more cultural offerings of Goa. Panaji itself is a pleasant, easy-going town which could have been in Portugal or South America, with broad streets and squares ornamented by statues. But it was to Old Goa that I was whisked. 'You must see it before the light fails,' I was told. 'Panaji is more fun when it has.'

Goa was the first important Christian colony in the East but back in the 15th century it was the starting point for Indian pilgrims *en route* to Mecca. It was also a bone of contention among the English, Dutch and Portuguese, who were vying for its possession. The Portuguese, in the person of Alfonso de Albuquerque, won.

This was the beginning of Goa's glory as a trading centre – spices from Malaya, coral and pearls from Persia, porcelain and silk from China. St Francis of Xavier, on an evangelical mission, arrived, as did Gareia da Orta, the famed botanist, and the poet Luis de Camoes. Everybody who was anybody set up home there.

Then Goa's decline began. The Inquisition was set up in the late 16th century – a grim reflection of the religious fanaticism that was sweeping Europe, instituting a 250-year reign of terror. Then, in 1655, a disastrous plague wiped out 200,000 people. In 1834 the seat of power was moved six miles down the Mandovi River to Panaji, and a year later Old Goa was abandoned altogether.

Portugal's days of glory in India were coming to a close too. Time and time again her colonists found themselves in skirmishes not only with the Dutch, Spanish, French and English, but with the Goans themselves. After India became independent, the French handed over the territories they occupied, leaving only Goa and the Portuguese – the first and now the last European intruder on Indian soil. Approaches were made to Salazar but he flatly refused to depart, so in 1961 Nehru ordered his army to invade. Hence Goa was liberated and is now an integral part of India, though it still exhibits a strong Iberian flavour.

In Old Goa, dense jungle has smothered all that remains of the opulent mansions of the old aristocracy. Round the deserted square, with moss growing between the paving stones, is a cluster of churches, monasteries and convents, the best known of all being the Church of Bom Jesus; this holds the tomb of St Francis Xavier, whose body for many years remained in a perfect state of preservation but which has now shrunk to the size of a mummy.

Grass pushes up through the Avenida da Brasil, where the Grandees took their evening stroll; one fights through the matted creepers to reach the Palace of the Inquisition and watch for snakes in the nave of the Sé Cathedral.

Returning to Panaji, I found a town come to life. The market stalls, heaped with shrimps, crabs, giant prawns, lobsters and mussels, were doing a roaring trade and the bars were full of Goans effervescently exhibiting their love of music and drink, if not of work. There is little poverty here; nothing on the scale of that in the rest of the country. In a downtown bar, Mr Kandhalar and I partook of a couple of glasses of the local firewater, *fenny*, distilled from cashew nuts, and eased ourselves into a spirited conversation with the garrulous patrons who plied us with more.

My hotel was across the Mandovi River estuary, traversed by two ferries working in conjunction since the new concrete bridge upstream had fallen down. The ferries cross and recross non-stop, dodging the dhows and barges, which drift on the tide, laden with sardines, pomfret, herrings, manganese and iron ore. The jungle laps at the edge of the town and in a year or two it could take over the tree-lined avenues, the formal square and the bland baroque facades as easily as it has in Old Goa.

Next day I found my way back to Vasco-de-Gama and caught the early morning train – the Mandovi Express I think it was – towards Bombay, the brief holiday over – or that's how it felt. The biggest diesel I have ever seen pulled us out of the station and out of Goa with contemptuous ease. I pretended not to see the slums of Londra and scores of Indians squatting by the tracks emptying their bowels with enormous concentration. From medium gauge to broad gauge, a change of trains at Miraj and I was on the overnight Mahalazmi Express bound for Pune and Bombay VT (Victoria Terminus, one of the city's two main stations). No sneaking into a suburb with this train but, with no berth reservation, it could offer me no more than a night on the tiles. Which, perhaps, was just as well since arrival at Pune was scheduled at four in the morning and I intended dallying there for a while.

Darkness hid the Deccan plain, a basalt plateau stretching for hundreds of miles, featureless and keening with heat. On the edge of it sits the old Maratha capital and former summer quarters of the Governor of Bombay, Pune – Poona of barrack-room legend. Immediately I alighted from the train, I realized why the governor – and lesser mortals – found the city attractive, for the humidity of the coast had evaporated and the temperature was comfortable. Pune retains its place in military annuals, being the headquarters of the army's southern command but, in Indian eyes, its fame lies in it being the childhood home of Shivaji, the revered and warlike leader whose statue graces the heart of the city. The British came into the picture when Pune fell into their hands at the Battle of Kirkee in 1817. Under them it developed into the 'monsoon capital' of Bombay Province and a sizeable military centre.

As a town it is one aware of its martial history and containing vestiges of 18th century warfare; the gates are fortified with spikes against elephant charges. I witnessed its awakening streets, treated myself to fried eggs and chips in a cafe-bar whose elderly owner told me he had served this fare to many a British soldier in his time, and then wended my way back to the railway station.

My subsequent train was the Sahyadhi Express (where do they get these expressive names?) which, on its idling jaunt towards Bombay, stopped at the township of Neral. It was mid-morning, we were only two hours short of the city and there were a number of later trains, so I emerged from my compartment to investigate the Matheran Mountain Railway. And there it was, just as I had expected, a narrow-gauge, somewhat rickety line wandering off in the direction of the only hill for miles around. On another platform, a tiny toy train of squat, brightly-painted wagons awaited my pleasure.

It is a bumpy ride as the miniature train drags itself across mostly barren and oft-sheer cliffs from stifling heat into chilly, goose-pimpling jungle by way of tunnels and excruciatingly sharp curves. Boys hop aboard to sell you *jambul*, a small, purple tree-fruit, while black and red-faced monkeys watch your passing with hungry interest.

Matheran itself came into being when an Englishman, Hugh Mallet, district administrator of nearby Thana, proclaimed the hill a fine place for shady walks. A number of tribes lived scattered about the region, and they are still there, augmenting their agricultural living by profiting from their visitors. There are no cars and the greatest charm of the place is its tranquillity and slow pace of life. From the summit of the hill can be seen the environs of Bombay disappearing into the heat haze.

For some reason my new mainline train chose to go no further into the city than the suburb of Dadar after all. However, I found no trouble at all reaching Bombay Central via an efficient suburban train service, though I started off on the wrong foot by entering a 'Ladies Only' compartment to be shooed out just as the doors closed. But just five stops on the next train and I was there.

As well as a *laissez-passer* to Welcomgroup Hotels, I also possessed similar facilities for a gratis stay at the Oberoi in Bombay; in fact, the two Oberois in Bombay since they stand side by side and are, in effect, one. Though I had spoilt myself at Bangalore, I decided it wouldn't hurt to repeat the process in Bombay. So, from the city's Central Railway station I caught a cab to Nariman Point, the hotel's situation, which was decidedly on the right side of the tracks.

There are no motor rickshaws in central Bombay: they have long been banished to the suburbs in an effort to alleviate the chronic traffic situation. Instead there are 16,000 taxis, and they all seemed to be coming down the same street. The one thing kept in good repair around here is the taxi horn, and no taxi-driver would dream of going more than a few yards without sounding it. The result is a day-long and unrelenting cacophony. And hardly had we left the station forecourt than we were almost flattened between the sides of two uncaring buses.

The heart of Bombay is by no means all high-rise office blocks. Solid architectural legacies of the British presence contribute to the city's distinctive character: the municipal buildings, courts museums, fort, churches and clubs. The style of some of them is Imperial Preposterous, and gothic piles like the Victoria Terminus Railway Station are impressive. Everywhere, huge gaudy hoardings advertising the latest films form an integral part of the cityscape, art forms in their own right and evidence of the largest movie industry in the world, the great provider of the stuff of dreams and romance.

I was dropped, safe and sound, outside the double Oberoi. Fountains splashed against marble walls in the Albert Hall-sized lobby; nine restaurants, from Indian through European to Polynesian, beckoned me via a three-level shopping centre, and bedroom suites costing thousands of rupees a night enveloped me. A butler entered my room, introduced himself and offered to unpack my luggage and lay out my evening attire. I hid my minuscule rucksack behind me and fought a compulsive desire to flee. A little later, a flunky entered with my personally engraved notepaper – and I knew I was hooked.

From my eighth-floor window was an incredible panoramic view of the wide sweep of the bay; assuredly I was seeing the best of the city. It looks better from a distance. Here, in this second city of India, you will find the extremes of sophisticated wealth and terrible poverty, ugly in unison.

The original trading post of the East India Company was at Surat, 150 miles up the coast. Bombay was ceded by the Portuguese in 1662 as part of her dowry when Catherine of Braganza was married to Charles II. Chronically hard up, he leased it to the Company for the modest rental of ten pounds a year, plus, of course, a substantial sum in cash. It consisted of a string of small, malarial islands set in a network of creeks. Forty years later, the Company moved its headquarters there and set about linking the whole together to establish what has become one of the largest ports in Asia. It is now a city of more than eight million inhabitants; Parsis, Gujeratis, Sindhi bankers from Karachi, Goanese, Maharastrians, Sikhs and Pathans. All are drawn there by the notion that its streets are paved with gold; a notion given impetus by the fact that the city is the one in all India that is nearest to Western tastes. Hollywood, New York and London all rolled into one would describe one aspect of Bombay.

My sojourn at the Bombay Oberoi was hardly painful. I endured rather than enjoyed the extravagant and ostentatious attentions lavished upon me. I was induced to sample each of the grandiose restaurants, where the fare looked better than it tasted (even in the Oberoi, Indians seem incapable of serving tender meat). And I found it hard to reconcile this whole vast cathedral of opulence, replete with its battalions of butlers, lift boys in natty white soldier uniforms, beautiful PR ladies in flowing saris and miscellaneous staff garbed far more expensively than any of the guests, with that other sight out of my window – of the down-and-out human flotsam asleep (or dead) beneath the promenade benches.

Yet this kind of reasoning helps nobody. Business folk and their families, as well as tourists, come to such hotels because they want to. Thus there is a need for such establishments the world over. And because of this all luxury hotels create both money and employment beneficial to everyone. As I had already observed, it is not easy to distinguish between what, by Indian standards, is plain simplicity of living (in a country with less need of the trappings of European living) or real poverty. Alas, in India, poverty is the norm. One is stunned by it, one accepts it, one ceases to notice it. Like the presence of the perpetual Indian sun, poverty is simply taken for granted.

From the Oberoi Hotel, I proceeded on the standard tour of the city. An insincere young man, clearly more interested in amassing his company's income than of showing off his hometown, led us from one landmark to another. The Gateway of India – a massive archway built to commemorate the visit in 1911 by King George V and Queen Mary. The Prince of Wales Museum of Art commemorating the same event. The Victoria Museum concerned only with the history of the city and commemorating nobody. Bombay University with its familiar English clocktower. The Victoria Railway Terminus looking remarkably like St Pancras and, across the bay on Malabar Hill, the Hanging Gardens remarkable – to me – for their mediocrity together with the Towers (which they are not) of Silence. The Parsis hold that they must not profane the sacred elements of fire or earth by burning or burying their dead so they expose them to be devoured by birds of prey. For ghouls like me, there is nothing to see except a permanent flock of vultures soaring, expectantly, on the thermals of a cloudless sky. The tour ended with brief visits to the Jain Temple and the Mahatma Gandhi residence.

Back at Bombay Central Station two days later, I made my way to the departure platform of the Rajdhani Express bound for Delhi. Bombay Central has not the charisma of Victoria Terminus but there is a certain expectation generated even here by the impending departure of a crack express train, as there used to be at London's Victoria Station for the direct Orient Express. The Rajdhani is an all-air-conditioned train with a waiting list of potential passengers as long as your arm. I was pleased – and again, not a little surprised – that the good Mr Dev's magic had worked: my name, spelt correctly as well, reposed smudgily upon the list of the chosen few. Railway staff fussed around the exceedingly plain coaches, cleaning their windows and loading aboard insulated containers of provisions. Two passengers-to-be engaged me in conversation on the platform as we waited to entrain and we found that we were assigned to the same coach. 'We'll celebrate when we've left Bombay,' they told me, but what there was to celebrate was not immediately clear to me.

We left on the dot of four and straightaway attained a speed I have seldom experienced before on an Indian train. It sped along the coast at a most satisfactory rate and, until the environs of Delhi, abided by its promise of but three stops *en route*. Afternoon tea with unappetising European-type sandwiches and cake came round at once and a curry dinner followed after dusk. Full of Oberoi fare, I gave both a miss even though all meals on the Rajdhani Express are included in the fare.

With nightfall our seats were turned into beds and, glory be, the full regalia of bedding – sheets, blankets and even pillows – were distributed and made-up by well-practised attendants. No do-it-yourself caper here.

Before turning in, my two friends arrived to invite me to the 'celebration', leading me out of the compartment to the attendant's kitchenette at the further end of the coach. And for a hilarious hour the three of us, together with several members of the train crew, consumed between us a bottle and a half of Indian whisky beneath a stern Indian Railways notice proclaiming 'No alcoholic beverage whatsoever may be consumed on the train'.

The first stop was at Vadodara, the junction for Ahmadabad and the western end of the state of Rajasthan, where we replenished the whisky stocks. My new friends were hungry for knowledge of my earlier Indian travels so I told them about a journey I had made a few years before, one at the luxurious end of the spectrum (and one which I was to relate in detail in my own book *The Great Travelling Adventure*). It was appropriate too, for the Rajdhani Express in its dash to Delhi, runs a parallel course to that of the delectable 'Palace on Wheels'.

* * *

Rajasthan is the obvious choice of states through which to run a Maharajah's train. It is a land of rock and desert, lakes and gardens and enchanting fairy-tale forts and palaces.

From the human angle, Rajasthan is a region that is still living in its historic past, despite the changes of the last few years. Home of the Rajputs of ancient lineage, it is the legendary land of chivalry and knightly prowess. Its very name means 'Abode of Kings'. Palace and fort, garden and lake, they speak of love and loyalty, of proud prestige and deeds of derring-do. Rajasthan has a stirring story indeed writ large upon the embattled walls of its cities. Resisting every invader since the time of Harsha in the 7th century, the feudal lords and princes of Rajasthan valiantly defended their independence and, in this, they were helped by the British, for whom its colourful peoples maintain a high regard.

The prestigious tour train, the 'Palace on Wheels', introduced to present this evocative area to visitors, hides its light under a bushel. The long line of dun-coloured coaches gives little impression of a palace, wheeled or otherwise, though its colour might initiate the notion of a golden train. The windows, set low, are the usual barred variety and there is no corridor. The train's chief power unit is the steam engine and this, externally, is where its grandeur lies. In my day there were two such locomotives, magnificent monsters both, each bearing a golden coat of arms and the proud names *Desert Queen* and *Fort of Jodhpur*.

The outside of the coaches may have been unimpressive but

inside was another story. Upon being ushered into my own private coach – in its time it had borne both the Maharajah of Bikaner and Mrs Indira Gandhi – I gazed in awe upon the spacious sleeping compartment replete with wardrobe and double bed, plus refinements such as table lamps, fans and a telephone. The lounge contained a sofa and armchairs of quality brocade, the walls were lined with heavy polished mahogany. A well-fitted-out toilet and bathroom and a further two smaller bedrooms completed the suite of rooms, beyond which lay the servants' quarters, the domain of two most gracious Rajashanis attired in crimson and gold tunics and turbans to match, their sole object over the ensuing week being to wait upon me hand and foot. Further along the train, the restaurant car was a reflection of what I can remember of the one-time *Brighton Belle*: pink lampshades at each window, the tables agleam with monogrammed china and cutlery, while the lounge car was plentifully endowed with soft cushions around long, low divans and oblong coffee tables of polished carved oak; the whole menage tastefully encased by the luxuriant folds of curtains glittering with gold thread. An end section housed a bar and a library, each well stocked with its particular requisites.

Indian Railways it was that carried out this major refurbishment of rolling stock rescued, item by item, from railway sheds and disused sidings at remote railway stations all over India. Saved from the grave, but rusted from the monsoons and bleached by the sun, they were assembled and painstakingly restored to their former glory, or rebuilt from a basic framework.

The first meal in the restaurant car was representative of them all. There was a choice of meat or fish between the usual ancillary items, but the paramount attraction of that particular meal was vested in the assembly of its consumers; the gathering of the clan. Across the soup, the veal cutlets, the halibut and the creme caramel, we eyed one another in critical appraisal, pondered upon the type of person who would choose a train for a holiday and launched into a fever of introductions. Thus, with the coffee and mints, I was able to discern that our numbers included lawyers and doctors, stockbrokers and company directors, a naval captain and a nuclear scientist. That such an upper stratum of society should be so strongly represented was surprising only in that it showed who is the most adventurous class – so long as the adventure is diluted with comfort and there is the money to embark upon it. The coffee and liqueurs concluded, we bade one another goodnight and scurried to our respective bedchambers to await the maharajan movement.

And indeed, the maharajan movement took us all over Rajasthan. At Jaipur, the 'pink city', we were greeted by a cavalcade of elephants, not pink but vivid nevertheless in glittering head-dress; a band of folk-musicians warbling boisterously, and the first of seven marigold garland welcomes from smiling girls of exotic allure.

There was a perfect tonal harmony about the salmon-pink dawn breaking over the faded red-ochre sandstone of the city that owes its name and symmetry to Maharajah Jai Singh II. Encircled on all sides – except the south – by rugged hills surmounted by forts, Jaipur is enclosed by battlemented walls. Within them is medieval bedlam. The *Hawa Mahal* – Palace of the Winds – is the landmark of the city, though its elaborate, fanciful, pink facade stands amid the high street chaos of clogged roads and rude dwellings.

At Amber came the scheduled elephant ride on which we progressed regally up the hill, musically escorted, to the deserted Moghul edifice before a lesson on sundials at the Jantar Mantar Observatory, tea on a Maharajan terrace and dinner among the floodlit remains of the ruined fort of Nahargarh.

Came Udapur, another sprawling city, this one given a romantic air by the steel-blue waters of a lake. Moated Udaipur, ethereal, unreal, holds island palaces galore that sparkle with pinnacles of coloured glass, of amber and pale jade created by Maharajah Udai Singh in the 16th century. His palace-fort, massively bastioned and gated, erupts from the crest of a ridge and is the largest such pile in Rajasthan. In the less sombre palace that takes up the whole of an island in the artificial lake, we lunched very adequately on asparagus and venison.

'Island in the Sun' describes the next port of call, and for most of us it was the most fascinating city of all. In a scarred, romantic land amidst shifting sands, barren ridges and jutting rocks of sandstone, limestone and flint under a brazen sun lies Jaisalmer, a forgotten feudal outpost where palaces, temples and bazaars created a magical medieval city of the Orient. At every turn there are glimpses of an older, fiercer way of life, a life made hard and vital by its remote and austere setting. Proud, turbaned figures, impressive faces atop slow, swaying camels; graceful *panharis* walking from the village wells, brass water pots balanced on their heads; the clamour and clangour and colour of bazaars; kohl-rimmed eyes, bangles, ankle bells; a hundred ancient secrets kept behind fortress gates among the streets and alleys of the teeming city.

Jaisalmer's history dates back to the 12th century when it became an important trading post between east and west. The discovery of the sea route to India by the Portuguese three centuries later nullified its commercial raison d'être, but successive flamboyant maharajahs maintained its splendour with temples and palaces, all encrusted with stone carvings. Only in the last decades has this exotic city become accessible with the construction of both road and railway.

On camels now, we sauntered eastwards in single file across stony expanses and over dunes towards the Pakistani border, each of us perched uncomfortably on the blanket-covered wooden saddles as the animals rocked back and forth. Our return looped southwards over parched earth framed by a featureless horizon, our mounts maintaining their air of haughty indifference, contemptuous of their desert joyriders.

Northwards, still on the railway, lies Bikaner. 'Out of the silken darkness of a desert dawn emerged the dream of Bikaner.' For thirty years after leaving his father's capital of Jodhpur, Rao Bhika and his followers lived from skirmish to skirmish on the edge of life in a hostile land. Gujars, Pratiharas, Chauhans, Afhgans, Bhattis and Rajputs fought with one another for supremacy and here, in a wilderness of sand, Bhika won a kingdom for himself and ruled as 'Lord of the Desert of Bikaner'.

And so to the last city, Jodhpur, once the capital of the state of Marwar, built upon the brow of a low sandstone hill again in the heart of the desert. A rocky eminence immediately behind dominates it from the sand that stretches away on all sides, and at its summit soars a massive fortress, its towers and bastions standing out like tough sinews gleaming with a copper tinge where the rock itself was hewn to form the walls and ramparts. From these the view commands the horizon; indeed, on a clear day may be seen the tower of Khumbhalgarth, 80 miles to the south.

These then were the cities of the tour, plus Bharatpur with its Keoladeo Ghana bird sanctuary, an ornithologist's paradise and, as a grand finale, the jewel of the Taj Mahal at Agra. But for me, the height of evocation came with my repeated transfers from the luxurious splendour of the mobile abode of the Maharajah of Bikaner to the sooty confines of the cab of the locomotives. Here, my eyes full of smut and a tummy full of sweet, oily tea, I rediscovered a joy of travel that was in danger of eclipse beneath a welter of high living. Within a shuddering cab full of dials and levers, I was back in a corner of real India and in the company of Indians, together sharing the whiff of steam, the searing blast of heat from a raging furnace, the ear-splitting scream of the whistle and the sheer exhilaration of riding a mechanical animal vibrating with unleashed power. On the last morning aboard the *Desert Queen*, I was given a revisionary lesson by an appreciative crew on the rudiments of an old-fashioned semaphore signalling procedure and in, in farewell, received a big hug from the driver and his fireman who had tolerated – even aided and abetted – my numerous incursions into their domain. We were an hour late into Delhi but nobody minded. Back at New Delhi station, there were no garlands: we were maharajahs no more.

* * *

The Rajdhani Express is never late into Delhi. Nor early either, I was given to understand by the train commander as he made the morning rounds. With breakfast brought to our compartments, both sets of windows – mesh and glass – were pulled up and our bedding removed. As well as the steel bars, there are double windows, both lockable, on all trains. It is still common, apparently, for bandits to hold up a train, strip the richer passengers of their valuables and make their getaway by truck. Here we were nowhere near dacoit country but old habits and old fears die hard. On my outward journey on the Kerala Express I had travelled all night with both windows open such had been the heat – and had survived to tell the tale.

In the suburbs of Delhi we slowed, halted, moved off and halted again, then slid into the platform at New Delhi Station on the stroke of 9.15 a.m.. The fragile bonhomie generated within the compartment faltered and fell asunder as we went our ways.

Chapter Four

My train was again the Rajdhani Express, but this one plied a
different route. There are, in fact, two Rajdhani Expresses: one
plying between Delhi and Bombay, the other between Delhi and
Calcutta. It is four years later – 1991 – and, on this occasion, I was
heading east.

This rail journey threatened to be somewhat of a sheltered and
overscheduled one, pre-programmed by the Indian Government
Tourist Office in London, who, as my host, wanted me to see
specific locations and archaeological edifices upon learning I had
my eyes set upon the less-frequented eastern end of their country.
However, my idea of 'eastern end' had been Assam and beyond,
whilst they had the closer and more accessible provinces of Orissa
and New Bengal in mind. In fact, they positively blanched when I
revealed a desire to investigate Assam and the so-called hill states
which, of course, had the effect of increasing my curiosity. 'If you
go there you're on your own,' they declared, fondly imagining this
to be a threat.

But, *en route* to Assam, I was well content to take a look at the
renowned temples of Orissa and to sample the famed 'toy train'
ride up the Himalayan foothills to Darjeeling; in fact, this second
detour featured in my own plans – as did a sojourn in Calcutta,
India's largest city, though this not without inexplicable dread.
And what's more, so far as Orissa was concerned, a journey there
would entail back-tracking on the Madras line towards a point
which would close my full circuit of India's periphery. An
unimportant fragment of accomplishment perhaps, but one that
gave satisfaction to a tidy-minded traveller.

For my eastern journey I was equipped with not only the
necessary permit for entering Assam but also a full set of Indrail
reservations covering virtually the whole of my itinerary, thanks to

the insistence of the good Dr Dandapani, UK representative of Indian Railways. And at various stages of my route I would be met, hosted and accommodated by representatives of various goverment tourist offices, which promised a trouble-free if unadventurous trip. So far as accommodation was concerned I had stipulated the use of middle-grade hotels; I'd had enough of the overblown pampering of the super-luxury gin palaces.

The Calcutta-bound Rajdhani Express rolled out of New Delhi station on its appointed minute and, snug but sleepless through the night, I merely heard Danpur and Allahadbad and glimpsed the momentary dazzle of their stations. No lying abed permitted on this train and, with the tea and biscuits, our bedding was speedily removed. I'm not a fussy person but I do tend to become conservative at breakfast; curry at eight in the morning doesn't really appeal.

On the run-up to our midday arrival we slid through a series of suburban stations well-patronised by passengers waiting for commuter services. My neighbour in the compartment, guessing I was a newcomer to the city, issued a warning. 'You're in for a shock, you know. Hope you're prepared for it.' My apprehension increased alarmingly as Calcutta's reputation as an urban horror story struck home.

But my introduction to one of the world's most populous and allegedly poverty-displaying cities was lessened by the driver and car that awaited me at Howrah station though, such was the scrum on the arrival platform, I nearly missed them.

We inched over the Hooghly river on the famous Howrah Bridge, the most utilised bridge on earth, and my eyes were everywhere, keenly aware of looking upon something already familiar from photographs and literature. On the other side of the huge iron structure my driver used the universal technique of swerving and hooting to negotiate the solid mass of humanity, vehicles, beasts and carts compressed into the street, a street partly excavated because of the new underground railway being constructed.

The density of traffic in those streets was greater than I had seen anywhere else in India. Bordering them, buildings rose higgledy-piggledy from the dust. Wobbly verandas leant out from upper storeys, incredibly dirty windows were half obsured by corrugated iron or enormous cinema hoardings; power and telephone cables looped and dangled from leaning posts and rusty hooks. It all looked decayed and old but strangely English which, of course, it was. The mementos of the British Raj are not just the solid Victoria Memorial, the prim St. Paul's Cathedral and Dalhousie Square.

The beginnings of Calcutta were humble enough. Three villages – Sutanuti, Gorindapur and Kalikata – lay on the banks of the Hooghly river. From them the road to Kalighat meandered. Here was a place of pilgrimage, infested with wild animals and ruthless dacoits. Though mythical associations of Kalighat go back to Shiva himself, history records no references to this temple before the 17th century.

If Kalighat, with its halo of fierce divinity, lent a focal point to the growth of Calcutta, so did the mundane reaches of commerce. Chittagong, in present-day Bangladesh, and Saptagram in the west were the two great centres of trade when the Portuguese and Dutch first began to frequent the shores of Bengal in about 1530. The Hooghly was then easily navigable and it became their anchoring point. Weaving, a yarn market, business transactions between the Portuguese and Dutch, and later involvement of the East India Company all contributed to drawing the trio of villages together into what eventually became the city of Calcutta.

The seeds of British imperialism were sown with Job Charnock's decision to set up a factory at Sutanuti, and between the 17th and early 20th centuries the British Raj came to represent Calcutta's history. From the confines of Fort William, built by the British, it spread its wings. Construction proceeded at a hectic pace. The majestic buildings on Chowringhee and in Dalhousie Square are symbols from the past, evoking nostalgia of days gone by. And the Victoria Memorial, Lord Curzon's imaginative blending of the Taj Mahal with St Paul's Cathedral in London, is still carefully preserved.

From my base at a modest hostelry, the Lytton Hotel in Sudder Street, I was given a whirlwind tour of the city that only served to confuse my senses the more. The small churchyard of St John, which includes the octagonal mausoleum of Job Charnock; St Paul's Cathedral full of Raj memorabilia, the huge statue of Queen Victoria looking decidedly not amused; the Tollyunge

Club still reeking of a class distinction imported by ourselves; and Kali Temple, athrob with praying well-fed priests who appeared to want nothing to do with Mother Teresa's hostel next door, where a few dedicated Indian and European volunteers were donating crumbs of dignity to the dying. Dalhousie Square, where all indications of Calcutta's infamous black hole have been painstakingly removed; the Paresnath Jain Temple and the Maiden, this last a large green expanse where cricket, tennis and football are played, cows graze and citizens of all ranks partake of yoga sessions or defecate.

The comparatively few tourists who come to Calcutta usually give it half a day before moving on. Seldom do they take the trouble to wander into the mean pulsating streets containing the workshops of the *kumars*, or potters, who labour throughout the year preparing clay effigies – life-size and larger – around cones of bamboo and straw. The vividly painted, oft-startling idols of gods and goddesses – particularly of Durga on her lion slaying the demon Asura – are for the *pujas*, or festivals, the clay images usually unbaked since they are immersed in the holy river Hooghly at the culmination of the festival. As the time of the *puja* approaches, thousands of these giant figures, brightly painted and gaudily dressed, can be seen being stacked away to await the final finishing touch by the master painter prior to being trundled away to join the multiple processions. I was to return to Calcutta within a week and so would be present to witness the most important Hindu festival of Bengal, the *Durga Puja*. In the meantime I was happy to wander from one *kumar* to another, taking photographs, talking with the ever-cheerful craftsmen and being shown their special creations.

I left the city on the afternoon Coromandel Express, which plies the line to Madras via Bhubneshwar, largest city of the province of Orissa, a journey of 270 miles. My company was a livelier, more entertaining one than that of my earlier train. A young couple with two toddlers sat near me for much of the way, the woman being as beautiful as she was fat, and when she sat cross-legged her lap made the perfect cradle for the smallest child. I was inveigled into a game of Ludo in return for which they shared with me ill-tasting morsels bought at stops along the line. As dusk fell the countryside became criss-crossed by irrigation canals and awash with paddy fields but I was not allowed to do much window-gazing through the demands of Ludo.

We reached Bhubneshwar a few minutes early – a rare occurrence for an Indian train – and a car took me to the Hotel Kalinga Ashok classed as three-star. Such hotels display impressive reception areas, though the bedrooms are something of a let-down with off-white bedlinen and cracked bathroom tiles. Costs of such establishments work out at between £8 and £12 a night with a cooked English-type breakfast for about a pound. But why-oh-why can't Indians make decent toast or desist from the habit of bringing everything – tea, cereals, grill and toast – all at once so that the eggs and bacon are congealed and cold before you've got to them.

Orissa's hazy past focuses with the reign of Kalinga. In 260 BC he was defeated by Ashoka, the great Indian emperor, but the bloody battle left such a bitter taste with Ashoka that he converted to Buddhism and spread that gentle religion far and wide. Buddhism soon declined in Orissa, however, and Jainism held sway under the Jain King Kharavela until his dynasty likewise declined in about the 2nd century AD to be replaced again by Buddhism.

The zenith of Orissan civilisation was reached between the 4th and 13th centuries under the great builders – the Kesari and the Ganga kings. During their reigns literally thousands of temples and monuments rose up all over the land. But the ambitious Muslims, whose sultans by that time reigned from Delhi over much of India, could not be held back from Orissa forever, finally subduing the country in the 16th century – and with typical bigotry, destroying as many of the temples as they could. Of the 7,000 edifices in and around Bhubaneshwar some 500 remain in different stages of preservation or dilapidation.

Even so, you will never see elsewhere temples in such profusion. Those of Bhubaneshwar, along with others at Puri and Konarak, represent a remarkably full record of the development of Orissan architecture from the 7th to the 13th century AD. Although some have suffered structural damage, a number of them fast decaying almost to extinction, many are virtually intact – even in everyday use.

I was raced by car around the Bhubaneshwar-Konarak-Puri

'triangle', rich with the heaviest concentration of temples – my ears bombarded with legend, dates and history, my eyes confused by sights extraordinary. The climax of the spectacle is Konarak, perhaps the most vivid of all architectural treasures of Hindu India. No longer does it stand as a landmark on the sea shore since the sea has receded some two miles, and despite the fact that the 'black pagoda', as it was called by European sailors, now lies in ruin it is a substantial ruin still magnificent, the culmination of Orissan art.

With tremendous originality Konarak was conceived as the sun-god's own chariot. It stands on 24 enormous stone wheels and is pulled by seven straining stone horses. Each structural feature of the temple has a hidden meaning: the seven horses represent the seven days of the week, the 24 wheels are the 24 fortnights of the Indian year, and the eight spokes of each wheel are the eight *pahars* into which the ancients divided night and day. Some say that if Konarak had not stood in almost total obscurity until the beginning of this century it would have taken the place of the Taj Mahal as one of the seven wonders of the world.

Nearby Puri not only yields a 12th-century temple – the enormous Jagannath, Shrine of the 'Lord of the Universe' – but also a fine stretch of golden sand fronting a long promenade lined with cheap hotels. The seafront offers a greater impression of a poor man's Blackpool than of being one of India's holiest cities – though what you are likely to find on such Indian beaches would hardly equate it with either.

A gigantic market in the spacious square close to the temple draws the crowds to rows of stalls selling an assortment of junk, though my preference in Puri was for the thatched fishing villages on the edge of town where the fisherfolk were launching clumsy wooden outrigger craft into the heavy breakers of the Bengal Sea. One such village was close to the Hotel Toshali Sands, a group of individual chalets and a swimming pool, mostly occupied the nights I was there by a coach-load of Cossack Russians – the noisiest of bed-fellows.

The myriad edifices of Bhubaneshwar filled my second and third day. The Orissan capital is known as the 'Cathedral City of India' and though guidebooks describe the town as 'fabulous' I would reserve this adjective strictly for its temples; the town itself is unremarkably like Canterbury or Salisbury. After Konarak even the most ornate of Bhubaneshwar's shrines makes tame viewing though, assuredly, all are worth seeing, even those crumbling to dust amongst the refuse of private backyards. The Bhaskavesvara, the Parasuramestara, the Muktesvara, the great Lingaraja, the Rajavani, the Siddhjesvara; the roll call of names is endless, the designs multifarious, the settings contrasting.

My fourth Orissan day I won a holiday from temples. Instead, the fare was an indigestable one of a Japanese-built, spaceship-like Shanti stupa at Dhauli (near the battlefield of the Kalinga war), the Jain caves of Udayagiri and Khandagiri providing historical evidence of a dynasty known as the Chedis, and a zoo – that of Nandan Khanan – to see the rare white tiger. My overnight Puri Express back to Calcutta at the end of it all provided, relatively speaking, an oasis of serenity – a description I rarely bestow upon an Indian train.

But I hadn't quite finished with temples. Though half an hour late into Howrah there was no escaping Dakshineswar and, back into Calcutta proper across a lorry-blocked Vivekananda Bridge, the Belur Math, headquarters of the Ramnakrishna Mission, where I was reprimanded for attempting to photograph its solid, if sacred, exterior.

There is no riverside city I know so poorly served by river crossings. Calcutta has but two with a third currently under construction by an Italian concern. The enormous Howrah Bridge dominates the city and from any distance looks as if it was trying to crush the life out of everything beneath. It is a graceless thing, a huge fretworked grid of steel built solely to bear road, tram tracks and footpaths and certainly not to beautify a skyline. There are many bridges in the world constructed upon similar principles and they usually seem to lean across an intervening space with a spring of their own. But this one has merely been clamped down over the city and looks every ounce of its 27,000 tons. Yet its very ugliness generates a certain grudging attraction.

The contradiction fits this city. By visiting Calcutta in the autumn I was probably seeing its fairest face. Religious fervour grips the populace as they render homage to the goddess Durga and for ten days the place becomes a radiant centre of light, joy and hope. Not that even this can hide the hideous poverty –

though, paradoxically again, Calcutta is one of the richest cities in all India. Being poor in Britain, it has been said, means not having a second TV set; being rich in India means having enough to eat. But being poor in Calcutta is to be one of those miserable wretches lying under the blistering sun virtually naked, hair matted, sinews clearly visible, skin the texture of parchment. They die like that and the kites which forever swing lazily in the skies overhead congregate in a swirling circle high above the corpse, waiting for it to be alone.

It is, I suppose, the easiest thing in the world to come close to despair in Calcutta. Yet, even after just a few days arises a splendid truth about the city. Hand-in-hand with so much misery is an abundance of life. Especially during the Durga Festival, it pulsates and churns around you; it swirls in every direction, warming with its humanity. On the penultimate day of the *Puja*, a human deluge sweeps Calcutta as thousands of gaily dressed citizens take to the streets to participate. Garlands festoon each district's individual procession of effigies of the gods and goddesses as it winds along the packed streets towards the river to the accompaniment of a cacophony of drum-beating, blaring loudspeakers, chanting voices and firecrackers.

I carried a kaleidoscope of images to take with me on my forthcoming journey to the north but Calcutta doesn't get rid of its visitors so easily. My train, the Kanrup Express, to New Jalpaiguri was inexplicably rescheduled from late afternoon to the early hours of the following morning, thus presenting me with most of a night on the tiles at, of all places, Howrah.

It was not a relaxing night by any manner of means. Against the continuing symphony of exploding firecrackers and sounds of revelry was the ceaseless turbulence of untold thousands of permanent and temporary residents of what is undoubtedly the world's most populated railway station. Every inch of floor space was carpeted by prostrate bodies, every waiting room of whatever class a congested dormitory, and all the while, even within the station confines, the noise of train whistles, taxi hooting and engine-revving. Periodically I felt obliged to go and check the new departure time of the Kanrup Express, so losing my hard-won square inches of floor.

My northbound train, exasperating to the last, even managed to depart half an hour later than its rescheduled time but, once aboard, I was content to stretch out on my corridor bunk, draw the curtains and wallow in relative comfort. But it was daylight almost immediately as the train crawled through a flat featureless terrain of rice paddies and jute, and by the time we jerked to a stop at New Jalpaiguri, at heaven knows what hour, the attraction of my bunk had long turned sour.

I was met by a tall, thin Bengali who was to become my driver for the ensuing few days. Poor fellow, he had not been told of the delaying of my train so had been waiting all day under a boiling sun.

It is a sad fact that, more often than not at certain times of the year, the mountain line up to Darjeeling is closed by landslides for all or part of its 54-mile length, necessitating a hairy three-hour drive in place of the eight-and-a-half hours taken by the little steam-hauled train. This may seem a blessing in disguise for non-railway minded souls; yet surely one of the great attractions of Darjeeling is its tiny blue-painted trundle of a train, which takes one indefatigably chugging up through forests and tea gardens. However, I was pleased to learn that the line was open from Kurseong onwards, which would at least give me thirty miles of trundle.

Through the urban confusion of New Jalpaiguri and neighbouring Siliguri we drove towards what I initially had thought were storm clouds but which materialized through the heat haze into the foothills of the mighty Himalayas. After a long dose of flat terrain the sight of mountains was exhilarating, and as we began to climb the oppressive heat lifted with every yard of altitude.

There are two roads to Darjeeling, one longer but easier; the other, hairpin and landslide-prone. We chose the latter, and with an Indian as driver it was also disturbing – the Asian habit of depending upon instinct for what lay round each blind corner providing the disturbance. At several points landslides had removed half the road, forcing us to crawl alongside yawning gaps overlooking sheer drops and stupendous views across the lush vegetation and creeper-strewn hillside to the infinity of West Bengal.

At Kurseong, built upon a series of shelves, we stopped for tea and to await the departure of the 'toy train' for Darjeeling. It was distinctly cool now and I was again regretting my shorts – though for different reasons. The trains contribute to the usual traffic hazards in this particular town since the track also shares the main street.

The Darjeeling line is operated by the North East Frontier Railway and began life as a steam tramway in 1880 following the route of a cart road built by military engineers in 1861. Until the opening of the line, all provisions for Darjeeling had to be humped up this road by bullock cart, which was not only slow but expensive. The .610-metre-gauge railway, operated by natty little B class 0-4-OST locomotives, is an ingenious feat of engineering that incorporates four complete loops and five switchbacks to reach 2,259 metres at Ghum before a descent by means of another double loop into Darjeeling.

The train looks like something any small boy would like in his Christmas stocking; usually three coaches and the huffing, puffing and tooting locomotive. On such a vehicle I ground through Kurseong and out into the steep-sided countryside at a heady ten miles an hour following the road which kept appearing on one side and then the other. Youths and children took the opportunity of a free ride by jumping onto the running boards of the coaches, even climbing into them if train staff weren't looking. In a sweat of steam the train halts at Ghum station for re-watering before continuing on a less tortuous section of line into Darjeeling.

The town that day was entertaining another visitor besides me, the president of India having arrived there by road. The result was a horrific traffic jam throughout all its streets with police blocking every move. To make matters worse the clouds had descended, it was raining and it was cold. Somehow I found my way to the Central Hotel where, in my cell of a bedroom, I donned every item of clothing I possessed.

Like Kurseong, the town is spread in layers along a narrow ridge with deep gorges on either side. Yet Darjeeling is not at all the typical Indian urban centre; I found it, swirled about by cloud, curiously self-contained, a town magically reduced in scale – like its trains – and shut off from the world by vapour and high hills. Jan Morris in her book *Among the Cities* describes it as a 'tiny trinket of a town' and I can't do better than that.

To quote her again: 'To see Kanchenjunga and its peers from Darjeeling is one of the noblest experiences of travel' – though it must be said that it is an experience involving a 4.00 a.m. rise and a draughty jeep ride to Tiger Hill about seven miles away. If one is lucky, not only the majestic peak of Kanchenjunga can be seen emerging into the dawn sunrise but occasionally the faint outline of Everest 140 miles distant.

The layers of the town, joined by flights of steps and well-nigh vertical lanes, make for fascinating exploring. The 'top floor' is reserved mainly for visitors and contains the Mall where, of an afternoon, most of Darjeeling turns out for a stroll along the triangular piazza. The 'middle floor' is Indian in flavour: a profusion of bazaars, guesthouses and small restaurants. The 'ground floor' is where the working population – Nepalese, Tibetans, Bhutias and Lepchas – live in a compacted huddle of homes.

During my four days in and around Darjeeling I was introduced to many of its blandishments. Monastery Hill – ablaze with prayer flags – in which two religions operate side by side in perfect harmony; Sonada Monastery, where Tibetan refugee monks and their families form a self-help community around a temple containing the visible embalmed body of Lama Kalu Rinpoche; a clutch of further Tibetan centres, there to meet the most charming of little people – all smiles and appreciation; the Himalayan Institute – all climbers and statistics; and, not my choice, another zoo – though this one made palatable by a botanical garden of orchids.

An enigmatic booklet I found in my hotel with the title of 'Bliss in a Swirling Mist' has this to say about Darjeeling.

'Nearly everything can be reached on foot; narrow alleys are crowded with the exotic, the hybrid, the familiar and the never-to-be-seen-again. Cultures merge and exhibit a high fluidity as the town borders the Bengal Plains, the erstwhile Kingdom of Sikkim, Nepal, Royal Bhutan and is less than a hundred miles from the Chinese border as well as being close to Tibet. Darjeeling has the exciting mobility of a frontier settlement.'

On my last night I was invited to dinner at the Windamere Hotel. The Windamere could be – and is – described as a time

capsule. In the face of today's uniformity, the hotel has simply
stood still over the decades, elbowing change away with gentle
insistence. It was run by a deceptively fragile-looking Tibetan lady
in her eighties, Mrs Tenduf-La, who was very much in the centre
of things in the days when Raj officialdom patronised the town to
escape the heat and humidity of the plains. Friend of royalty,
celebrities, captains of industry and names that whisper of
vanished epochs, I found her and her son to be the most
enchanting of hosts – seeming even to enjoy the company of a
nonentity.

Fortified by an exotic cuisine, several brace of gins and good
French brandy, I bid farewell to this strange corner of Alpine India
to be conveyed back into the cauldron of the plains below.

At New Jalpaiguri station it was just like old times. My
eastward-bound North East Express from Delhi would be five
hours late, I was informed, and would not be arriving until well
into the night. Nobody seemed the slightest put out except me and
my irritation was further increased when a man behind the ticket
grill, to whom I had reported to confirm my onward reservation,
announced with a dreadful finality: 'You can't go to Assam.
There's been trouble there.'

'But I have a permit,' I countered and showed him the addition
to my Indian visa. He wasn't impressed.

'Go to the police control point on platform 1,' I was told,
'they'll tell you the same thing.'

A uniformed personage behind a counter was unable to reveal
the extent of any new trouble in Assam but assured me that
foreigners were not permitted to go there. He took note of my
particulars in an outsize ledger but was adamant about the
prohibition.

I decided to ignore it. After all, India – like the world in
general – is full of civil strife. Even Darjeeling was in a restricted
zone, having only recently been declared free of agitation
following an uneasy agreement between the central government,
the Gorkhaland National Liberation Front and the Marxist West
Bengal government. And wasn't full-scale rioting and even
fighting going on in Kashmir and the Punjab? Surely a little
unrest in Assam needn't be cause to turn its few visitors away.
The platforms were less crowded than those of Howrah so I lay

down on the parapet of a wall contemplating a blood-red sunset and, indulging in a favourite Indian pastime, waited.

Had I not wanted to visit Darjeeling there was still no practical alternative method of reaching Assam by rail from Calcutta other than via New Jalpaiguri. There's no short cut across Bangladesh – even though the then-East Pakistan had been Indian before Partition. It's not a question of politics; the railway system of Bangladesh – attuned to the watery geography of that country – is simply unable to oblige. All the way from Calcutta to New Jalpaiguri, and from there into Assam, the Indian line skirts the border. As I relaxed on my wall I remembered my one and only visit to Bangladesh a few years previously.

* * *

A wide, empty beach – seventy-five miles of it – of clean, silvery sand backed by coconut palms or low cliffs might sound almost too good to be true but here, spreading out in both directions from Cox's Bazaar, is just one surprising aspect of Bangladesh.

This comparatively new country is full of paradoxes. Despite being subject to natural disaster on a scale unsurpassed elsewhere the population continues not only to survive but to expand. Although today the majority of its people are among the world's poorest it is also the most densely populated, while the deltic lowlands are among the richest of the earth's environments.

For 300 years Bangladesh existed as an independent state of Bengal, after which the Moghuls claimed it for their own. Two centuries later the British followed suit and, after them, the Pakistan majority whose then-Eastern Pakistan began to suffer economic exploitation by its western half until finally breaking free – at terrible cost – in 1971. Since then Bangladesh has remained an independent country but one seldom devoid of political upheaval, with one president after another suffering assassination – a state of affairs which does little to further that nation's yearning for democracy.

I arrived in Dhaka, the capital, by air from Kathmandu, Nepal, with a group of half a dozen journalists. The city's extensive Moghul edifices give it a distinct similarity to Delhi, as does a chronic traffic congestion – though here it is mostly composed of motorised rickshaws in uncountable and uncontrollable numbers.

The chief landmark is the Lalbagh Fort, a massive building erected in 1678 by the Moghul Prince Mohammed Azam, son of Emperor Autangzeb. Inside is the Pari Bibi tomb, that of the daughter of Nawab Shaista Khan, Viceroy of Bengal, who succeeded Prince Mohammed Khan. Built of marble, black basalt and sandstone, the tomb flaunts overtones of India's Taj Mahal.

Our guide was a kindly little man, by name Mr Abdul, and plainly this was his first experience of dealing with obtuse journalists. Very early in our acquaintanceship he fell foul of our thirst for the truth about Bangladeshi politics. 'Yes, of course we have democracy' he declared, his small chest puffing out with pride, 'but the president has complete control.'

Escaping from the choking atmosphere generated by the mammoth rickshaw jams we flew south to Chittagong through a violet sunset flecked with clouds. Chittagong is the country's main port and second largest city, once described, so Mr Abdul vouchsafed, as 'a sleeping beauty emerging from mists and water' though our initial impression was that the good lady had aged somewhat and none-too gracefully at that. But I liked what can only be described as the village green near the centre upon which eternal cricket matches are played with a deadly earnestness. Outside of town is a military cemetery where are buried many hundreds of British and Commonwealth and Japanese soldiers who fell in the Burma campaign of the Second World War. I was struck by what one of my colleagues subsequently wrote when he remarked on their dying in this remote, faraway land in so permanent a resting place surrounded by the impermanence that hangs over life in Bangladesh.

On the beach of Cox's Bazaar the enormous carpet of firm sand encourages jeep racing and, against the natural instincts of Mr Abdul, one of our members borrowed the minibus and raced off into the horizon. As time went on the poor man was reduced to panic, convinced that both his guest and vehicle had been lost in the ocean. Upon their eventual return Mr Abdul was to be seen on his knees in the sand thanking Allah for their salvation.

Another peculiarity of the country, to me, was the character of the Bangladeshi people themselves. And with something like a hundred million of them there's no shortage. Hospitable and friendly they are in common with their Indian neighbours but never have I come across such a disconcerting mass *passiveness* in a race. Lie down for a sunbathe on that empty beach with not a soul in sight for miles around and you'll wake up a few minutes later to find several dozen dark-skinned little Bangladeshis squatting in a half circle around you; silent, undemanding, intense; passively waiting to see what you do.

On the way to see a Buddhist temple at Rumu standing forgotten and deserted close to the Burma border, Mr Abdul finally met his nemesis. Our inexperienced driver, attempting to cross a narrow bridge before an oncoming truck, lost control, skidded, nose-dived through the parapet and hurtled down a steep bank – the vehicle ending up with its nose embedded in soft earth and water. Had we overturned *en route* the consequences could have been fatal but Allah was with us that day. None of us was seriously hurt though I sustained a badly cut finger from which blood flowed copiously. But Mr Abdul, after vomiting into the bank, ended up once more on his knees in shock and mortification. While we struggled out of the half-submerged minibus and up the incline, at least a hundred Bangladeshis materialised to stand looking at us but offering no assistance; not even a helping arm. The blood of my wound staunched with a toilet paper, we continued our sightseeing prior to flying back to Dkaka.

Our final destination was Sylhet, in the north of the country. Gently hilly, its rich soil promotes a heavy crop of tea as well as tropical forest abounding in game. Sylhet itself presents a picture of an English riverside market town deflecting the eye away from the more unappealing Bangladeshi features. On the road to Shillong, in the far-eastern corner of India, is a decidedly un-English lake, that of Haripur, which forms part of a natural gas-field, and one of the few places I know where can be found burning water.

As we left this phenomenon I gazed wistfully up the road. Shillong. Now there was a place I always wanted to go.

* * *

The rail journey from New Jalpaiguri to Guwahati, the chief city of Assam, takes all of eleven hours and the fact that my North East Express was late into the former at least saved me from a pre-dawn arrival at the latter. Instead, I was pitched into the humidity and chaos of Guwahati station at noon. And so accustomed had I become to being met and hosted I all but experienced a moment of panic. Suddenly I was my own. Then my spirit of individuality returned and I began to revel in the prospect.

Crossing a rusty footbridge spanning a maze of tracks, I found myself in a street utilised as a bus departure point with drivers touting loudly for custom, chanting their respective destinations in sing-song voices. 'Chillo, Chillo, Chillooo' reverberated in my ears, rising to a crescendo at the realisation that a rare foreigner was in town. Chillo. Where the hell was Chillo, I wondered, and then it struck home: Shillong. The place, for no good reason I could fathom, I had long wanted to visit. I had toyed with the idea of continuing by rail to the very end of the easternbound line at Dibrugarh but the notion of another fifteen hours on a train failed to hold great attraction just at that moment. And since Shillong was railwayless, a bus, however compacted, would at least offer a change of movement.

So, without further ado, I purchased a ticket and within 20 minutes we were away. Our vehicle was British Leyland, elderly but serviceable. Neither was it full by Indian standards which, in other words, meant there weren't too many passengers standing in the aisle. My neighbour was an army officer who aired his surprise at my nationality. 'We don't get many of your breed here these days,' he said with a smile.

The city I'd hardly seen but would come back to gave way to country looking equally industrious. In the villages and in the fields scores of people toiled in groups. I saw monkeys, and exotic birds; some tall and graceful with red heads, and flocks of green parrots flapping from tree to tree. For a while the road was level and then began to climb, the pine-covered hills more pronounced with every mile. I realized that we were already out of Assam and into the smaller state of Meghalaya.

This north-east region is the most varied and at the same time the least-visited part of India. Originally the whole was known as Assam province but it was subsequently split into five separate states and two union territories – Mizoram and Arunachal Pradesh. Assam and these neighbouring hill states have little in common with West Bengal from where I had come. The latter is now comparatively urbanised, industrialised and rich in culture but

Assam remains an unsophisticated, untamed land characterised by a largely tribal population and wildly beautiful scenery. There is no love lost between the Assamese and the Bengalis; the Assamese feel the Bengalis are exploiting them – the old story – and this simmering resentment boiled over in the 1970s to reach a climax, in the early '80s, of violence and terrorism. Coupled to this is the fact that, with the Burmese and Chinese borders close by, the area is essentially a sensitive one at the best of times. At present the hostilities are only spasmodic but the Indian government does not encourage visits by the likes of me. Only Assam and Meghalaya are permitted reluctantly to foreign visitors; the remaining states of Manipur, Nagaland, Tripura, Arun Pradesh and Mizoram emphatically not.

One fact that is well-known about these states is that they are the 'home' of the monsoon. Cherrapunji, quite close to Shillong, is reputed to be the wettest area on earth with 426 inches as the average annual rainfall total though, in 1861, it reached an incredible 906 inches. I asked my companion what it was like to live under the shadow of such a period of downpour.

The chap was a rich source of information. He told me that the tension as the clouds built up and the heat increased was tangible, communicating itself to man and beast. In the cities the streets empty; everyone seems to be under the spell of some psychological preoccupation. Then, with startling regularity, the first storms break. In their wake, first the insect world, then crops, plants and trees jerk into life. After the first deluge the clouds roll on; there may be days, even weeks of tantalising waiting before the next downpour. Or the rain may fall incessantly flooding fields, streets, villages and roads. One wonders if it will ever stop. My informant caught me searching the clear skies over a range of hills and laughed. 'Don't worry,' he assured me, 'We've already had this year's monsoon.'

We drove into Shillong in the early evening. The bus driver, ticket collector and his boy assistant all clamoured for my patronage on the return trip to Gawahati so I arranged things then and there. Hardly into Shillong's centre and I had fallen for the place; it's strange how first impressions fall into categories – either good, indifferent or bad. Gawahati had fallen into the indifference bracket, though I was to revise my opinion later, but Shillong made a hit with me from the very start.

Assuredly I'm not the only one captivated by Meghalaya's capital. Set at 1,500 metres its temperate climate alone makes it one of India's favourite resort towns and, for a Brit, the recognisable bits of very English architecture about the place make one feel at home in the same manner as once did Simla and 'Ooty'. Again I was looked upon as a rarity in the town and treated accordingly, with folk coming up to ask me my nationality but in a much less aggressive manner than usual.

The people hereabouts belong mostly to the Khasi tribe, one of the few societies in the world where the power and land are inherited only through the women. The Christian missionaries who have converted many Assamese, notably among the Nagas, did not get very far with the Khasis – they still erect monolithic stones to their ancestors and tell the future by breaking eggs.

Much of the town is of fairly recent origin, many of the earlier buildings falling to an earthquake in 1897. My guesthouse, where I spent the night, had seemingly survived it but was falling about my ears while I slept. The owners were a delightful pair who insisted I have my evening intake of curry with them in their tiny living quarters.

My bus crew gave me a rousing welcome as well as the front seat for the run back to Guwahati and, as the temperature rose again with the reduction of altitude, they repeatedly insisted I take swigs of a horrible-tasting Indian cola – lukewarm into the bargain – which I'd previously sworn would never pass my lips again.

They asked me where I wanted to be dropped in Guwahati and since I knew of no landmarks except the railway station I suggested the tourist office. At least I might be able to pick up a town plan there. They were as good as their word and that's how I came upon the good Mr Kamal Lochen Das.

A small, bustling man, he greeted me as if I was his long-lost son. 'We expected you yesterday,' he told me in worried tones. 'We had somebody to meet you at the station but the train was late.' I failed to mention that I had been to Shillong though surely he didn't believe the train to be *that* late!

I was taken aback. 'But how did you know I was coming?' I asked.

'My good friend and colleague in Calcutta phoned me,' he explained. 'We used to be in the same office together. And when he told me an English writer was coming I straightaway arranged a programme for you.'

So I was not to escape, even here, the kindly tentacles of Indian hospitality. But Mr Das and his colleagues of the tiny office were so sincere and pleased to see me I could hardly decline.

I was taken to the Brahmaputra Ashok Hotel and a suite of rooms that was a far superior pad than anything that had gone before on this trip. Not quite in the Bombay Oberoi class perhaps but the view of the great Brahmaputra river, over a mile wide, from my window was astounding. After a sumptuous lunch in the elegant dining room I was pitchforked into a whistle-stop tour of Guwahati city.

Actually, the administrative centre of Assam is Nispur, a smaller, undistinguished town a mile or two distant but Guwahati is by far the biggest city of all the North East Hill states. Probably its top attraction stems from it being situated on the bank of the enormous Brahmaputra, a name meaning 'Son of Brahma', which is in its own way the Lord of the Universe of the Assamese, for like a god it dispenses life and death. During the rains the river may rise 40 feet and flood hundreds of square miles. Sometimes this natural irrigation may leave lush harvests of jute, rice and mustard, but just as often it leaves only destruction in its wake. It was a disturbing, awe-inspiring waterway to look at, even when it was calm.

The town itself grows on you, or at least it did on me. A city of temples – though nothing on the scale of Bhubaneswar – it has one in the very centre, the Janardham of Buddhist origins. Another – the Shiva Umananda – stands on Peacock Island in the middle of the river, while the best known of them – Kamakshya – is the topping on Nilachetal Hill, six miles away. I was to be conducted around all of them in due course. In the meantime I had to make do with a couple of museums and a craft shop, the day having run out of hours.

Next morning Mr Das and I set out for a day in the country. We drove across the river on the great one-and-a-half-mile-long, British-constructed Saraighat Bridge and into a fertile land of coconut palms, jute fields, small lily-swamped lakes and

minuscule thatched villages that looked more African than Indian.
Our initial destination was the archeological site of Madan
Kamdev, set in a simple garden park, close to a township called
Baihata Charial. A sacred place this, of ancient stones carved with
exotic – and erotic – designs of aeons past. We were almost the
only people there in this peaceful haven surrounded by trees, the
sounds of nature and the feathery touch of long-dead spirits. We
took tea with the lone supervisor and departed.

I asked to look at one of the tribal villages I could see in the
pine forests so we halted and walked among the mud-walled,
frond-roofed houses. We were given a touching welcome, all the
children emerging to see the blond-haired being from outer space
and not displaying the least awe or fear. The ladies competed to
show us inside their simple homes, all spotlessly clean so far as
dried mud will allow; the implements of cooking unchanged since
the Middle Ages. It occured to me that here, in such villages and
even the towns of this far eastern corner of the Indian
subcontinent, the besmirching hand of commercialism had not yet
spread. I rarely saw a beggar in the province and few signs of
abject poverty.

The silk-weaving community of Sualkuchi was on the fledgling
tourist circuit but, again, I found no commercialism; simply a
desire to show a visitor the tools, products and handiwork of their
labours. The largest village in Assam, the secrets of its weaving
skills are handed down through the generations. Escorted from
house to house, workshop to workshop, I was shown every facet
of the weaver's trade including some striking examples of made-
up material rich with intricate gold thread. Mr Das had relatives in
the village so we ended our tour in their house to take tea and
delicious coconut-based sweetmeats. I was presented with a
locally-made scarf and an expensively-bound book in a manner of
a royal prince receiving the homage of his subjects.

The following day we 'did' the temples in and around
Guwahati, the most memorable of which, for me, was that on
Peacock Island. This was not so much for the temple itself but the
manner of my visiting it on one of the big vehicle ferries I had
seen anchored at the quayside. This was put entirely at my
disposal and following a landing on the tree-covered island we
steamed upstream for a dozen miles to permit me views of the

idyllic countryside stretching away from both banks of the river.
Here and there, men, women and children bathed and splashed
where the strong current allowed it, some completely immersing
themselves and coming up squirting out brown mouthfuls of
Brahmaputra.

Assamese sunsets are on a scale of those in the far south of the
country and the one I witnessed atop the sacred Nilachal Hill,
believed to be an ancient Khasi sacrificial site, was sensational, the
blood red sky reflected in the huge spread of the river below. Such
a sunset could have made an appropriate finale to my brief sojourn
in Assam but no, Mr Das had other ideas. Following a restful
interlude in his home among his enchanting family we repaired to
the Nandan Hotel for what can only be described as a banquet.
Fatigue pure and simple denied me the ability to do full justice to it
and what the good Mr Das's assembly of newspaper editors and
local radio programme presenters must have thought when my
head kept falling into my soup as they plied me with questions I
shudder to think.

It was well past midnight before I was able to return to the hotel
through empty streets. They were empty again when I rose a few
hours later to catch the westbound North East Express at the
station. It left half an hour late of course; held up by the late arrival
of the Dibrugarh connecting train but as we finally slid away,
leaving Mr Das and his entire staff waving on the platform, I felt a
jab of home-sickness, the highest compliment I can give to Assam.
One day, God willing, I shall return.

Before me loomed a near forty-hour journey which, for once, I
failed to relish. However, I had a most pleasant Assamese
companion who would be with me throughout it. 'This train is
never on time,' he told me.

And he was right. Once an Indian train has missed its appointed
slot in the system it loses its priority with the result that our so-
called express had to give way to every Tom, Dick and Harry of a
local. Hold-ups in the middle of nowhere became increasingly
frequent and the speed at the best of times was often no more than
twenty miles and hour. I slept intermittently.

At Moghal Sarai, beyond Patna, we switched to electric traction
and the speed picked up a little though the inexplicable halts
continued. And it was somewhere about then too that I became

aware of a growing pain in the upper reaches of my thigh that precluded further sleep and persisted whether I lay down, sat up or stood. I subsequently learnt the cause of my distress was a compressed nerve and the pain reached agonising proportions as we clattered into the suburbs of the Indian capital many hours behind schedule. At the time my own diagnosis of the symptoms was 'railway cramp'.

I have arrived in Delhi in various ways but never before have I had to emerge from a train virtually on hands and knees.

PART 3 – OUT OF INDIA

Chapter One

Over the recent years, I had travelled relatively comfortably and unadventurously many thousands of miles through central, southern and eastern India for the simple purpose of observing both the country and its passenger rail system at a cost well within the means of any European visitor. In my opening chapters, and now with my closing ones, I offer another picture of Indian and Indian subcontinental rail and public transport travel; a picture I gained admittedly fourteen years earlier but one that still haunts the prospective traveller from Europe or North America to the subcontinent. I do this not to deflect anyone away from the railway; far from it, for I am anxious that everyone should want to sample the priceless rewards of riding them, but because the experience I gained became adventure pure and simple – and all the world loves an adventure story.

So far as Indian Railways are concerned, one is prepared to forgive them their superficial failings and shortcomings. The romance of riding the Frontier Mail, the Kerala Express, the Varamasi Express and others, and of hearing the steam engines chugging past in the night, is matched only by the insight afforded by the railways into Indian and Pakistani ways of life. Every station remains a microcosm of the town or village it serves and of the families who live in them. Some of my recollections are so vivid that they come to eclipse all others. Out of tens of thousands of miles covered in the reassuring familiarity of the trains of the subcontinent, one journey stands out above all others. It was my 1973 journey home.

I left New Delhi by the Frontier Mail bound for Amritsar and the border with Pakistan. Even today there is but a single direct rail link with Pakistan and this was the line upon which I had entered India. Initially my northbound journey on it evolved into a re-run of my southbound one. The train was still filling minutes before departure; intending passengers – with or without tickets – clambering through open windows and using their baggage as battering rams against intense resistance from their fellows already installed in the compartments. The assault was still in progress as the train slid away from the platform but the opposition never weakened. How nobody was killed in the mêlée I shall never understand for the mood was ugly. Children were being trampled and men aimed blows at women who fought back with feline savagery. For me, standing pinned by the sweaty press of humanity, my prospects for the ensuing nine hours were bleak.

Again, numbers in the third class compartment were over-subscribed by at least 500 per cent; even the luggage racks were two-deep with bodies. After a while, the crush lessened slightly when, to use a grocery term, 'the contents settled'. During the next five hours of misery, my surreptitious movements towards the door rewarded me with a 'seat' on the floor, sharing a step at the open door with an amiable Afghan, our feet dangling out of the train. Our route now skirted the base of the foothills of the Himalayas, this greatest natural barrier on earth seeing to it that no railway ever gets too close to the mountain border states in the north. At Ambala is the junction of the line to Kalka and the end of the broad gauge – leaving a narrow gauge light railway to tiptoe into the heaving ranges of the foothills.

* * *

It was in 1981 that my wife Anna – on her first trip to India – and I came here to join a trekking group in those same foothills. From the Simla Mail we had transferred at Kalka to the white-painted Viceroy's railcar for the five-hour haul up through the green hills to Simla. As we stepped into our carriage, and had rugs wrapped around our legs, we might have been the viceroy and vicereine ourselves, though five in the morning is not an hour for viceregal airs and graces.

For much of the way, the line runs close to the road, their paths crossing at frequent intervals. To enable trains to climb the 5,000 feet to Simla, two miles of viaducts and 107 tunnels had to be constructed over a track length of sixty miles, such is the terrain. Two hours out, and we halted at the little station of Barog where the railcar waits while its passengers partake of a leisurely breakfast before setting off again into the tumbling cloud. Occasionally the cloud and mist were rent by shafts of light to reveal a valley floor thousands of feet below, ignored by the busy railcar with more than views on its mind as it hooted indignantly at buffalo and goats straying onto the track.

Solan Brewery Halt is both a brewery and a railway station. But the station came afterwards, the brewery having been erected in the 19th century by a British company which found good spring water here in the hills of Himachal Pradesh. In 1904 when the railway was built, the line cut right through the brewery, and passengers thereafter were treated to the rich aroma of malt and hops at the station approaches.

With its meadows of asphodel, of hyacinth and celandine, of carmine rhododendron trees surrounded by solemn forests of deodar and towering pine, Simla retains the ghost of bygone splendours. Golf and cricket are still played and the town's architecture is an uncharacteristic mix of late-Victorian colonial, mock-Tudor and modern spa resort. Higgledy-piggledy, it lurches up and over the steep slopes, one ramshackle building piled upon another. The Ridge is the centre where the sallow Christ Church and mock-Tudor library provide the tourist-acceptable face of Simla. The precipitous back alleys and narrow passages between the houses are, however, pure India. The Viceregal Lodge itself is a splendidly over-the-top baronial affair and from Scandal Point, where a European lady is said to have been abducted by a maharajah, the town can be seen wreathed in the smoke of thousands of cooking fires pungent in the chill morning air.

Anna and I based ourselves for a couple of days at the elegant Woodville Guesthouse, a rajah's former residence, while we explored this smiling caricature of an English county town and its district. Then we were off into the hills where no railway dared venture.

* * *

The last town of substance before Amritsar on the main line out of India is Jalandhar. Another junction, this one serves the extreme north and a line that peters out in the rugged territory of Kashmir. The railhead here is Jammu, the closest one can get by train to Srinagar and the high peaks of the Indian Himalayas.

* * *

It was 1986 when I came to follow the 223-mile-long highway between Srinagar and the Ladakh capital, Leh, deep in its mountain fastness. As with the Karakorum Highway further to the north, the road to Leh held a magnetism for me that I could not ignore.

Pages of my notes taken at the time read: 'Kargil – second town of Ladakh – is the halfway point; the place where the coaches, buses and lorries take refuge from the storm of rock. A solitary street, merchant shops, traders and cheap hotels. The atmosphere is a strange blend between the sleazy decadence of a medieval Kandhar and the vigorous through somewhat monotonous precision of the army. The military's red and white brick walls and creamy gravelled drives have, however, barely mitigated the confusion and clangour of the market place. Chaos thrives. Slim, fine-boned Baltis with hennaed beards and skull caps walk pensively along the widening streets as the muezzin's call cuts through the chill morning air. A handful of darker, squarely built Dards, Sikhs, Kashmiris and Ladakhis complete the improbable ethnic pot-pourri. A hundred years ago, this very town straddled three bustling trade routes linking the Indian Empire to Russia and China – the legendary Silk Route. Today it is a village, diminished in stature, straining to regain its historic importance and position.

8.00am. A late start. From 4.00 a.m. onwards, civil trucks bound for the remote vastness of the Zanskar valley to the south-east have been rumbling out of town. The air remains cool but not chilly. Beyond lies the realm of crimson-robed Buddhist lamas, awesome monasteries and towering vistas.

My little Morris Ambassador taxicab snarls into life. The hills rise sharply above the muddy Suru River swirling like a chocolate fantasy. Close by, the Suru meets the cold waters of the Dras before their confluence with the Indus. Our chief obstacle is behind us, the impressive inevitability of the Zoji-La Pass, 11,578 feet high, a dominant threat no longer – at least until the return journey.

The road reopened after its six-month winter closure only the day before and negotiating it, fighting a maelstrom of melting ice walls, floods, landslides, crumbling snowfields, mud and fissured rock is starkly fresh in my mind. With the thaw further advanced, coming back should be easier. Perhaps.

We – the driver and I – make our way towards the second pass of the three that bar the highway to Leh. The air is astonishingly clear. The absence of dust plays tricks upon the senses and remote mountains appear to be within a hand's reach. Gigantic streaks of purple, rust, maroon and deep blue criss-crossed the ranges in spectacular seriations like the handiwork of some surrealist artist. The sun climbs into the azure sky as the heat builds up. The landscape turns increasingly barren save for slivers of cultivation alongside the riverbanks.

Road dust envelops the vehicle like a smoke screen as the tyres bite into sand, sending pebbles ricocheting off the hillsides like angry missiles. With each passing vehicle a fresh coat of dust settles on our skins and the sun burns with vicious intensity, sending rivulets of sweat coursing down the face. Once a day, the army sends through a convoy of upward of a hundred trucks carrying provisions for their garrison at Leh guarding a hostile border with Pakistan and China. They move in great serpents of brown smoke, grinding along the single-track road. The military have priority over all other traffic so that civil buses, cars and lorries are daily held up for hours at special laagers to await their passing. Those civil vehicles going in the same direction then have the daunting task of attempting to pass each slow-moving, unyielding truck on what is little more than a country lane edging through hostile shale.

The mountains are stark and jagged, almost Tolkienesque – lurching in fantastic shapes and forms, the valleys sweeping bowls of grey rubble, magnificent in their desolation. The temperature has dropped sharply with the climb to 12,200 foot Namila-La but it is a 'dry' crossing as it is with Fatu-La at 13,430 feet seared by a fiend of a wind. Each successive village displays its *chortens* and many walls of inscribed stones, often bedecked with flags and bunting. The road twists and drops to the valley below, sheer and precipitous. There are signs to exhort a driver to proceed with caution though few take heed: 'Safety first, luck afterwards', 'Take your time, not your life', 'Better late than never'. The chief danger on the eastbound route, when the drop is on one's own side of the road, is from the driver of the oncoming vehicle which sweeps round blind corners at speed. There are also impenetrable herds of goats, sheep and horses to be negotiated. Mixed among the herds are women and children and great St Bernard-like dogs. The people are Gujars – nomads – who come over the passes from Pakistan to feed their flocks and herds. Villages, with their smoke-blackened chai houses, offer unsavoury but welcome refuge from the desolation – the hot, sweet, milky tea a balm to dry throats. Drass, proud of its reputation as the coldest township on earth, is sweltering in a hundred degrees of heat. Mulbekh displays its rock-carved Buddha. Lamayaru pulls one off the road to stare at its gompa as does Spitk, Finag and other monasteries along the way.

One approaches Leh, even in a 20th-century taxi, with something of an ancient traveller's ardour not dimmed even by the rows of military hutments that make up the suburbs. Beneath the dominating semi-ruin of the castle-palace, designed along the lines of Lhasa's Potala – the old city's narrow, twisting lanes are reminiscent of any medieval town; nondescript yet enchanting. Inscrutable yaks meditate in the market place and gorgeously attired women wearing triangular *peraks* bring back some of the fading charm. Perched high above the palace on Namgyal Peak is the windowless Avalokitesvara Temple reached by a centuries-old path that is a real test of one's ability to walk uphill at the 12,000-feet level.

The road along the Indus from Leh to the Hemis Gompa is remarkable in being a straight black line; a fresh typewriter ribbon rolled across a sandy waste of foolscap. Prayer flags flutter in the villages and large copper prayer wheels, driven by wind and water, creak mournfully. Shey Gompa is a stark outline against the blue sky. The township below is agog with brightly caparisoned chortens and cheerful old men swilling *chhang* (rice beer).

At Hemis, the largest and most famous of Ladakhi gompas, I am privileged to witness the annual *mela* or festival of the Lamas; grotesquely masked in mass procession. Their strange dances to sounds emitting from long, straight horns continue into the next day, and to see this bizarre, colourful spectacle is alone worth every tortured mile of the journey.

On the return drive some days later, the Zoji-La pass lay in wait. Its negotiation this time was a test of strength and driving ability as we manhandled the little car through lakes of freezing water hiding stones and boulders large enough to tear the innards out of any vehicle. The ice-walls – streaming melted water – were on the verge of collapse as we painfully pushed and guided our gallant little Hillman through this lethal avenue and extreme example of the retribution of nature. All in all, the road to Leh makes for quite a ride.

* * *

We drew thankfully into Amritsar and again, its station took on euphoric qualities; the cup of tea in the first class buffet was ambrosial. On this high note, I took my leave of India.

The Pakistan Western Railway has been overtaken by history. Its once eastern section, then the pride of the one-time East Pakistan, had been lost to Bangladesh, though for many years it obstinately remained PWR as it was when I made this journey. Today it cuts its losses and calls itself, unprovocatively, Pakistan Railways.

Like Indian Railways, Pakistan Railways boasts three classes today: air-conditioned, first and second. In 1973, unlike India, the now obsolete third class seats and berths were, surprisingly, reservable. However, I never managed to reach a departure station in time to make a reservation, so never managed to prove this for myself.

Second impressions of a place are, to my way of thinking, the dangerous ones. You see it through a veil of familiarity and the glories look less glorious the second time round; only subsequent observations can restore the balance. But my second visit to Lahore did nothing to detract from the image of the intensity of life in the streets. It was still early when I reached the city, and the sun had not yet subdued the fervent activities in which everyone appeared to be engaged. Barbers clipping and scraping at clients in the gutters, sugar-cane dispensers clicking and squeezing green liquid into thirsty mouths; madmen gesticulating fiendishly;

vendors persuasively selling anything remotely sellable; open-air 'factories' full of little men producing everything under the sun or repairing objects we would have long since relegated to the dustbin; taxi drivers, scooter drivers, buggy drivers, bullock cart drivers, all courting death in the cluttered streets, and policemen standing at crossroads surveying the ill-tempered traffic with dismal impotence. Flitting apologetically along the pavement, as if aware they had no right to be there, the veiled women. And, very much in evidence, clean children, dirty children, noisy children, beggar children, working animals, lame animals, dead animals and over everything, a rich ambience of noise and smell. The station was a seething ants' nest but it held, for me, an irresistible attraction. Through it lay the way out of Lahore.

Since Pakistan Railways offered a limited network my choice of route was simple. If I did not want to return the way I had come then the only direction available to me was that westwards to Quetta and across the Baluchistan Desert to Zahedan and southern Iran. Then homewards by way of Isfahan, Khorramshahr and Iraq, Syria and Turkey.

The vehicle taking me out of Lahore was the Quetta Mail and again, there was the problem of getting on it, but I was learning. Selecting the toughest of the many red-jacketed porters I offered him a rupee if he got me a seat; two if it was a window seat. The train came in late from Rawalpindi and long before it stopped, my porter had taken a header into a third class coach and was defending a corner seat with his life. His two rupees were well earned.

Even then I got a seat only because half a dozen men already occupying the hard wooden bench squeezed themselves even tighter to make room for me. Before we had been under way five minutes, we were sweating heavily from this bodily contact, and the train was not moving fast enough to turn the air rushing in through the window from warm to cool.

My companions were a rum lot. When it was time for prayer, a soldier sat with both hands open in front of him as though reading from an invisible book; his husky voice became a private mutter as he recited the prescribed version of his faith. From above my head, a second soldier, prompted no doubt by his colleague, commenced his devotions on the luggage rack, where there was space to undertake some of the attendant movements, and I was full of admiration for his sense of balance over the tricky bits. Another passenger was singing to himself in the far corner (but he could, likewise, have been praying). A fourth member of the congregation lay on the floor between the benches quite oblivious to the fact that everyone else had their feet on him. Most squatted, cross-legged, on the wooden slats, a position I find excruciating after very few minutes. All were Pakistanis but from a variety of regions of this sizeable country.

We halted for unexplained reasons in the outer suburbs of Lahore amidst a tent-cum-shanty town. The dwellings were built right up to the edge of great black scummy lakes of filth and the horror of what I saw then has not left me. Draped figures sat in the foul mud or slithered along on some unimaginable errand. Children sheltered under decaying scraps of canvas. Poverty, even other people's poverty, can sear the soul in its awfulness. I was thankful when the train moved forwards again.

The line ran straight as a die for a hundred miles over a flat, well-cultivated landscape. Our electric locomotive was effortlessly efficient and when it was forced to stop by signals, half the occupants of its coaches spilt out onto the trackbed as much for curiosity as well as to escape the heat. Station halts were an excuse to lay siege to the buffets in an effort to acquire tea, fruit or whatever else was going. I kept losing my seat when I followed suit so after the third hassle I stayed put and awaited the arrival of the inevitable vendors. Whenever I bought out my pad to scribble a note my nearest neighbours crowded round to look at what I was writing, a habit that dried up any glimmerings of inspirational prose faster than blotting paper.

The line we were travelling was that of the old Indus Valley State Railway, which formed part of an undertaking, started in 1853, to link Karachi with Calcutta. Its introduction formed part of a still larger transport complex to improve transit between Britain and Calcutta. The original route lay across Egypt – something of a daunting prospect in those days – to the Gulf of Suez and an almost unendurable long hot voyage through the Red Sea. The new idea, however, was to cross Asia Minor to the navigable waters of the Euphrates, then by a succession of steamers across Mesopotamia, through the Persian Gulf and into the Arabian Sea,

800 miles up country on the Indus and its tributaries, overland to Delhi and finally by further steamers on the Jumma and Ganges rivers to Calcutta.

Sufferers from sea-sickness were probably the only travellers to benefit from the overland route. Though decidedly shorter, the speed of accomplishment was hardly quicker than the passage by steamer around Africa. Nevertheless, in spite of the opening of the Suez Canal in 1869 and such matters as the difference in gauge between European and Asian railways putting an end to a subsequent dream of through-carriages on trains from Calais to Calcutta, the Indus route never sank into oblivion.

At first it was the Indus itself that was put to work. By 1858 the flotilla of boats consisted of fifteen steamers and thirty barges until the opening of the Indus Valley State Railway twenty years later. This was the last link to be forged in the chain of railways giving through connection right across the country to Calcutta. The only break was the crossing of the great river at Sukkar, where a ferry conveying wagons and passengers sufficed until the opening of the Lansdown Bridge in 1889, then the longest cantilever span in the world.

The Indus Valley State Railway became the Scinde, Punjab and Delhi Railway until its amalgamation with the state-owned systems north of Delhi. Then came August 1947 and Partition. The boundary between the new India and West Pakistan cut clean across the tracks and, as I had seen, no longer is the Karachi to Calcutta through-coach a fact of life. To me, as it must be to everyone who cherishes the flourishing of railways, this step backward is a sad reflection of our time.

Multan, the town at which we halted as cooling night relieved the pressures of the day, lay not upon the Indus but a large tributary, the Chenab. The whole of north-eastern Pakistan is a skein of large rivers all funnelling into the mighty Indus below Multan. Road and rail communications are subservient to them and, though often out of sight, we followed these waterways right down to Sukkur in the south. At Sukkur we were to sheer away from rivers to enter brown, dry Baluchistan but at Sukkur the Indus changes course too, splits into fragments and fans out in a broad delta to enter the Arabian Sea close to Karachi.

Today, the greater portion of the Indus runs through dry and barren desert where, for centuries, man has been struggling to irrigate the unfriendly soil by diverting the flood waters of the river. The enormous Lloyd Barrage at Sukkur, completed in 1932, assured control of the wild waters. One of the world's largest single irrigation works of its kind, the headworks below the great cantilever bridge regulate the take-off of a team of canals and so makes possible the irrigation and cultivation of millions of acres.

I was to see nothing of either town. Multan, whose four claims to fame are alleged to revolve around heat, dust, cemeteries and a stubborn defence against the British in the Second Sikh War, was obscured by the dusk. Sukkur was but a sprinkling of lights in the night. Only the dull roar, the swishing echo of steel girders and stabs of light reflected in a great expanse of water below, gave away the presence of the Lansdown Bridge.

If my eyes had found the terrain of the Punjab flat and dull I was in for considerable contrast in Baluchistan. Very soon after Sukkur had faded away, the dawn illuminated a countryside ugly with desolation. Here was a great brown desert with the occasional mud village hanging onto life and crying out for succour, a cry that found expression in the beseeching arms of stunted, broken trees.

We had begun the crossing of the Kachhi, the desert of eastern Baluchistan which merges with the desert of Upper Sind. The line was now to run dead straight for more than a hundred miles to Sibi and beyond. As in all the best desert traditions, camels emerged to form part of the scenery, plodding one after the other in columns of up to a score at a time, each beast's tail attached by rope to the muzzle of the one following along a road which ran parallel to the railway. They paced in their indolent fashion against a background of flat emptiness, apart from a string of telegraph wires and the occasional tortured tree shimmering in the haze that flared off the earth. Somewhere around here, I was told gleefully by one of my companions, 130 degrees Fahrenheit in the shade was once measured; one of the highest natural temperatures ever recorded by man. I wondered where they found the shade under which to measure it.

The Quetta Mail's deflection northwards had allowed it to escape the worst of the Sind Desert, a flat expanse of sand and scrub, winnowed by hot winds and scoured by limitless horizons. But this didn't mean we had escaped the dust. It piled up against the doors and window ledges and tiny avalanches slithered to the floor at every stopping place. A grey film covered everything and my tongue felt like sandpaper. The affliction of spitting increased ten-fold and for once, there was good reason. But these Pakistanis were hopeless spitters. Twice in a few hours I had to wipe myself clean and audibly proclaim my disgust. I have an international spitting table for my travels. To date, Romania takes top honours for accuracy but Pakistan is at the bottom of the league.

Huge shoulders, escarpments and battlements of rock dappled by the morning sun lay against the railway, ridge upon ridge, layer upon layer, forged into fantastic patterns for mile after mile. Vast slopes of gravel, known locally as *dhamem*, fringed the foothills and spread out like fingers from the hands of arms sloping upwards in great colonnades of rock. Scatterings of palm trees in tiny valleys scooped out of granite, velvety blue cacti and delicate candles of olive were living alien features in a land that was surely dead.

The train struggled up the steep gradient and felt its tortuous way through a labyrinth of rock sculptured by the waves of seas that lay over it 400 million years ago. Once upon a time the greater part of Asia lay immersed beneath a warm, clear sea and these massive outcroppings, now dried out by a savage sun, have long forgotten the pull of the tides and the abrasive drag of water on sand. Yet in Baluchistan, there is an incredible sense of agelessness pervading the whole seared landscape that creeps into the hurrying train. In my compartment, I noticed for the first time that many of my fellow travellers had changed. The Punjabis had become swarthy-faced Baluchis with fierce bushy eyebrows and beards. They stared at me with prolonged and disconcerting intensity, and when they spoke their questions were sharp and to the point. Why have I come to Baluchistan they ask, as if my incursion into their ancient and terrible land is a grotesque anachronism.

Sibi sits on a junction of the line and is said to be the hottest place in Pakistan. For some reason we had to change trains here; a delay of two hours.

The few houses and scattering of streets cowered under the merciless heat, serving a railway that is as grotesque an anachronism into this ancient territory as myself. All work in the township is completed by noon, after which all activity ceases and nothing stirs. In the late afternoon, when the fiercest heat has passed, Sibi stirs its stumps once more. Tailors appear on the pavements embroidering the Marri jackets worn by local tribesmen, the grinders of knives ply their trade to an audience of onlookers who must have seen it all before. Sugar-cane sellers become suddenly activated into a frenzy of selling. I bought some expensive oranges at a fruit stall and ate the lot non-stop.

While waiting on the station platform following my brief excursion, a friendly Baluchi came and sat beside me to put me wise as to his version of the reasons for the continuing unrest that gripped his land. Pakistan was, of course, the source of all evil. His spit was one of hate rather than habit or a sandy mouth. The lack of water and food was Pakistan's fault. I was a little unsure as to what Pakistan could do that God couldn't but it seemed that a lot of rash promises had been made and not kept concerning sundry irrigation schemes and food distribution projects. And so his fellow villagers were dying, the animals were dying and everything was dying because of an uncaring government. Thus the friction and the feuding, and if the odd Pakistani military patrol got itself wiped out among the defiles it was just tit for tat to show that Pakistanis could do a little dying too. 'Damn their promises,' ejaculated my friend with another spit, 'promises like that lake over there.' And he pointed to the shimmering waters on the horizon that I'd thought to be my own private mirage.

I detected the approaching train only because nothing else moved in the liquid undulation of the heat haze above the plain; the thing was wriggling slowly towards us, a tiny centipede curving across the land. Imperceptibly it grew larger, straightened, became five coaches hauled by a steam engine and then was audible at last. As it cruised towards the platform, heads were to be seen craning between the bars of every open window. I girded my loins for another fight to the death for a seat.

At close intervals all along the track PWR markers, carefully framed in whitewashed stones, showed a devotion to duty by some past generation of railway staff. Many looked as if the job had been carried out only yesterday. Maybe so, for boredom in this land of nothing must be as potent a force as loyalty. Even the ballast of the track itself showed a tidiness to the point of ridicule.

Before, long before, it became PWR in 1947, this line had been the Kandahar State Railway. The story of its construction has no parallel in the whole of the history of the railways of the Indian subcontinent. It is a tale of appalling muddle in the beginning, of extreme privations in the face of frightful heat and bitter cold, and of success achieved through sheer determination to force a route through some of the most forbidding territory in the world. Much of the line was built in record time; the original construction was to suffer destruction by floods and devastation from landslides and earthquakes, and the line kept open today, even in the face of Baluchi hostility, is evidence of a quality of engineering endeavour unsurpassed anywhere.

During the second half of the 19th century, the history of north-west India is dominated by the fear of Russian invasion through Afghanistan. So when, for purely strategic reasons, the government in 1876 determined to take measures to keep open at all times and seasons at least one route from India into Afghanistan, orders were issued for the immediate construction of a railway to Quetta and beyond to the Afghan border. The threat receded but the line remains. And those little whitewashed stones, so carefully laid, could equally be gestures of pride.

Beyond Sibi, the railway reaches a climax of engineering accomplishment. Through the historic Bolan Pass, where General Roberts bade farewell to his troops after his epic march from Kabul to Kandahar, the present line is the third to have been constructed since the original was laid along the stony bed of the gorge. Fifty-nine miles long, it cost a prodigious sum since most of it is either tunnel or bridge. Its existence is a tribute to victory over cholera, flood and earthquake that stalked the history of this remarkable railway.

I watched the approach of the mountains, my head stuck out of the window. There was nothing particularly dramatic about their outline since no one peak dominated the others. The summits appeared to form an endless and serrated ridge which eventually curved down into the horizon at both extremities, many miles away. The drama lay in the existence of this high barricade, flung so abruptly along a whole side of the immense desert we had been crossing, unimpeded for so long. The nearer the mountains came, the illusion of one endless ridge gave way to the sight of a whole series of ridges, one behind the other, each overlapping its neighbour in front and behind. Even so, there appeared to be no gap through which a path, road or railway might enter; somewhere, amongst that maze of ridges, must be a gorge.

The gorge is that of the Bolan. It is three times as long as the Khyber Pass away to the north. Alexander the Great marched his army into India this way, back in 329 BC and he was followed by hordes of other invaders through the centuries. The British had no doubts at all of the Bolan's strategic importance in their scheme of things and from the moment their Great Game with Russia began, they could see the control of the pass mattered more than most strategies they might or must adopt. Hold it, and they commanded the only route out of India an army could take if it were bent on attacking Herat and Kandahar, just as the Khyber was the key to a direct advance on Kabul. It was to secure the Bolan, more than anything else, that the British fought the Baluchis for so long. And when they first used the pass aggressively in 1839, early in the First Afghan War, the operation was to end disastrously with the loss of 16,500 soldiers slaughtered while retreating from Kabul.

Between Hirok and Kolpur lies the Bolan Pass proper with its narrow winding defiles. The track crosses the ravine nine times within four miles to burrow into the rocky crags that tower above the stony bed. It is as if man and nature were in competition for the grandeur of those hidden bridges, and the structural appearance of each tunnel mouth matches the awesome majesty of this sinister place.

The grey walls were old when Alexander marched his Greeks along the Indus by the devil coast of Baluchistan to Babylon. Caravans of camels and horsemen, not much slower than the hard working train, filtered through the pass where a century and a quarter before, the British, diverted from their passage across the Punjab, entered Baluchistan. From time immemorial, migratory tribes, rich merchants and conquering armies have poured over the Iranian plateau to sweep through the Bolan Pass into the fertile plains beyond. With so pungent a history and geography to digest in these last exciting miles, to enter the relative calm of Quetta cantonment is like time off from school.

Formerly the capital of Baluchistan, its name is a variation of the word *kwat-kot*, meaning a fortress. It is quite a small town with little of the concentrated bustle of other Pakistan cities and none of the grandeur. The cantonment is the most pretentious neighbourhood with its avenues of chinar trees, the Residency and the Commissioner's Secretariat exuding an air of English upper middle class from lush stockades and moat-like gardens meticulously tended. The town itself brings you down to earth but is still a well-planned community with roads running parallel in clean and uninspiring neatness. The further end of Quetta goes classy again with a bevy of expensive hotels and a monument to the British resident victims of the 1935 earthquake that was one of the worst in world history; 23,000 people died in the city alone, but only the Christians are formally remembered.

I found myself with a hotel problem. A resident wishing to air an Oxford accent came to my aid.

'Regrettably you've timed your arrival with a busload of tourists,' he explained, 'but have you tried the Lourds Hotel?'

This establishment was one of the multi-star shakedowns in Staff College Road. I didn't think they'd have me in my condition even if I'd been willing to raise the money. I made a sour face and established the level of accommodation required.

'Perhaps you would do me the honour of staying under my humble roof?' he went on, encouraged, no doubt, by the fact I was not aiming high. I accepted gratefully, pleased at the prospect of a home instead of a hotel, and was led to a wooden bungalow behind the bazaar. The first rain of the journey began to fall in wet, solid drops.

I waited in a little porch while my new friend went to find his wife. I heard voices raised and I thought I detected female anger, oddly out of place in Muslim territory. The man returned, crestfallen.

'I am extremely sorry but my wife doesn't want anyone else in the house,' he explained, and I admired him for not wrapping up her rejection of me in a tissue of excuses and white lies.

The chap could have stayed in the dry and left me to fend for myself but no, his outraged sense of hospitality ensured he was game to the bitter end. From doss-house to doss-house we went but there was no room at the inn. I challenged an American hippy couple in the main street. 'Come to our pad, man,' they said. 'It's a snake-pit but if we frighten some of the bugs out there's room for the three of us.'

So my first night in Quetta I spent in a hippy couple's bed. The 'pad' was a row of cabins surrounding a pigsty of a courtyard and when we shut the door of our little room, it was pitch-dark for there was no window. A stove had once formed the only other item of equipment besides the bed. This had disappeared together with its flue pipe and a hole in the roof was the only evidence of their passing. Through this the water poured as if the rain outside was being funnelled straight into it. Next morning we were castaways on a desert island as we struggled into our clothes and rescued damp portions of baggage from a flood that covered the floor. The proprietor conceded that the quality of his accommodation left much to be desired and offered me my own room, free of charge, the subsequent night.

Meanwhile, I explored Quetta and its district. Bicycles weaved uncertainly down Jinnah Road for the average Pakistani has never really mastered the art of balance, hampered as he is by his *lunghi*. Around the bazaars, bullock carts strained their clumsy way between the leisurely crowd of shoppers and in the park a military band played *The Dashing White Sergeant* with enormous gusto. In the cool of the evening, a *tonga* creaked and rattled me to Hanna Lake with its dam rising out of the water like the battlements of a fort. There were suddenly trees everywhere, turning a dense green in the short twilight and my eyes feasted upon them after the diet of granite and sand. But there was little of a holiday atmosphere. Maybe it was because I was out of season; more likely, it was the threat that lay heavy on the sultry air. Baluchistan was a territory in revolt and police and soldiers squatted, waiting and ready, behind sandbag emplacements at every strategic point.

On the third day, the holiday was over. I bought a third-class ticket to Mirjaveh on the Iran border for 25 rupees, and a knowing porter ensconced me in a second class coach. There wasn't even standing room in the third-class coaches and I was lucky to acquire even a second-class seat. The morning sun beat down upon the roof turning the steam-hauled train into a mobile oven. The trouble was, it wasn't very mobile either since at every station, we stopped for lengthy periods. It was but a once a week service and in each village the locals had things organised. Each could raise a football team and they had captive opponents for their weekly 'home' matches whenever the train came through. Being a single track line, the delays were necessary to allow an approaching train to pass by and I'm convinced that the signalling system was geared to the football schedules rather than the needs of the train services. Watching the untutored footwork going on at the stationside pitches, I could but admire the energy if not the skill. In Quetta it had been cricket that was all the rage but here, in the sticks, football reigned supreme.

This lonely line was once known as the Nushki Extension Railway though it runs hundreds of miles past Nushki, across the border and fifty miles into southern Iran. It leaves the Quetta line at Spezand, the home ground of the first football match of the series, and continues parallel with the mountain range forming the frontier with Afghanistan. The railway was built during the First World War when the British and Russians 'policed' the territory between the Caspian Sea and the Persian Gulf.

Between Dalbandin and Nok Kundi, a distance of 104 miles, the region is wholly without habitation, virtually devoid of vegetation and is a hell upon earth. The line crosses long stretches of *dasht* covered with sharp black stones broken only by patches of coarse sand. For eight months of the year, the heat is intense and the '120-day wind' whips this sand into tight little desert whirlwinds that lacerate the skin. The whole desert is coated with sulphur, dust and water – when it is obtainable – is a concentrated mixture of common and Epsom salts. When there is any rain the year's fall may occur within an hour. The river beds, bone dry for ninety-nine out of a hundred days, then hurl the water, laced with quantities of stone, at the exposed railway. To overcome this disconcerting obstacle, the engineers built Irish bridges or 'dips', and the drivers of the steam-hauled trains crossing them were expected to use their discretion as to whether they could pass through without the water getting into their fire-boxes and putting the fire out.

This is not all. There is also the *do-reg*, or marching sandhills. These are crescent-shaped sandhills formed by the wind and constantly on the move. Again the line is the target and, from time to time, diversionary track has to be laid to take the railway round the back of the *do-reg* to avoid several thousand tons of sand. The sandhills move in parallel lines for many miles across the *dasht*. Their speed is between 500 and 600 yards per year so that the duplicated tracks are left in position and trains use the one that is clear of sand at the particular time.

These, then, were just some of the vicissitudes of my trans-Baluchistan desert journey. Another was to come. Having dodged the ticket-collector for the whole day, I was caught out during a doze and banished to third class. With every seat occupied, every conceivable space filled, I took refuge during the prolonged halt at Nushki in the cab of the locomotive. An Englishman was a rarity it transpired, and I was welcomed aboard the old American oil-burner of 1930s' vintage on account of my novelty value. Joining it was, in a way, like jumping from the frying pan into the fire for the heat from its roaring boiler matched that of the sun.

My companions on the footplate were a pair of Baluchis of most agreeable temperament. One wore the pillbox Sindhi cap; the other had his head swathed in the elaborate *pugri* of the Baluchis, a turban that can consist of up to twenty yards of muslin. The Baluchis, who inhabit one of the hottest regions on earth, are notable among other things for the amounts of cloth they use in their dress to provide long flowing garments that keep them as cool as can possibly be achieved in great heat. We Europeans could learn a lot about dressing for hot-weather travel from such people but all I could think of doing to make life bearable was to remove my sweat-soaked singlet which left me attired in no more than sandals and the briefest of shorts. This failed to worry my new friends who slapped me warmly on the back and wrung my hand.

I observed no signal and heard no whistle to instigate our departure; we just upped and left, seemingly at the will of Nadir, the driver, who with a flourish of steam, coaxed the locomotive into motion. Away from the cluster of mean houses that was Nushki, his fireman, whose name sounded like Zir, alternated his duties between staring earnestly ahead as if looking for non-existent signals and feeding the raging furnace. Aware that I ought to earn my keep, I volunteered my services and was straightaway accepted into the brotherhood of Baluchi engine-drivers.

My attempt to transfer most of the coal per shovel into the open maw of the firebox was, initially, disastrous. In the confined space,

either the long handle of the shovel kn
tipping most of its contents onto the floo
firebox door with the same result. Thus I s
hour chasing errant lumps of coal about the ruction
amusement of my associates. But practice ma he
eventually I got the hang of things until sweat ru
eyes blinded me.

On these occasions Zir took over and I would rev
onerous task of hanging out of the side of the cab stan
for what, I was never quite sure since not once did I see
arm. But the action of looking gave excuse for catching th
remnants of a breeze and that was good enough reason for n
With an ever-increasing rapidity, glasses of sweet, oily tea we
the rounds and this served to lubricate my parched and dried-up
throat.

We never made much speed; often the train slowed to walking
pace over sections of track that were pronounced 'poor', by which
was meant 'worn almost to non-existence'. And seldom have I
ridden such badly-laid track as that of the old Nushki Extension.
For this state of affairs, the extremes of weather must be blamed
but plainly the line was not high on the Pakistan Administration's
list of priorities. With so few trains this was perhaps
understandable but it provided another thorn with which the
Baluchi could goad their government.

At every decrease in speed, male passengers jumped out of their
coaches to answer the call of nature and then scrambled back in
again. Some even took to walking beside the line. The
environment became more austere still, the terrible landscape
unrolling into eternity, its horizons shimmering in the heat
generated by sun and hot sand. Evening contributed a delicious
coolness and a sensational sunset that brought the horizon into
stark relief. Caravans of camels wound their way to nameless
destinations. Tiny lights emanating from dung cooking fires sprang
up along the way like fireflies pitting their feeble illumination
against the great suffusion of vermilion and gold that lapped the
earth. All at once it was dark.

I returned to my coach at about midnight, my usefulness at an
end for the time being. With the greatest difficulty I found and
cleared a space on the floor amongst a morass of limp limbs and

g. My exhaustion was such that I actually dropped
instant I got my head down but scuffling legs and
kept knocking me back into wakefulness. The stench
d bodies was bearable since they matched that of my
was, additionally, well-begrimed with coal dust. At
had an hour-long halt at a station serving no visible
but which boasted a water appliance and so became a
iunal bathroom; everyone dousing themselves as soon as the
ty locomotive had received its fill.

Refreshed, if hardly rested, I returned for another spell on the
footplate to discover another crew on duty. The new men plainly
expected me, the good pair providing me with breakfast of
chapatti smeared with a revolting goat's cheese and what looked
like sump oil. The sunrise was as spectacular as the sunset had
been and, again, the temperature was perfection. I made the most
of it, knowing that all too soon we would be wilting under a blast
furnace.

The new crew – I never got to know their names, so stuck to the
ones of yesterday – were kindly rogues who took full advantage of
a source of free cigarettes. In return, I was not permitted to exert
myself unduly at the chore of coal-shovelling so increased my stint
as observer. And it was while I was so engaged that I found out
what it was I was supposed to be observing.

I had already noticed lengths of spare rail, discarded I thought
at the time of construction or reconstruction of the line, at many
points along the route. This, I was informed, was reserve track for
use when the line became buried by sandstorm or action of the
wind on the *do-reg* or, more commonly, when operational rail
buckled under the relentless action of the sun. With no regular
inspection carried out on the railway, detection of such hazards
rested with the train crews who were expected to maintain a
lookout for trouble. Aware now of the true nature of my
contribution to Pakistan Railways, I took my responsibilities rather
more seriously.

On down gradients we managed surprising bursts of speed in
spite of the atrocious track. At such moments, I waited in agony
for the wildly swaying locomotive to leap the rails and plough into
the soft sand dragging the coaches with it. Swallowing my fears, I
firmly kept my eyes on the line ahead endeavouring to reduce the

risks from one hazard even if we met disaster from another. Nadir and Zir plainly enjoyed these probably forbidden 'aberrations of acceleration', Zir shovelling coal as if his life depended upon it. Gripping handholds wherever I could find them, I clung on grimly trying not to dash myself to pieces against hot metal pipes, iron protrusions and rivetted steel plates from which jets of steam issued for no reason that my simple mind could fathom.

As the sun rose in the sky to pour its wrath upon the burning wasteland surrounding us on every side, I stripped down to my shorts once more and prepared to endure another day of purgatory. But no, not quite, for I have to say that I was enjoying myself. Maybe I'm a masochist but even purgatory – within limits – can be fun. I accepted the second glass of tea of the morning, cracked a joke with Zir and resumed my station. And that was when I spotted the distorted rail.

I shouted a warning, not quite sure if I was over-reacting and making a fool of myself. The crew rushed to the sides of the cab to follow my gaze. It seemed I had taken the correct action for Nadir immediately released steam, slammed on the brake then put the locomotive into reverse so that the thing slithered along the track, the coaches buffeting into each other for all the world like a demented caterpillar. We stopped well short of the damaged rail.

Our council of war around the ruptured track was, within minutes, enlarged to League of Nations proportions by many of the inmates of the train. And, like the League of Nations, everyone had different ideas as to how to rectify the situation.

It was a colourful scene. In a variety of dress – flowing Muslim and tight-fitting pseudo-European, or a mixture of the two – was a potential workforce of Sikhs, Punjabis, Baluchis, Dogras and Pathans, a martial selection mainly from the North-West territories, fiercely combative, independent of spirit and proudly unsubmissive. Some wore cartridge bandoliers festooned from their shoulders and their fierceness of visage was more potent than any weapon that may have lain concealed in the folds of their robes.

Nobody exhibited the slightest concern for our predicament, however, and it occurred to me that the event was a regular one; being stranded out in the middle of a white-hot desert where only death could blossom. Instead, the only topic under discussion was

who should do what to rectify matters. And with the workforce –
albeit unskilled – of hundreds on tap, the job required no more
than firm supervision by those who knew what to do.

Nadir and Zir were in their element. They despatched several
dozen passengers to the nearest stock of spare rail a few hundred
yards distant while another knot of bystanders were press-ganged
into removing the offending rail. For this operation Nadir had
produced a pair of long-handled chair-bolt spanners from the
tender which confirmed my presumption that such incidents as this
were not uncommon. The rest of the crowd acted as a kind of
supporters club, offering advice and encouragement from the
terraces, while a fourth contingent moved away from the scene to
initiate the inevitable football match.

Having made my contribution to the morning's activities, I felt
no compunction to participate in the scrum so wandered off in the
opposite direction to that of the footballers. In the distance I had
espied a village, a collection of adobe huts and framed nomad
dwellings, and my interest was aroused. Calculating a good two
hours' delay, I thought I could put the time to educational
advantage. I was to pay for my nosiness. I had been made aware
that foreigners were not particularly welcome in Baluchistan, that
parts of it were out of bounds to them as well as to even ordinary
Pakistanis, but had never bothered to elicit details. In a land that
was supposedly seething with revolution and racial enmity, I had
met with no more than kindness and acceptance and this had
placated any symptoms of unease I might otherwise have nursed.
As I neared the settlement, however, I did begin to recollect that
somebody, somewhere, had advised me that it would be unwise to
venture off the roads without a Baluchi companion.

What transpired could have happened anywhere no doubt, but
in Baluchistan it was assuredly the more likely. The bearded
nomad who came towards me as if to head me off from his
community was carrying a gun, a fact that did not pass completely
unnoticed by me. I slowed and smiled with cherubic innocence,
changing course obligingly to meet him.

The man grunted as we met and I replied neutrally in English,
seeing that some sort of exchange was expected. He grunted again,
a series of monosyllabic noises and then brought up his ancient
long-barrelled rifle in a kind of charade of gun-toting that would

have been a howl for devotees of the Wild West. I laughed and extended my hand in greeting but the piercing dark eyes that were the only noticeable feature of his face, which was swathed in cloth, showed no amusement. Slowly it got through to me that the chap wanted something from me and not just the pleasure of my company.

My adversary wore a dirty pair of pantaloons that made his legs appear stubby like those of a duck, and his tunic was patched with pieces of material from a variety of sources. On his head was a Sindi cap; around the edges of this, his greasy black hair curled in unkempt abandon. At intervals he removed one hand from his gun and made snapping noises with his fingers in what I took to be the accepted gesture that went with a demand for money. With the other hand, he prodded me in the navel with the gun barrel, in an impatient manner as if he was dealing with an imbecile.

So I had fallen victim now to armed robbery. The fact took time to register in my tired mind. I was more annoyed than frightened. I'd been caught once in Kabul. Now I was about to be the fall guy in Baluchistan. Any sympathy I might have had for the residents of this dried-up land began draining away. I told him not to play the fool and tried to push past but the gun barrel stayed firmly in my stomach. I shrugged and started fumbling in my visible pickets for a few rupees and hoped he wouldn't instigate a body search. Round my waist my money belt felt abruptly conspicuous. I wondered what this second robbery was going to look like on the insurance claim: 'Type of weapon used?' I didn't recognize it as anything out of my fire-arm repertoire and I couldn't very well ask the owner for its serial number. I threw about fifty rupees on the ground so that he'd have to pick them up. An idea came to me that I would belt him one as he did so.

In the nick of time came intervention. A woman's shout shivered across the dry air. Baluchis are renowned for courage and ferocity but my scourge must have been the runt of the litter. His eyes widened, his face turned white under the suntan and he obediently turned and lumbered off the way he'd come. Swiftly, I retrieved my largesse and scurried back to the train. For the second time in 36 hours, I had witnessed the vanquishing of my own sex. It was becoming increasingly clear who wore the trousers in Baluchistan.

The company of my fellows took on a rosier hue, adding to a tightening of a community spirit triggered by the unscheduled delay. Suddenly the mass of people blossomed into individuals exhibiting characteristics that became exaggerated and grotesque. The two identical brothers wearing identical orange and black suits as if one was a reflection of the other; the 'funny man' who, at the slightest instigation, acted drunk although I failed to see how he could attain such a condition unless the water in his clay gourd (part of the standard equipment of travel in Pakistan) was heavily laced with un-Islamic rum; two morose Australians ever-spoiling for a fight and frequently having to be dragged apart; an old man invariably asleep with a pair of cockerels tied to his feet, and the first class passenger who now abandoned his exalted comfort to sit with me with our backs to the locomotives driving wheels. This worthy gave me three oranges – payment for acting as his bodyguard in territory he alleged was inhabited by murderers – that increased to four when I confirmed his worst fears by telling him of my encounter. The little world of the train became a cosy one all our own: strangers were strangers no more. As we waited for the repairs to be effected amidst the shimmering heat, I felt a strange contentment and an affinity with my fellow-men that, earlier, had been an angry condemnation. On the horizon, I steadfastly ignored the enticing lake that was the standard mirage but which looked real enough to dive into.

Three hours after my shouted warning, we moved off again, inching gingerly across the replaced rail. As dusk fell that second evening, the topic of conversation was the hardly original one of how late we were going to be arriving at Zehedan. There should not, according to the timetable, have been a second evening on the train at all. Even without the enforced delay caused by the buckled rail, the train journey I was making could chalk up one solid accomplishment. Without doubt it was the slowest in the world.

At Mirjaveh came the Iranian border, a long passport check and a general evacuation to the hut that issued Iranian railway tickets for the final fifty miles on Iranian track. It was the middle of the night, the office ran out of change and, halfway through the ill-tempered proceedings, a power cut plunged everything into darkness. The half of us still in the queue for tickets consigned the regulations to hell and returned, ticketless, to the train. And when, subsequently, an inspector with two soldiers to enforce his authority came round demanding sight of our tickets, he was consigned to hell likewise. The trio sized up the strength and mood of the opposition, decided that 50 to 3 was dangerously over the odds and prudently retired.

The train belched, jerked forward and crawled across a barren landscape touched by the grey shrouds of dawn. The faint outline of a live volcano – the sometimes smoking Koh-i-Taftan – was remarkable only because it differed from the flat surroundings. The Nushki Extension, in the beginning, was purely a strategic line; it held few pretensions to be anything else.

Chapter Two

For a town on the edge of eternity, Zahedan was surprisingly congenial. It is an oasis in the midst of purgatory and its simple amenities are all the more remarkable for it. My mile-and-a-half walk from the station to the centre took in a cosy little airport, pleasant tree-lined streets amidst neat suburbs and quite the most civilised shops since Lahore.

In spite of this, the populace appeared to have but one object in life. This was to get out of Zahedan. There were four bus companies in the town and all were under siege by hundreds of intending travellers. Harassed booking clerks rendered the same dismal prospect: 'It'll be at least three days before a seat is available. Come back again then.' At first I was perplexed. Why the exodus? Part of it, of course, may have been the sudden increase of the populace occasioned by our late-arriving train but that was not all. Then I too caught the fever. It wasn't just the burning shafts of brilliance that bounded at you from white buildings or the stupor that afflicted the squares as the sun climbed high in a remorselessly clear sky. It couldn't, surely, be the barren mountains that stood respectfully at bay on the horizon encircling the town. Or was it? North, south, east and west, that awful lunar landscape spread its clammy presence filtered, like the eddies of dust, into the little community that had tried to shut out the sight with a few belts of wilting evergreens. Most of those clamouring for a bus were, indeed, my fellow travellers of the weekly train but the atmosphere of evacuation had caught my nostrils too. I joined the aggressive Australians in trying to hire first a minibus, then a taxi, to anywhere north or west of the town but the owners shook their heads. Go to the petrol station, they suggested, and beg a lift. So we did, and for hours on end we waved at, cajoled and entreated the few vehicles that did come our way.

Then I had a brainwave. Being a frontier district, Zahedan has a sizeable garrison and I had noticed a number of barracks. A big one, crammed with impressive rows of armoured cars and lorries, was just down the road. To the startled sentry on the main gate, I announced that I was a serving British Army officer – which was stretching it a bit – and that I required to see the duty officer forthwith on an urgent matter. To an equally startled lieutenant, I made my request for transportation towards Kerman on the road to Isfahan. I reinforced the request with the explanation that I was a serving officer of the Territorial Army and that, being a British soldier and they Iranian soldiers, weren't we all soldiers together so what were they going to do about it. Through an interpreter, I made this recitation five times before puzzled officers of increasing rank and stature to whom I correspondingly jacked up my own seniority. Sceptical my interviewers may have been but I seemed to be getting somewhere in spite of my dishevelled appearance. The fifth recitation was to a full colonel, who invited me to tea and made a lot of encouraging noises into a telephone. Finally I was instructed to go and wait in the guardroom to which a vehicle was being dispatched.

A military car of Russian origin all to myself. I could hardly believe my luck. Kerman was all of 326 miles distant and I was on my way in style with a driver and a sergeant for company. We swept out of Zahedan, capital of Persian Baluchistan, brooding among its empty hills.

Two miles out of town at a road junction and an army checkpoint, I was brought down to earth. 'This is as far as we go,' announced the sergeant, 'but we'll fix you up with a lift.' And by the simple expedient of blocking the road with his steel-sided vehicle did just that.

My new mode of onward travel turned out to be hardly compatible to my self-initiated rank but even brigadiers cannot always be choosers. A high-sided lorry, three Baluchis crowded into the cab, came to a reluctant halt following a very long wait when nothing showed up on the dirt road. The soldiers spoke to the driver asking which road he was taking. 'Kerman,' he replied, and I was ushered out of my staff car and pushed up the vertical wall of the back of the lorry. Waiting expectantly within the cavernous interior were some three score sheep and goats, a

Baluchi herdsman, a bearded tribesman of indeterminate
nationality, and an English youth from Leamington Spa.

I shall never forget that ride. The driver was in a hurry and put
his foot down hard. The road led into the satanic hills and
commenced a series of hairpin bends which we took at a good 70
miles an hour, the sparseness of traffic being the driver's
presumption for there being nothing coming from the opposite
direction round each successive bend. A heavy cloud of dust
billowed from the wheels to throttle us and provide a thick coating
to our sweat-laden skins. This could also, I suppose, be construed
as beneficial since it acted as a screen and filter against the direct
rays of the blistering sun. Besides equally filthy humans and
animals in the lorry's back, there were diverse items of cargo such
as the two long rolls of straw matting which kept falling from the
cab roof onto our heads, a number of old rubber tyres to ensnare
one's feet and some sacks filled with a soft and sittable-upon
substance which provoked screams of rage from the cab crew
whenever one of them espied in the mirror their precious cargo
being utilised as a seat.

But the most exasperating of companions were the sheep.
Friendly, smelly and stupid, their herdsman had his work cut out
hauling them, at regular intervals, out of postures of suffocation. In
this operation the rest of us felt obliged to lend a hand. At every
corner everything would fall down, and on the occasions the driver
stood upon his brakes, which he did with unnerving frequency
when there *was* something around the bend, all sixty beasts jack-
knifed into us and we were up to our ears in filthy wool. All the
time both sheep and goats were treading and relieving themselves
on our feet, which is all the more depressing if you're wearing
open sandals. Once in a while the road decided to take a straight
course and, thankfully, I would sink down upon the soft
unresisting bags only to be galvanised back onto my feet by a snarl
of fury emanating from the cab.

Our tribesman was the best equipped of all of us for such a
journey. Here more than anywhere on my current travels could I
appreciate to the full the reason for Islamic modes of dress. From
him I was to learn the technique of dust protection. Whenever our
own or other vehicle's generated dust reached the consistency of
solid fog, he would wind the long flowing end of his turban round

the mouth and nose excluding from those organs the fine powdery particles that had the rest of us in choking paroxysms. Even the women's *chadari* seemed not so ridiculous a garment on such occasions.

Like those in nearby Afghanistan, the mountains, stubby and brittle, rose dramatically from the flat lands that surrounded them. Outcrops of rock smirked at our passing and received our dust cloud in their faces. Later, the mountains subsided, the territory deflated into a series of defiant ruts, and villages gave the lie to what had been shown on maps as uninhabited tracts. We stopped at several of these villages to become the event of the week as dozens of amused peasants clambered up the lorry sides to prod and stare.

Twice we disembarked to be shyly offered tea and yoghurt for these were kindly folk in spite of their aggressive curiosity. I tried to elicit the lorry's destination and learnt that it was indeed Kerman though I doubted whether we would be tolerated that far.

Evening brought relief from the sun though not much else. The tribesman spent the evening alternately effecting his devotions and hugging me for, quite early in the ride, he had developed a fancy towards myself. Secreted about his person were dirty little morsels of rancid cheese which he unearthed and surreptitiously passed to me. Equally surreptitiously, I fed them to the sheep which was only to encourage their unwelcome friendliness.

The driver's toleration lasted to Bam, a town 205 miles from Zahedan but still 124 miles short of Kerman. In the high street, he slammed on the brakes and indicated the ride was over. I offered him a 100 rial note as both payment and bribe to match that proffered by the tribesman but, to my surprise, he would accept nothing.

I made a brief exploration of the little town seeing nothing of its fortress – the Ark, as it's called – in the company of half a dozen smartly dressed youths who found in me more Saturday night entertainment than in forbidden female company or a male-dominated disco. One of them spoke good English. He suggested a hotel but the others vouchsafed it was closed. I asked if there was an overnight bus to Kerman or beyond. Yes, said one. No, said another. 'But don't sleep alone out in the fields,' I was warned, which was disconcerting for it was what I was intending to do. I asked why. 'Last week, a man was robbed and beaten to death doing that,' I was told with relish.

In an unsavoury restaurant, I purchased a double helping of eggs and chips (it was that or the inevitable kebab), drank three jugs of iced water and learnt there really was a bus at midnight. 'It comes from Zahedan, takes in petrol at the garage up the street and continues to Kerman. There will be a place on it for you.' My new informant was the sloppiest soldier I have ever seen in any army. The good Schweik was a gleaming guardsman in comparison. He was cross-eyed, unbuttoned and he had an unfortunate habit of urinating in the most public of places. But he was friendly, so I forgave him everything. With hours to spare we moved from restaurant to restaurant, he smoking my cigarettes and I knocking back the iced water.

The last restaurant closed at ten but it remained open longer for my benefit. Over the rows of empty tables the proprietor, his deformed son, my military lap-dog and I played a game of 'What's My Line' utilising additional skill in fathoming what the hell the other was talking about. The restaurant was alive with vermin and when I visited the toilet, all sorts of things furry, feathered and scaly scurried into hiding. In a sink piled high with unwashed crockery, I succeeded in sluicing the top film of encrusted dirt from my hands, face and neck.

The soldier decided that he too was for Kerman and, towards midnight, we marched together through the empty, silent streets to the one and only petrol station. Here we found three other lost souls destined for the same goal and by two o'clock, we were still waiting. By common accord, it was decided that the bus was not coming so we retired each to an empty car standing in the forecourt. I managed an hour's sleep hunched up with one leg over the steering wheel though, judging from the snore emitting from the Moskvitch next door, my soldier did better. Uncertain of the next move, I awaited the general awakening and when this occurred we moved back into town the soldier contentedly urinating over the pavement as we walked.

One of the bus companies was open and, glory be, I was able to buy a ticket right through to Isfahan. I consumed seven glasses of tea plus a packet of Persian *petit beurres* and, eventually, boarded the coach. My seat was well away from that of the soldier and nothing he could do would alter the situation. The driver winked at me and went out of his way to ensure my well-being. I didn't know it then but this was the point of a transfer of affections.

A new road was being driven through the flatter country beyond Bam, making the existing dirt road the dirtier. But in a coach, the dust clouds were of little consequence so long as the windows stayed shut and the sun remained low in the sky. We rattled along at great speed, our safe arrival at the destination guaranteed by the communal prayers transmitted to Allah in chorus before we left the garage. In the distance, snow-capped mountains began to appear over the shoulders of the stubby brown foothills.

A fleck of deepest green, crowned by a pin-head blue dome and a cluster of needle minarets abruptly produced a recognisable landmark. The saintly Ni'matollah, whose bones the shrine at Mahan encloses, was a protégé of Shah Rokh. In 1406 he arrived to spend the last quarter of his life in the town, thus making it very much his own. The buildings and gardens that make up the shrine complex offer an exquisite paradise of leafy coolness in an unrepentant land. A prophet was Ni'matollah and among his luckier prediction was the Indian mutiny, a piece of visionary inspiration that earned him the title of the 'Nostradamus of Iran.'

Three courts comprise the shrine. Roses, lofty cypresses and pines stand guard over a pool the shape of a cross which reflects the two minarets and the dome with uncanny perfection. A giant plane tree once stood in the inner court but only a protected stump remains. The magic of Mahan, its cool, shady precincts and glitter of blue tiles, spreads outwards to encompass the small town with its richness.

Kerman is but 25 miles away. The road suddenly pulls itself together, as if remembering it will soon be approaching the skirts of civilisation, and turns to tarmac. The sensual hiss of tyres was countered only by a waking sun mindful of its duty.

Though larger than Mahan, the provincial capital looked an unprepossessing place as we drove through endless suburbs of baked mud. But gradually it developed into a more or less presentable place worthy of investigation. The bus bowled happily into its company garage and I learnt that I had, in fact, all the rest of the day to effect the investigating. The same coach and the same driver were to leave in the evening for the overnight run to Isfahan.

The complement of the vehicle drained into town and I was ready to do likewise but my driver, freed of his responsibilities for seven hours, came to the conclusion that I was in need of care and protection. Holding me in place by the simple expedient of giving me the freedom of the coach refrigerator full of ice-cold Coke, he filled in his forms and was then ready to accompany me into Kerman.

Not a penny was I allowed to contribute towards a substantial lunch, nor to the ecstasy of a Persian bath where two youngsters alternately scrubbed and dowsed me for a full hour. The bazaars differed not at all from those elsewhere but they were one of the sights of Kerman so had to be seen. They were, perhaps, more full of maimed beggars than usual and where the original bazaar ended, newer ones extended under corrugated iron.

My friend's name was Momeny and although he was the very epitome of generosity, there was something about him that caused me unease. Conversation was an exercise in explicit gesture and I was considerably older than him. Yet he hung onto me, refused to let me out of his sight and went out of his way to display his affection to a degree that was embarrassing. On the other hand I was relieved to note that the few young and visible Persian females we saw drew his healthy stares and vocal appreciation in no uncertain manner.

With continued misgivings, I allowed Momeny to cart me round the rest of the town, finding reason every few minutes for disengaging my arm or hand from his. The clay walls of Kerman had long fallen down, leaving a residue that might have been anything. The Friday mosque, the Masjid-i-Malik, was likewise inclined to crumble although I was assured that it had been restored. A tile fell from the roof while I was there and the clatter was excuse for a protective embrace.

The long-distance coaches of Iran are meticulous about punctual departure even if this means leaving a percentage of their clientele behind. Angry scenes developed when we emerged from the yard as ticket-waving late arrivals exchanged heated invective with drivers and staff and threw themselves aboard in a welter of luggage. Their veiled womenfolk clambered after them clucking plaintively. Momeny had ensured that I had a front seat close to him and soon after departure, I was inveigled into occupying the co-driver's seat.

Before a captive audience Momeny was in his element. The jokes at my expense came thick and fast but soon I began to detect a veneer of hostility all round me and especially from the second driver who displayed open derision. My neighbour had presented me with handfuls of pistachio nuts as far as Yazd but these abruptly dried up. At the tea stops I was cold-shouldered. Hardly could I conceive it to be a case of mass jealousy but that was how it appeared.

The Yazd stop gave me opportunity to avoid more unpleasantness and see something of the night-cloaked town. And it is a worthy place to see. Since Sassanian times Yazd has been famous for beautiful silk textiles. Together with Kerman its shawls rival even those of Kashmir. Many of the inhabitants of the town are descended from the Parsis who took refuge there when the Arabs invaded Persia. No longer permitted to practise their ancient custom – as in Bombay – of exposing their dead on the flat-topped Towers of Silence, the Parsis have to be content with more conventional rites in their Parsi temple. It is quite a modern building equipped with an undying flame and hideous tubular metal and plastic chairs.

The skyline of Yazd is reputed to be the most picturesque in all Iran, containing as it does the highest minarets in the country as well as some interesting surviving medieval fortifications. The middle of the night, however, is not the best time to see it. The 14th-century mosque is also one of the finest buildings in Iran and the newly constructed approach sets it off magnificently. Painted friezes retain their freshness in the dry air, but perhaps the most intriguing thing for me was the many wind towers or *badgirs* devised to collect and convey moving air down to the many small chambers that alone make the intense heat of summer bearable in Yazd. I was not unaware that, with Yazd, we were back in railway country. The single track running south-east towards Kerman then ended at Bafq, some 62 miles east and through which we had driven. There is nothing significant in Bafq. It was only that this small and isolated town was as far as the new line had got when I was there. Today it extends to Kerman.

From Yazd the line runs, in the other direction, to Kashan, Qom and Teheran. At Qom, there is a branch running south of and into Isfahan but it is a freight line only. Since Isfahan was firmly established in my mind as a place to see there was no alternative but to grit my teeth and continue with the nauseating coach journey.

Sleep, even the cat-nap variety obtainable in my reclining high-backed passenger seat, was denied me while I was forced to humour my 'sponsor' by sitting alongside him. He even tried to persuade me to drive the coach but this I firmly resisted. To end up with my seething companions in the ditch or wrapped around another vehicle was a decidedly unenviable proposition. But in the early hours Momeny was relieved by his co-driver and withdrew to the rear of the coach. Pointedly ignored by one and all, I watched the dawn tint the fields of opium.

The desert counter-attacked soon after Ardakan and big drifts of sand threatened the road. The sand was smooth and firm like a hard tennis court which I would have thought made the road something of an expensive superfluity. At Na'in rivers of dried salt, white as fallen snow, traversed the plain and nothing relieved the utter monotony except an occasional crumbling village with its *badgir* masquerading as a mosque.

On the outskirts of Isfahan, a police check delayed us nearly an hour. All baggage on the roof of the coach was searched but nobody appeared the slightest bit put out even though only one in three other vehicles entering Isfahan were being singled out for similar treatment. In an unappetising suburb, the relief driver, in a fit of pique, chose to eject me from the coach. I remonstrated for a moment expecting to be taken to the company garage but I met nothing but a howl of protest. How was I to know the confounded coach was, in fact, going straight on to Teheran? But my efforts to retrieve my bag from beneath the rear seat were equally resisted and for a very different reason. Wasn't my incursion to the back of the coach for the sole purpose of re-establishing contact with Momeny? Eventually, my baggage was handed forward to me amongst a flounder of waving arms and indignant, jabbering faces and I disembarked as haughtily as I could manage it. God, what children these Persians can be!

With Isfahan on the tourist circuit, I underwent certain

reservations about staying in the place. but there is no smoke without fire, and I'd been told that I *must* see Isfahan if I saw nothing else in Iran. Such vigorous praise, as I've said, usually results in a bit of a back-hander after you've done the rounds and found the praise to be more overwhelming than the subject. It all depends on the individual of course but Isfahan, to me, was a gentle slap in the face.

The one-time Aspadan of Ptolemy, the city was formerly the capital of Persia. References to it have been found in documents recording a period between 3,000 and 2,000 BC but it was under Shah Abbas I that Isfahan attained its greatest prosperity. This magnificence gave rise to the saying *Isfahan misf-i-jahan* (Isfahan is half the world) while Lord Curzon, whose utterances have become the very fount of wisdom, speaks of the Maidan of Isfahan as 'the most impressive square in the world' in spite of the fact that he says the same of the Registan at Samarkand. But although present-day Isfahan is something of a city of vanished glory, it remains a centre of remarkable beauty.

It appeared with a splendid array of turquoise cupolas and minarets outlined against an azure sky. Along the main street of respectable shops giving off an air of Bond Street, slender poplars stood guard between the quadruple highway. The slightest breath of wind caused the leaves to rustle and glitter like silver. This is the Chahar Bagh, a fine thoroughfare interrupted at intervals by squares overhung with rose hedges and jasmine. At the Zayinda Rud, the usual disappointing trickle that goes for a river in these parts, the street crosses the bridge of Allah Verdi Khan. A delicious structure this of arcades and alcoves that is more imposing than any bridge I have seen in Rome or Florence. On the other side lies the Armenian suburb of Julfa, a place of formal gardens and modern hotels.

In a fit of extravagance, I took tea in one of the Chahar Bagh's *kefekhanas* or coffee saloons. This may sound a bit Irish but until about a hundred years ago, the Persians drank nothing but coffee; only through contact with the heathen British and Russians have they been converted to tea. A customer came over to talk to me. I told him of my woeful ignorance about the heritage of Isfahan so he proceeded to fill more gaps in my education. The city, it appeared, had influenced the culture of an alien race and what these invaders learnt followed in the wake of their conquering armies. 'Look at the fountains of the Alhambra in Spain, the mosaic-ornamented palaces of Baghdad, the marble observatories of Samarkand, even the philosophy of Al-Azhar University in Cairo,' he exclaimed, and I realized he was talking about the Arabs. 'Why, even your sherry, or *Jerez*, which you get from Spain was originally an imitation of the grape wine once produced in Shiraz just south of here.' I was suitably impressed and departed to take a closer look at the source of all this inspiration.

The Maidan and Royal Mosque is the crowning architectural achievement of Shah Abbas. The Great Square is seven times the size of that of St Mark's in Venice and walled by arcades and towering portals. The curve and swell of the turquoise dome of the mosque is beautiful, if anything in the world is beautiful. The court of the *madreseh* is lined with student's cells and makes a fine sight but, to me, Islamic mosque and sacred college construction has a depressing similarity about it. The European cathedral, on the other hand, offers a variety of architectural richness apparent to the most casual eye.

Surprise is probably the first emotion that arises within the breast of the first-time visitor to the Maidan. Here, Shah Abbas and his courtiers played polo and for centuries it remained a vast, dusty open square, probably the largest in the world. Isfahan could have made something of this priceless site but instead the municipal authorities rose to the occasion by producing an unkempt park of soulless geraniums set about with broken seats occupied mostly by down-and-outs. But I suppose this was better than the block of flats that once threatened the square and I must admit to a pleasant hour spent dozing there beneath the morning sun.

Against the west wall rises the Ali Qapu, the pavilion, leading to the royal palace from whose shady terrace Abbas used to watch the pageantry of the Maidan. It is full of little frescoed rooms of utmost loveliness as was the little Shaikh Lotfollah Mosque east of the square with its cafe-au-lait-tinted dome and an interior of subtle colours. Off the Chahar Bagh, the *madreseh* Mader-i-Shah Sultan Hussain was built for the training of mullahs and dervishes. Lord Curzon uttered his pearls of wisdom again here describing it as 'one of the stateliest ruins in Persia' and it has since been beautifully restored. To the north-east of the city, along a road leading through a suburb of vaulted bazaars, lies the great Masjid-i-Jami, or Cathedral mosque, which historically and architecturally carries top honours in Isfahan. It is impressive in its isolation from other remarkable buildings and is an ensemble of pride and age. Scores of superbly constructed rib vaults and two magnificent Seljuk dome chambers were being used by children for play and the odd adult for prayer. It appeared neglected by tourists, who preferred the concentrated attractions of the Maidan. Every show-city has to have its gimmick and Isfahan keeps hers at arm's length, six miles distant. No scientist has ever been able to fathom the reason why, when one minaret of the Menar Jomban is shaken, the other moves in unison. Long may this ignorance remain. I never beheld the interesting phenomenon but I'm tourist enough to revel in a good mystery.

Two days in Isfahan was enough for me. Having to pay to enter every building, holy or otherwise, irritated me beyond measure and my second night in a small but luxury hotel I slept badly because I was too comfortable! My last call in the city was to the offices of the British Council where, over a cup of exclusively British nescafé, I enjoyed a rewarding chat with the director.

My departure from Isfahan was accompanied by a woeful essay in mispronunciation and a good hoisting by my own petard. My original intention was to take a bus north to Qom and catch one of the two trains a day southwards to Khorramshahr close to the southern border with Iraq. Then I learnt of a coach travelling direct to Khorramshahr and my firm resolve to stick to trains where railways existed clattered to the floor. Stamping firmly on my conscience, I purchased a ticket, and a good half hour after leaving Isfahan, discovered the morning sun to be shining the wrong side of the bus. Thus I learnt I was on my way to Kermanshah, 420 miles in the wrong direction! I could have abandoned ship but, no, I would see this out. The elusive railway line ran through Arak, its nearest point to Kermanshah, some 170 miles east of that town and I would take a bus there in the morning. A prolonged diet of distances affect travellers like this. One's mind slips into overdrive. At home, I could hardly see myself travelling from London to Glasgow and halfway back again simply for the joy of catching a train from Newcastle.

In the event, my erratic detour became a pleasant excursion. As far as Hamadan, I had a companion who was British to the core. She was a one-time schoolmistress as if I couldn't have guessed. She was elderly, determined and aggressive. She was holidaying alone in Iran bent on discovering how the country ticked. I applauded her purpose but not her method. She was staying in top luxury hotels between which she was commuting in local buses and the abrupt transformation from high living to low was wearing her down. All this came out in a torrent of mortification; the dreadful price of the hotels, the unsuitable food and, when she was with the 'proletariat', as she called it, the dirt and the squalor. It all sounded the odder too coming from a self-confessed disciple of socialism.

Up to this point, our conversation had been rational. The good lady had made an arch-enemy of the coach driver right from the start by poking him in the back with her umbrella every time he increased the volume of his radio. This developed into open conflict during which our conversation, held in louder and louder voices, was pitched against an ever-expanding blast of Iranian pop. At intervals, the umbrella snaked out to deliver a blow to the enemy's rear and the grimaces we drew in retaliation were ferocious.

Then it suddenly dawned upon the driver that I did not share the views of my compatriot and the result was immediate. He turned down his radio and treated me to the widest of conspiratorial grins plus an enormous wink. Unaware that the opposition had subsided, the good lady continued proclaiming her views on life with shouted fervour for all to enjoy.

And enjoy it I'm sure they did. A smartly dressed English-speaking Iranian invited me to breakfast at the first meal halt. My companion was included in the invitation but she refused it on the grounds that the eating house looked dirty. It was, but produced a first class breakfast all the same, and the Iranian was a charmer. He asked if the lady was my girlfriend and all but provoked a war.

It was pleasant and relaxing to the senses to be driving through a gently rolling, easily cultivated land. Early morning bathed the romping countryside in a fetching shade of mauve. In the far distance, the snow summits of mountains announced their impending presence.

I think it was Borujerd where we had lunch. A fair-sized town it produced a large contingent of children to gape at two rare birds of passage and a number of beggars to fleece them. Leaving my erstwhile companion to consume her daintily packed hotel fare, I took refuge in the restaurant. While I consumed my kebab and rice she was so bold as to join me at the table and after sampling a yoghurt, pronounced it to be the best she had tasted.

After Hamadan I was alone again and not at all dismayed. The school-teacher's departure from the field of battle was accomplished via a round of back-slappings and assurances that 'all was forgiven' by the driver and those in the front seats of the coach. A trifle dazedly, she moved off in the direction the Grand Hotel was meant to be. I would have been happy to stay a day or two in Hamadan myself in spite of the unpropitious appearance of the town.

But its interest lies outside Once it bore the significant name Amadana, meaning 'place of meeting of many ways' and Semiramis is supposed to have built a Summer Palace there in 800 BC. Hamadan was the capital of the Medes in the 6th and 7th centuries BC and is the Ecbatana of the Bible. Herodotus described the city as enclosed in 'seven round walls of increasing height with battlements painted in white, black, purple, lapis blue, orange; the last two plated with gold' and that, in the centre, was the royal treasury housing the combined wealth of Ninevah and Croesus. It was reputed to have had a thousand treasure chambers and eight double iron doors, each 30 feet high. The mediocre town of today with its extensive bazaars, tortuous streets and rash of Coca Cola advertisements hardly added up to Herodotus's build-up.

Excavations continue to unearth the remains of great temples, palaces and stone tablets of Darius and Xerxes. A famous relic is the colossal, badly damaged stone lion that once guarded a gate destroyed in AD 931. It stands, still regarded as a potent talisman against hunger and cold, staring blindly out towards the 12,000 foot high granite peak of Mount Alvand.

From Hamadan the way to Kermanshah was spectacular. A fine road ran straight over the range of mountains offering magnificent views across a fertile plain cradled in yet more mountains, these displaying skirts of green and sharp peaks of alpine perfection.

Again, they wore their undoubted desolation with quiet dignity and beauty. A village, with its terraced fields drawn tightly around it at the foot of the descent into the plain, put me in mind of broken slabs of chocolate.

With a spectacular flourish of gear-changing, the coach skidded to a halt at its Kermanshah depot. Feeling like the famous train passenger who got carried on to Crewe, I poured out my predicament to the office staff. They simply couldn't understand how I could have mixed up Khorramshahr and Kermanshah. I was given an elocution lesson and the office became a hubbub of resounding vowels and guttural growls. My teachers became practical and prescribed an overnight coach to Khorramshahr leaving in four hours. They also volunteered buses to Khorramabad, Kanagavar and Karand but this was just to confuse the issue. I was sorely tempted by the Khorramshahr service as I was equally by the suggestion that, with the Iraqi border not much more than two hours away, I could be in Baghdad in the morning with a good night's sleep into the bargain.

But my stubborn streak was showing again. Nothing was going to stop me undertaking that bit by rail. I spread my map over the counter and customers and staff all huddled round to look. A kind of Dutch auction commenced: 'Anything tonight for Dorood?' I enquired, stabbing the nearest point on the railway. There was a murmur of voices and representatives were found for the other bus companies with depots in Khorramshahr. 'No, nothing for Dorood,' I was told. 'What about Andimeshk, Azna, Arak?' I volunteered hopefully and there was a general shaking of heads. 'Not tonight at any rate,' came the verdict. 'I'm going to Qom this evening,' said a still small voice, 'you can drop off at Arak if you like or come with me to Qom and catch the afternoon train.' I banged the desk as if with a mythical gavel. 'You're on,' I cried, 'but what's your vehicle?' I had a momentary vision of a lorry full of sheep. 'It's a postal van,' everyone vouchsafed in unison.

In spite of my transfer of allegiance to the postal service I felt a glow of admiration for the bus system of Iran. It had showed itself to be a first class institution of private enterprise and comprehensive complexity. Each town had half a dozen or more companies linking different routes and localities with major destinations often hundreds of miles distant. As in India, it was cheap and the coaches reasonably comfortable, fast and able to stand up to rough and constant usage. One was assured of a seat through an efficient system of booking that did not eliminate the casual pick-up if there was room to spare in a vehicle.

Having arranged to meet my benefactor, I still had four hours in hand to 'do' Kermanshah. It was a larger city than Hamadan and populated largely by Kurds. Architecturally I found it a pleasing town though, again, giving no hint of rich archeological treasures from prehistoric to Sumerian, Babylonian, Achaemenian, Parthian and Sassanian times to be found in the rocky terrain. As usual, it was crammed to capacity with people with nothing to do but stroll the pavements in the cool of the evening. A red sunset blooded the ramparts of still more mountains. I have nothing against Kurds in general but I found those of the younger generation of Kermanshah to be thoroughly objectionable. The display of hostility commenced in Mordad in the flashy part of town. Here, I became the butt of uncomplimentary remarks which a foreigner with his funny clothes and ways is wont to unloose amongst the less educated of townspeople anywhere. The chorus of abuse was taken up by a horde of youths and children. I held back, for an appreciable time, the righteous invective that rose to my lips but when eventually I let loose a torrent of retaliatory basic Anglo-Saxon, it was taken up on a wind of sneering mimicry that made my blood boil. Usually when such behaviour showed signs of developing, a responsible adult would step in to terminate it but nobody came to my aid in Kermanshah. Followed into a backstreet, I became the target not just for verbal abuse but also a barrage of stones. I took refuge behind the wall of a derelict house plentifully endowed with similar ammunition and made to give as good as I got. My antagonists, incensed, returned my fire tenfold; stones and half-bricks smacking into the wall above my head with the force of unleashed anger. Frightened, I attempted no further provocative action as I cringed against the protective wall. Then a misfire went through the window of an occupied house nearby and the tinkling of broken glass brought the affray to an inconclusive end. We all fled in different directions.

I do not, I fear, carry particularly happy memories of Kermanshah and, after dark, left it thankfully, ensconced in my mail van with three beakers of tea inside me generously donated by my chauffeur. You just can't generalise about people: one moment they are stoning you, the next astounding you with their kindness. The town disappeared behind a curtain of sickly coloured spray from the illuminated fountains, a recent and unfortunate innovation.

Half-filled mail bags make quite respectable mattresses if you discount the odd package or magazine roll. With a tea stop at Arak, I slept intermittently in the back of the van and we reached Qom as that city was stirring its stumps for another day. I was given more tea and an orange in the sorting room of the main post office for helping to unload the ever-so-slightly dented mail but my benefactor would take no monetary reward for the life he had given me.

Pronounced 'Gum', the city, which looks its age, is a place of pilgrimage second only to Meshed in importance. Fatima, sister of the Imam Reza, is buried here and, in consequence, it is full of pilgrims and infidels, the latter being no more popular than in Meshed. The Shrine of Fatima, with its golden dome and four blue minarets, excitingly oriental, is one of the visions of Persia.

All roads and alleyways lead eventually to the Shrine and my morning wanderings inevitably landed me up at its imposing portals. Once the mere presence of Christians in this city was frowned upon by devout Muslims but commercialism had won the day. Round the entrances to the court of the mosques were clustered countless booths selling pious junk and the fact that some four hundred saints are interred at Qom is made to look like a Guinness record. I was solemnly warned not to enter the court so I dutifully desisted from a repeat of my Meshed incursion. Muslim hypocrisy was making me not a little bored, and anyway I was getting hungry. Fly-blown holy cake and well-handled pilgrims' biscuits were not for me so I dived back into the alleyways in search of a good heathen restaurant.

I found one near the station after which I went to join my train. It was most satisfying to be back on the railway once more. Sometime around the morrow's dawn I would be in Khorramshahr – and upon the threshold of Iraq if I got my pronunciation right.

Chapter Three

I was seeing too many dawns for my liking. Another crept into my
weary eyes at Ahvaz, the one before last halt on the line to
Khorramshahr. The train had been excruciatingly slow and had
stopped at a variety of unscheduled points along the way. Even
though reasonably on time according to my timetable it induced
uncharitable thoughts concerning the efficiency of the Trans-
Iranian line upon which I was travelling. My impression was that
Iranian authority put most of its eggs in the other basket, the more
northerly east-west line I'd been riding on my outward journey
and known as the Trans-Caspian. Assuredly my journey then had
been a lot more comfortable; its diesel-hauled trains more
businesslike. Now, travelling south, we were being pulled by a
scruffy specimen of steam locomotion though this fact had nothing
to do with my dissatisfaction. Previously I had been riding an
Iranian express. This was an Iranian mail train. Maybe there lay
the rub.

Again the floor had become my bed; that of the compartment
instead of the corridor. We were an exclusively male fraternity
and, being slow on the uptake, I had lost the chance of a share of
the seat. But my companions had been a good-natured crowd and
saw to it that the bonier portions of my frame were carefully
padded with their discarded outer garments. For most of them the
prayer-stop was Ahvaz.

My map showed Ahvaz, Khorramshahr and Abadan sitting in a
segment of verdant green, one of the very few such segments to be
found on a map of Iran. What showed up with the dawn, however,
was dead flat terrain of burnt grass lapsing into bald patches of
sand for all the world as if a flame-thrower had been at work.*
The open plateau allowed both railway and road unobstructed
terrain, which was exhilarating after hours of winding about the

---

* My description was prophetic. This was the scene of heavy fighting
  in the Iran-Iraq war which broke out later.

Zagros Mountains bathed in the ethereal light of a full moon. Though I was not to see it, I could smell the sea of the Persian Gulf.

Ahvaz is a modern town of considerable size handling much cargo of the former Anglo-Iranian Oil Company, which became the National Iranian Oil Company. The terminus of the Trans-Iranian Railway is actually Banda Shapur, the port in the Persian Gulf though passenger trains ended up at Khorramshahr on the branch line from Ahvaz. Technically an island, Abadan, seat of the great oil pipe terminus and refinery, is a few miles further on.

Khorramshahr was a pleasant surprise. Something of a garden city; mimosa and luxurious flowering growth hung from every wall giving off a sweet smell that even the stench of the neighbouring oil tanks of Abadan were unable to overpower. The place came into prominence at the beginning of the 19th century when, as a village, it was demolished by the Turks on the grounds that its commercialism was a detriment to nearby Basra. The British and Russian governments stepped in to keep the peace by allocating territory to both sides with a view to a fair distribution of potential wealth. But they had reckoned without the Karun river, a tributary of the Shatt-al-Arab, which promptly upped and changed its course inserting a watery spanner into the works.

Basra is now, of course, firmly Iraqi but a hate – soon to erupt into war – was, even then, simmering between the two countries, though this had little to do with the 19th-century dispute. On that cool and peaceful morning, however, the land looked tranquil enough, sleeping amongst its mimosa and date palms. What conditions were like on the frontier, on the other hand, remained to be seen.

The oil tanks of Abadan flashed silver as I hailed a taxi and asked the driver to be taken to the border. 'Can't be done,' I was told, 'I'm a town taxi, but I'll take you to someone who can.' He drove me two blocks, indicated a garage and charged me ten rials when it should have been five. A large, florid individual with a face full of moustache said the border was closed and that he wasn't allowed into the frontier zone. 'Bang! Bang!' he added, 'Iraqi no good.'

'If you've not been there how do you know the border's

closed?' I demanded. My reasoning was a bit thin but I know something about taxi-drivers.

'I'll take you for 400 rials,' he said.

'Two hundred,' I replied.

'OK. Two hundred.'

His vehicle was a Packard and an antique. We made a circuit of the empty streets of Khorramshahr picking up three labourers and a soldier on the way. An ill-kept and little-used lane led us westwards and a signpost said 'Shalamcheh nine kilometres' without much conviction. The soldier dropped off a mile down the road and we made a detour across sand dunes, where there was no road at all, to a building site. Here the three labourers disembarked. To me fell the honour of subsidising the trip.

Back in the lane we came to a halt sign and ignored it. Further on, a soldier sitting in the road was more effective. The driver spoke words sounding like 'I've a mad Englishman who wants to go to Iraq,' and the solder shrugged but offered no opinions. Shalamcheh turned out to be a five-house community all five houses having been taken over by the military. I was dropped outside one that said 'Passports'.

Though nobody was in sight I detected an air of front line. Barbed wire entanglements ineffectively laid, clusters of military vehicles, broken fences and rubbish littered the neighbourhood. A dog approached, its fur bristling, to burst into paroxysms of barking. In the passport house a half-dressed civilian stamped my passport and, with a little prompting, donated a glass of tea.

The second house was 'customs' but the officer was in bed. From beneath the blankets he eyed my arrival without enthusiasm. 'You don't want to look at my bag, do you?' I enquired trying to be helpful. But no, duty had to be done. The officer rose from his bed displaying a pair of startling silk pyjamas. From a chair he took his revolver belt and Sam Browne and strapped them round his middle. He broke into his best authoritative voice to ask if I was carrying any hashish, firearms or precious metals on my person. I assured him I wasn't, whereupon he nodded good-bye, removed his belt and climbed back into bed.

At the third house nobody bothered to get out of bed at all. I was asked how much currency I possessed by a tousled head sticking out of a mound of blankets which offered the opinion that the Iraqis wouldn't let me through at their end. I foresaw the situation – as had once happened to me on the Libyan-Egyptian border – whereby I was likely to be spending a period of my life out in no-man's-land, the Iranian authorities having cancelled my Persian visa.

With the dog yapping at my heels I commenced the four-mile hike across open desert towards a dot in the far distance which I presumed to be the Iraqi customs house. I was alone in a hushed world thankful, at least, that I hadn't a couple of trunks to carry. It felt like the end of a film; the hero walking into the sunset. Except that it was the sunrise.

I held preconceived ideas about Iraq, even then. Its public relations hardly raise the country on a golden pedestal as far as Britain is concerned; the one facet we recollect about it being centred around magic carpets and public hangings from lampposts. The Iraqis, I told myself, were going to be a pain in the neck – which showed how wrong preconceptions can be. Not that the border people had a lot to do with my reappraisal.

But for the fact that it was an hour later in Iraq than it was in Iran they too would have been in bed. As it was, the military staff were in 'mixed dress': uniform trousers with pyjama tops for officers and dirty vests for other ranks. Only the guard outside the entrance to the customs house wore an air of combat efficiency: a one-man army festooned with Soviet automatic weaponry. Everyone suffered from the extremes of five o'clock shadow.

I was steadfastly ignored by the Iraqi officer on duty. A trio of Serbians had pipped me to the post from the other direction and their desire to cross into Iran for a day's outing had him all of a dither. Quite certainly he wanted to refuse their request; but as their nation was then a country of some substance and provided communist technical aid, its representatives had to be humoured. Four times he resorted to the telephone but no definite ruling was forthcoming. The Serbs, decked out in flamboyant suitings in anticipation of decadent pastimes they hoped to find in Khorramshahr, ignored me too – even when, after a surreptitious look at my *Lyall's Languages*, I said: 'Izvinite, koliko je sati?' which I hoped was a request for the time in Serbo-Croat and was rewarded with a grudging response.

But my sally initiated a brilliant stroke of compromise by the officer. It seemed the stumbling block of transit to Iran lay in numbers he was permitted to let through his post. Two, apparently, was the quota. Yet here was a determined unit of three making his life a misery. He glared at me and I perceived a personal repugnance of things British fight it out with expediency. I knew what was coming even before he put it into words. He would swap one incoming Brit for two outgoing Serbs. The ration, which implied that one of me was worth two of them, plainly annoyed him intensely as it probably would the Serbs if they'd understood, but it provided a solution. He banged stamps into their passports and the room emptied.

Revenge was sweet. The officer, flanked by two grinning subordinates, tipped out the contents of my bag and rummaged amongst them. From the untidy heap he extracted my portable electric shaver and his discovery of its two batteries had the whole post alive with suspicion. Here was a British infernal machine loaded with pro-Israel consequences. Everyone turned to me for enlightenment. Feeling rather like a company salesman I obliged, thinking that as I was due for a shave anyway so it may as well be now. But I was not allowed to complete the operation. Hostility gave way to a childish delight and, in order of seniority, all the available personnel of the post demanded a go. I sighed. Everywhere my shaver had gone the rounds. but the batteries were as tired as I was and Iraqi beards are the stuff of hedgehog quills. The shaver took a firm grip of the officer's stubble and gave up the ghost clinging resolutely to the hairs.

His yell of pain heralded the return of the hostility but they'd had enough of me. I removed the offending machine from the officer's visage and shovelled my belongings back into the bag while my already out-of-date visa was counter-stamped without scrutiny.

The driver of the one-and-only taxi was asleep in the shadow of his old Packard but was kicked awake by the guard who had been witness to my mechanical magic show. The ride to Basra would cost three dollars, I was informed, but I hadn't got three dollars; only travel cheques and a few pound notes. So I tendered one of the notes – a pound was worth nearly three dollars in those days – saying it was all I had until I could change a cheque. The driver sneered and I walked away hiding a profound dismay at the prospect of a 13-mile walk to Basra under an already powerful sun. However, the glimpse of my British bank-note had detonated the chap's interest. Please, please could he examine it. I waved it once more under his nose and his face creased into a smile as his eyes caught sight of the face of the Queen. He was evidently a romantic as well as a monarchist though his emotions had to be tempered with the more practical aspects of commercialism. 'Two,' he demanded and again I walked away. Chivalry won the day and I took my place in his battered vehicle.

We rattled over rutted tracks discussing 'Elizabet' and all she stood for in a world gone grey. He didn't actually criticise his own country's fanatical leadership but he would have liked a queen. Even the heathens next door in Iran had raised a minor one for a while, he bemoaned, by which I presumed he was referring to ex-Queen Farah and the one-time Peacock Throne of Persia.

As we progressed I was puzzled by the fact that no proper road existed between the border and Basra for, after all, the rift between both countries had not been going on for all that time. Eventually we came to a tarmac highway but it lay parallel with the border, its southern destination being Al Faw on the Persian Gulf. The way led through lush clusters of date palms and occasional primitive villages fighting for space amidst marching undergrowth.

I never made Basra by taxi. The wide Shatt-al-Arab river saw to that. Across it lay the city but the southern bank was as far as my taxi would or could go. There was no bridge; only a ferry and the ferryman could raise no enthusiasm for pounds sterling.

It is unwise to arrive penniless in an Islamic country on a Friday, the day the banks and offices are closed. An expedient bystander, full of desire to air his fluency of the English tongue, came to my rescue.

The solution to the new problem, it seemed, lay in the deluxe Shatt-al-Arab Hotel. There they will always change money I was told.

'How do I get there?' I asked.

'It is eight miles up the river and I will find you a boatman who will take you there and back very cheap,' explained my informant.

'Very cheap' turned out to be the equivalent of £2.50 which struck me as scandalous until later experience confirmed that I was no longer in one of the world's cheaper zones. But the voyage up-river, struggling against a strong current, was a restful experience and I was in need of such. I dangled my feet in the cool water, completed my shave and made spasmodic conversation with the boatman as we chugged past rows of Russian freighters on the north bank and a date palm jungle on the other.

A shock awaited me at the hotel. 'We change all travel cheques except those of the bank of Barclay,' declared a suave, sober-suited young man. My cheques, of course, were of the bank of Barclay.

I demanded explanations. 'This Barclay they have dealings with Israel,' he retorted darkly and that, for him, was final. I tried to change my Iran left-overs but rials were looked upon with equal scorn. So I changed my surviving sterling notes which would, at least, cover the sum required by my boatman and get me across the river.

In all, my 'cruise' lasted a full three hours. It was a most agreeable portion of the day and since my train to Baghdad would not be leaving until nightfall – or so my Cook's Timetables assured me – I was quite happy to prolong it. Accordingly, I expressed interest in the foliage-clad scenery of the left bank and was invited – as I hoped I would be – to sample one of the many inviting little creeks half-hidden by palms and exotic undergrowth.

The Shatt-Al-Arab River is a saw-blade of inlets at this point. It is a wide river – 400 yards or more here – and its creeks enter the palm belt to a depth of several miles. My boatman appeared to have a particular creek in mind and as we chugged into the narrow waterway I perceived a village – many of its log-cabin type houses on stilts in the water – amongst the trees.

We drew up at a shack at the water's edge and were greeted by a smiling woman, her face a mask of worn leather, together with a litter of eight curious children that were assuredly a contributory cause of their mother's rhinoceros-like hide. The boatman's limited English gave me to understand that the woman and the litter were his.

The boatman and I sat on pieces of carpet on the floor of the 'patio' overhanging the water. The woman and a convoy of children brought us tea and slabs of dates. Purists would have found fault with the number of dirty litle hands that fondled the fruit and the quantity of flies that wandered over its surface but I was hungry and I like dates. I was also offered a thick, grey yoghurt, rancid and vile but probably nutritious.

We talked of Basra's association with Britain, highlighted in both world wars when we occupied this strategic port and, though basically for own ends, enlarged it and improved it. There was fighting in the town during the second occupation when the Axis-inspired Iraqi rebels attempted to throw us out. But my friend had remained staunchly pro-British – or so he insisted. And, if so, he had backed the right horse for the port had brought prosperity to Basra. We toasted each other in lukewarm tea and munched dates until our jaws ached.

I was finally put ashore on the north bank and we parted to a charade of exaggerated salutation; exaggerated to me but normal to a well-disposed Iraqi. The heat of the day was at its peak as I meandered through the town with a vague idea of locating the railway station. But I hadn't got far before a youth accosted me, took my bag and guided me to a cafe where he insisted I joined him for a most welcome beer. Like the Shatt-al-Arab Hotel the station, I learned, was miles out of town but could be reached by a bus, wherupon – the bag between us – my new companion accompanied me to the terminal.

I found Basra to be more Arab than most of the towns in Iran I had seen and its good people much more disposed to help the lone stranger in their midst. An agglomeration of three towns and several large villages, Basra City lies two miles from its port at Ashar and spreads out into the country in the form of endless garden suburbs. Just as you think you are coming to the end, Basra starts up again with a different face and a different set of suburban subtitles like Jubaila, Manwe, Rubat Saghir and Maqil. Established in the time of Alexander the Great it has prospered and sunk to obscurity with see-saw regularity under Muslims, Zanj rebels, Carmathians, Mongols, Turks and Europeans. Everybody has left their mark on this not particularly beautiful hotch-pot of a city.

I lunched at a nondescript restaurant on egg and salad which I hoped would be cheaper than a meat dish. Maybe so but it bit deep into my ready cash reserves and I began to wonder not *if* I could reach Baghdad but *how far towards* Baghdad I could get before I was alone with my spurned travel cheques. In the late afternoon I entered the sizeable station building with the intention of finding out.

Basra Station gives itself no airs and graces even though it is the terminus for the third city of Iraq. It labels itself 'Maqil Street', which to a stranger means little. Trying to find a ticket office in the nearby empty concourse I blundered into the stationmaster's lair and, of course, was invited to tea and chat. The stationmaster was an educated man speaking good English and upon learning I was a disciple of the railway we got down to reviewing our combined thoughts on a through-rail service between London and India. Here, at Basra, was one of the gaps; a mere 30 miles including a substantial river and some temporary (we hoped) ill-feeling which, to neither of us, seemed so unsurmountable a set of obstacles to fulfilment of that dream. The Russians it was who had built the Baghdad-Basra line, and since that country were currently in a 'giving mood' we there and then designated a Russian extension from Basra to Khorramshahr.

The ticket office opened for business an hour before the departure of the Baghdad night express and I was escorted into the office itself by the stationmaster rather than be left to transact my business through the barred window like everyone else. I was a little taken-aback to learn that the night train to the capital was a deluxe, air-conditioned one for which a supplement was needed additional to the fare. However, the stationmaster insisted I categorise myself as a student at a rate considerably lower than a normal fare, which was surprisingly low anyway. My ticket and seat reservation were made out with due ceremony and the transaction sealed with a gratis Pepsi Cola. All this divested me of my last pounds and dinars but at least I would be able to reach Baghdad – and on a day that wasn't Friday.

The station began filling up as if in response to the Muezzin's call to prayer from a dozen mosques about the city. While waiting for the train to come in I was engaged in intricate political discussion by a man on the platform who introduced himself in the manner which comes so naturally to these Iraqis. He was, of course, violently anti-Israel but I played strictly neutral though not to the point of letting him get away with every Arab viewpoint. A dozen other people were soon involved in the verbal skirmish, the exchanges being good-natured but earnest.

Basra to Baghdad is 325 miles. This distance is covered in nine hours, which is good for a Middle-Eastern train. The soft, reclining seats were conducive to sleep but the attentions of an over-zealous ticket inspector and baggage-prodding operation by the military nullified the comfort. The single-track line keeps to the south bank of Lake Hammar and, after Ur junction, just two miles from the biblical city site and home for Abraham of Ur of the Chalees fame, follows the course of the Euphrates crossing it at Samawa. Deflected by a tributary, the Shatt-al-Hillah, it accompanies this to beyond Hillah before striking out on its own to Baghdad. All I saw in daylight was Hillah and beyond.

Hillah itself was transformed from unremarkable modernity to a city of magic with the help of the crimson glory of a picture-postcard sunrise. But the real magic city is just down the road. We rumbled by a wayside station bearing the name 'Babylon Halt' and I knew we must be near it. That 'the glory of kingdoms, the beauty of the Chaldee's excellency' should be heralded by no more than a 'halt', a place which even local trains pass with a derisive whistle, seemed to me as bitter as any part of the dark prophecies of Isaiah.

On every side were sandy mounds ethereal in the fiery dawn; some large enough to be called hills, others low ridges, and still more the merest risings and fallings of the earth. But for miles around the soil was blasted and unhappy with the memory of Babylon. So this was the city whose Hanging Gardens were among the Seven Wonders of the World, where four-horse chariots could pass along the walls and on one altar alone a thousand talents' worth of incense was consumed every year. Three accomplishments of a forgotten city that had been burnt into me decades ago when, for some school misdeed, I was sentenced to record the fact a hundred times in a copy plate hand.

It was the Euphrates that made Babylon what it became. Earlier the great river had flowed past Kish but changed its course to favour the then lesser town. And so Babylon rose to become, geographically, politically and spiritually, one of the most powerful cities of the world through a cavalcade of generations and centuries. Finally brought to its knees by Xerxes, the legendary city passed into ancient history. Its continuing dirge is the whistle of trains not bothering to stop at 'Babylon Halt'.

Stone and brick gave an air of prosperity to the villages at the approaches to Baghdad. Though similar in design to the mud dwellings of Persia and elsewhere they looked more solid and permanent and far less drab. Maybe the local mud was unsuitable for building. But I had judged too soon. Even in the very suburbs of the capital a few mud streets and habitations made an incongruous appearance amongst an untidy jungle of concrete and corrugated iron.

The West Station is the Grand Central of Baghdad. It is a massive building titivated by two clock towers, and it stands aggressively amongst a parkland of flowering shrubs and an antique Iraqi Railway steam locomotive not much older than some I saw operating. There is a North Station and an East Station but all the best trains arrive at and depart from the West. Yet in spite of its appearance there is no great echoing concourse like those of the railway cathedrals of Iran; even one befitting a capital. Instead its congregation are led in and out through a side entrance, the rest of the building being given over to administration offices and the corridors of power.

My immediate destination was the street of trans-desert buses. This is not a street designation but the street in which the offices and garages of the particular commodity can be found. Arab cities may often be rabbit warrens but they have a certain orderliness about them. Invariably there is the street of cobblers, the street of tin-smiths and the like. In Baghdad there is a street of trans-desert buses.

With willing help I found it. The best-known of these transport firms running regular services to Syria and Lebanon was then Nairns, which was founded by a Briton in 1923. For many years he ran his vehicles without benefit of a road, simply crossing the 560 miles of sand to Damascus guided by a line of posts. I had a cousin resident in Beirut who I never missed an opportunity of visiting, and here was an opportunity even if it meant an 1,120-mile round trip.

Accordingly, I negotiated the purchase of a ticket from a rival, lesser and cheaper concern calling itself Al-Iktisad Trans-desert Transport Company (Nairns had no services running that day) whose bus was scheduled to depart in the afternoon. I arranged to pay the fare in Syrian pounds (which they preferred to their own currency) as soon as the banks were open, putting my trust in the assumption that the banks of the capital would be more favourably inclined towards Messrs Barclays. The morning I gave over to exploring Baghdad in the knowledge that I would see it again within very few days and could do it more justice then. I was aware that I could have returned home by rail from Beirut but I had covered that route before so stuck to my principles of not going the same way twice where a new one existed.

The Tigris flows through Baghdad but the city shuns it. The Faisal Bridge offered a view of the river washing the backside of the town and lapping at some very evident refuse dumps that were a happy hunting ground for dogs and humans. Any remnants of magical notions I may have retained of an *Arabian Nights'* city promptly drained away. Baghdad may possess charms visible to the resident but to my newcomer's eyes it was no more than a large, dusty-brown, semi-modern city squatting on the banks of a mud-coloured waterway.

The poverty and inertia of this domain of a once-Turkish rule were still written on the face of the Iraqi capital. Modern technology has seeped into the expanding community and with it a new political awareness I found rather frightening. Iraqi politics are notoriously violent and one gets the feeling that neither the technology nor the politics have been given a chance to mature. Baghdad has expanded onto both banks of the river, the main city being on the east side though the original grew up on the west bank.

A traveller visiting the city in 1583 described it as being 'a towne not very greate but very populous and of great trafficke of strangers for that is the way to Persia, Turkie and Arabia.' Certainly it was its position on the caravan route to the East that brought Baghdad to the fore.

Since Sumerian times it has been a meeting point of the land routes of South-west Asia. At the height of its fame during the 9th century, Baghdad was the home of wealthy merchants and learned scholars who flourished under the auspices of an enlightened caliphate. That was the period when the Arabian Nights image had substance. Its downfall in 1258 was at the hands of the ubiquitous Mongols from which its strategic situation was not again fully realized until the 19th century. Its legendary fame and undoubted commercial possibilities led to the idea of a Baghdad railway to connect Central Europe with the Middle East together with its return to capitalship of an independent Arab state. For a brief period the city regained a measure of importance but it has since never really made it in the Middle-Eastern city stakes. Baghdad, full of undistinguished bits and pieces of other people's empires, remains in the wings of the world stage.

I had a mission in Baghdad additional to that of raising funds. I had designated it as one of the cities on my itinerary to whence *poste restante* letters could be sent me. There were scores of post offices in the place but none would admit to being a repository of letters. '*That* post office is elsewhere' I was repeatedly told and given long, explicit instructions on how to find it. At the fifth attempt I ran the correct establishment to earth – after a helpful police squad car had taken me to a wrong one – to learn that no mail, in fact, awaited me.

And if I have not been particularly complimentary to Baghdad this is no reflection upon the calibre of its inhabitants. Taking a snapshot of a market, I backed clumsily into a snack kiosk and was promptly invited to a hot-dog breakfast. Tea and sympathy was often the result of an enquiry for a certain street or post office. And at the final post office the chief cashier deserted his desk and took me for cream cakes at the cafe round the corner before changing my blacklisted cheques himself at an advantageous rate, so saving me the inevitable hassle that would have resulted at a bank.

Footsore and weary, I wandered back towards the Al-Iktisad Transport Company in a Salhya suburb through streets of little shops under cloisters that reminded me of Chester.

On the Faisal Bridge I paused to watch a mongoose join the refuse scavengers. Beneath the western parapet the crews of small boats dragged wriggling silver fish from the Tigris in vast, cleverly-manipulated nets and at the fish market itself, amongst the gore and the guts, clients were outnumbered by cats.

The Al-Iktisad bus was a heavy unattractive animal of indeterminate birth. It looked as if bits and pieces from a variety of sources had contributed to its construction. Even when stationary, with the engine running, the thing shook itself like a dog emerging from water. My seat was at the rear and an English-speaking Iraqi couple seeing off an elderly gentleman onto the vehicle elected me his nursemaid. My other companion was a flamboyant Frenchman who spoke not a word of English.

But for the fact that nearly everybody, inside and outside the bus, burst into tears as we left the terminal the journey commenced normally enough. The old man, who answered to the name of 'Jazz', half-asphyxiated me with the thick acrid smoke of cheap Arab cigarettes on the one side while the Frenchman, babbling staccato French into my ear, puffed away at his Gauloises on the other. We stopped for food at Habbaniyah, once a famous RAF base during the Second World War, where my charge, avoiding my outstretched arms, fell out of the bus and spreadeagled himself over the ground. My own distress was the more apparent but compensated for by the bowl of fruit yoghurt he insisted on buying for me. Beyond Ramadi we left the main road which had slavishly followed the Euphrates River and took to the open desert.

Thereafter, the texture of the excursion began to deteriorate. The dead straight track across the Syrian desert was beset with maniacally-designed bumps indistinguishable to the eye and so unavoidable, even had the driver felt so inclined. Running to a schedule, the bus proceeded on its way at a steady 80 m.p.h. and, because of its design, the back of the chassis yielded to the full effects of the bouncing gait. At intervals I felt obliged to change seats with the Frenchman whose seat was an oil drum and so undertake my stint of being thrown into the air on it. Passengers donated soft items of apparel to cushion some of the heavier landings but the cold of a desert night drove them to retrieve their contributions all too soon.

Battered and frozen, it was a relief to stop at the Syrian border post. I was granted a visa with no trouble at all until it was discovered that I had no Syrian currency to pay for it and there was no exchange office for hundreds of miles. The problem was solved by a whip-round amongst the passengers. The military then effected a search of our luggage, which was taken off the bus and strewn around in the dark outside. Soldiers with torches went the rounds, prodding amongst battered suitcases and shapeless bundles to an accompaniment of howling children, wailing women and feet-stamping men.

The episode recharged the vocal chords of the Frenchman who, with the vehicle underway again, released a monologue of French jokes and anecdotes. They must have been screamingly funny for he laughed until the tears ran down his face. I tried to smile politely but this hurt my lips, chapped by the sun and sand, and now blue with cold. On the other side of me 'Jazz' was suddenly sick and repaired to the box-like toilet that occupied a rear corner of the bus. Outside this cabin were piled pots and pans and the assorted paraphernalia that Arabs deem a necessary adjunct to travel; only the door remained unencumbered and even this failed to lock. On several occasions it had flown open at the behest of the bumpy track to the embarrassment of the user, both male and female. In consequence of one particularly violent lurch, a woman quietly going about her business was propelled out of the door to grovel around in the aisle clutching her outer and under garments about her amidst a scattering of pots and pans. The Marx Brothers couldn't have done it better.

Yet another dawn presented the Syrian desert as a plain of pink gravel coarsened with a stubble of tough grass. I could envisage nothing noble about it like the Sahara but then, maybe, I was not in the right frame of mind. Damascus had abruptly become a warm, immobile hunk of real estate where I wanted to be. But Damascus could offer small comfort. The early morning sun was purely ornamental as the Frenchman and I went in search of coffee to defreeze our intestines. My companion had been soliloquising about Damascus for hours; to be back in a civilised city where the French influence still held sway and the language was comprehensible was going to be euphoria indeed. We entered a café from which the aroma of French coffee wafted and I basked in my friend's moment of triumph as he broke into Gallic eloquence. Then came the great disillusionment. 'I do not understand,' beseeched *le Patron*, displaying all the right gestures, 'please to speak English.'

In my current itinerary, Damascus was not more than a change of road vehicle. I would forgo the jumble of narrow streets, the Temples of Jupiter, the Great Mosque of the Omayyads and the bazaars of the Street called Straight. I had 'done' the sights on a previous visit and would be doing them again before long. Suddenly the prospect of a sojourn in an Englishman's castle – the home of my cousin – made irrepressible demands that frosty morning. Impatiently, I caught a *servis* taxi across the Lebanese Mountains, out of Syria, into Lebanon and to the sprawling city of Beirut.

My arrival in the Lebanese capital coincided with the aftermath of an Israeli commando raid and the city was like a disturbed hornets' nest. I was searched, my arms high in the air, by Palestinian commandos and checked twice by armed Lebanese soldiers.

When I left, three days later, on my way back to Baghdad they closed the border behind me and it's hardly been open since.

Chapter Four

The idea of a through-carriage train service between London and Baghdad and Cairo was very much more substantial than the simple London-Delhi fantasising of a Basra stationmaster, an itinerant Englishman and others. Even if the gaps were finally closed, the notion of through-coaches to India is doomed by a host of other considerations. Yet the running of through-trains between Europe and the Middle East became an obsession amongst nations.

The Baghdad Railway was the name given to the preliminary project. Britain drew up the initial plans but lost interest in the whirl of excitement over the opening of the Suez Canal. Germany's 19th-century expansionist policies, however, were directed at the Levant and beyond. For her the implications of a line southwards from Istanbul were far-reaching and momentous. By the time Britain and other European powers had come down from the clouds Germany had formed the Anatolian Railway Company and was forging ahead with two routes via Ankara and Konya. Construction of the line onwards from Konya to Baghdad followed under the impressive label 'Imperial Ottoman Baghdad Railway Company.'

The outbreak of war in 1914 gave the part-completed line immense strategic importance and, under German military supervision, the work pressed forward. By the end of 1918 there was a continuous line from Haydarpasha to beyond Adana, and considerable sections outward from Aleppo and inwards from Baghdad. By that date the railway fell under the control of Britain by conquest and, after protracted negotiation, each country through which the line passed apportioned their section of track into their own railway administration.

On the surface this would seem to be a reasonable solution but, because the line runs into and out of Turkey twice, and into and out of Syria twice, problems quickly became apparent. The Franco-Turkish Convention of 1932 gave a certain degree of transit rights as far as Turkey and Syria were concerned and the dust was settling nicely when, early in the conflagration of the Second World War, British troops again were in occupation at the Syrian and Iraqi end.

Thus the Baghdad Railway never stood a chance from the start. It was single track and of low capacity anyway. A tool in the hands of statesmen, its importance lay in its political and strategic consequence.

In 1939 trains could run from Haydarpasha, the Asian terminus for Istanbul, to Musul, and to Tripoli in Lebanon, whence road services provided connections with the lines from Kirkuk to Baghdad and from Haifa to Cairo respectively. The completion of the Baghdad railway in 1940 and the Tripoli to Haifa line in 1941 made possible through-running from Haydarpasha to Baghdad and Cairo; only the projected Turkish train ferry across the Bosphorus being required to bring the dream to fruition. But the Bosphorus ferry was never built (though the fine new road bridges, very much more recently, were) and through the contingencies of war and later Middle-Eastern conflict the line below Beirut was permitted to die. National obsessions turned elsewhere and the railway dream of the 19th century finally capitulated to the potential of the airways. Just for a moment in history the London-to-Cairo train became an accomplished fact. Now the bones of its track lie rotting in the sun around Tyre and Sidon while the Baghdad leg, with its then thrice-weekly Taurus Express is, to be honest, no more than a joke.

But joke of a train or not, the Taurus has a place in my heart. Invariably my railway wanderings come to an end on this slow, dirty, magnificent, incredibly-behind-schedule, friendly train. I've joined it at Aleppo and Adana on a number of occasions but never have I managed the full three-day marathon, Baghdad to Istanbul's Haydarpasha. Now I had the chance.

It departed from Baghdad's West Station at the convenient hour of 9.00 p.m.* I arrived there early and so earned myself a corner seat. The train left on time, as it usually does from its terminal station, but this I knew to be a piece of pretence in support of an illusion of long-lost prestige. As it winds across the initially flat,

---

* This line is, at present, 'temporarily suspended' over portions of the full route.

later mountainous terrain of Iraq, Syria and Turkey towards Istanbul the train lags further and further behind schedule, a state of affairs not lost upon its regular clients along the line who simply time their respective boarding by the hours it is, habitually, late. Were the Taurus Express ever to keep to its official schedule there would be nobody along the route for it to pick up!

My new travelling companions were a familiar Taurus Express mixture. Iraqi, Syrian, Turk, Armenian, Kurd, Lebanese and, twinkling at me from the opposite seat, a giant tribesman of the desert. He looked naked without his camel, though 'naked' perhaps is not the word for he was swathed in a voluminous *djellabah* over which, for good measure, he had wound a carpet not much smaller than the one that covers my living room floor. It was cool to be sure, as desert nights invariably are, but looking at the amount of clothing worn by my companions it was I who was naked. And, as for baggage, my small grip had vanished beneath a high tide of bundles, parcels, blanket rolls and crates piled on the floor between us.

'You are going to a far country?' I enquired tentatively.

Someone seemed to understand. 'Yes,' I was told. 'We go to Al Mawsil.'

Mosul, of course, was still in Iraq, some 250 miles down the line. I let it pass.

'I go to Halep.' This information arrived in the form of a deep rumble from the belly of my sheik opposite. He was afforded instant respect. Here was one of the compartment truly going to a distant country. Aleppo. That was distance indeed. But the small Turk in the corner could cap that. *He* was going to Beydegirmen but as nobody had heard of it his pronouncement fell a mite flat.

Outside was velvet darkness. The diesel-powered train trotted contentedly along with no hills or other feats of negotiation to endure. Beside us, out of sight, flowed the Tigris and at Samara we stopped at a station of some reckoning though it appeared to have strayed from the town it served for no lights showed except those on the platforms.

The vital subject of the inner man and its satisfying arose. Came the great unswaddling of the bundles, parcels and crates. There was no restaurant car scheduled to join the train until the Turkish border but even had there been one earlier I would never have been permitted to use it. Not once yet have I even seen the inside of a Taurus Express dining car, such is the aggressive generosity of its clientele. But I was ready with my own contribution to the communal messing arrangements on this occasion having purchased some fruit and meat-based oddments in Baghdad. A few inches of space was cleared on the floor for the charcoal fires and soon we were feasting on grilled *kebab*, joints of cooked veal, home-made pasties and tart tenderly prepared by some unseen wife banished to a forgotten village. Bottles of a home-distilled liquid that could have been a by-product of petrol came from the Turkish corner. It was shunned by some but not by me. With three nights ahead of me I had no desire to remain *that* conscious. Smoke from the burning charcoal filled the compartment triggering bouts of coughing and expectorating.

Bedtime for the *fellahin* on the Taurus Express is an exercise in co-operation. One man's shoulder or thigh becomes another's pillow, legs are intertwined and sockless feet of every hue and fragrance find their way onto opposite laps. Nobody utilises the corridor for the simple reason it is full of crates and the wreckage of meals.

The morning produced a country of oil wells resembling standing skeletons on the plain. It also showed us the vicinity of Assur, an ancient capital, for a time, of Assyria and once a city belonging to the Kingdom of Ur, which had me pondering again upon my lack of attention during my schoolboy divinity classes. The Tigris was still with us as we entered Mosul.

What rang more bells for me than Assur was the *raison d'etre* of this city for it was built on the site of one called Nineveh. The capital of the Assyrian Empire was destroyed by the Medes in 612 BC and nothing more was heard of it until the Sassanid period, when the existence of the town of Budh Ardashir is recorded. Mosul, meaning 'confluence' – that of the Wadi Khosar and the Tigris – first appears in AD 636, as the name of the town on the right bank. It grew to a great city in the Abbasid period, a centre of commerce and industry, with fine mosques, markets and palaces. It remained so under successive dynasties until the destructive Mongols, and later Tamerlane, came along to spoil things. From these blows Mosul never fully recovered though its position in a fertile belt of oil-bearing land and on a main caravan route from Aleppo to Persia assures it a certain significance.

Before 1918 it had a reputation for dirt remarkable even in the Ottoman Empire, which is saying something. No doubt improvements have been made but I was unable to judge for myself. The railway skirts the city and goes on an excursion around the corporation cemeteries. I gazed at the distant mosques with interest, for one of them – the Great Mosque – has taken a leaf out of Pisa's book and is supposed to lean to commercial advantage. But either the train was on the tilt or my Turkish friend's firewater was more potent than I thought for every minaret in sight stood as straight as soldiers.

My gigantic tribesman unrolled himself from his carpet to take his leave at the station. He indicated his bedshirt with pride and I guessed he was attempting to tell me that Mosul had given the world the word 'muslin' from the days of its textile fame. We performed our bowing ceremonies on the platform and the train became lighter, emptier and the poorer for his going.

We were only an hour late at the Syrian border. I was sorry to be finally leaving Iraq. A comparatively new country, formed out of territory belonging to successive empires of Babylonia, Assyria, the Caliphate and Persia and Turkey, it had a stirring past. Its people are a hotch-potch of a dozen races and their memories of British occupation in two world wars – not to mention the short, sharp conflict since – are not all that happy though I was to find no rancour on this account.

On Syrian territory I ran out of passport. Three times in almost as many days I had entered the country from various points around its frontiers. I had often wondered what would happen when I arrived somewhere with a passport full to the brim with mauve ink. There had been occasions when the then-Soviet Union had refused to place their visa opposite that of the United States, and during the McCarthy era I had been denied an American visa solely on account of the presence, within the pages, of a hammer and sickle emblem of someone's people's republic. But I'd never run out of space. Now I was to discover how Syrian authority would react to the situation. It was no problem really. They simply altered the dates and details of the previous visa, re-stamped it, charged me double and delivered a homily on the folly of not having enough pages in a passport.

Syrian history overlaps, of course, with Iraqi history and the designation 'Syria' once applied to all over the place. In ancient times it was the fertile strip between the eastern coast of the Mediterranean and the Arabian desert, from the Gulf of Alexandretta to Sinai. Lebanon, Israel and Jordan were part of it. Hittites, Egyptians, Babylonians and Persians successively dominated it. Alexander of Macedon conquered it as did the Romans, the Arabs, Turks, Mongols and Mamelukes. Finally the French became the mandators of it. But in the process of all this it has shrunk in size. Jordan and Lebanon became what they are and Palestine what it was.

But hardly had I switched my mind upon things Syrian and gazed upon a desert that had changed not at all when, blow me, we were in Turkey. And we were to remain in Turkey skirting the border all night. My Turkish friend had ensconced himself opposite me and, on the territory of his own domain, had blossomed visibly. At the various halts he dashed out to purchase tit-bits from vendors, and when these gentry came aboard to sell their wares he was loud in his protestations at the slightest breach of overcharging. Meals dissolved into a continuous sampling of weird and wonderful tastes.

A second dawn found us at Akhterin, a border village back in Syria. We were all in a tangle of sleep and Syrian authority, likewise, not at its best so no-one bothered about tiresome subjects like visas and mauve stamps and where they could place them.

At Aleppo we were two hours late. The Taurus Express halts for a long and unexplained time in Syria's second city. I think the reason is because the Taurus Express from Haydarpasha likes to meet its counterpart here so that the respective drivers can swap notes and the current political gags from Baghdad and Istanbul. I took a stroll on the platform following farewell ceremonies accorded to more of my travelling companions leaving the train. I had twice stayed in the city, though such brief sojourns could never satisfy one's curiosity about a place like Aleppo.

It had been the citadel that had impressed me most. With the possible exception of the pyramids, this must surely be the largest man-made object on earth. Abraham may or may not have milked his cows on the summit but his name is the one most bandied about throughout its turbulent history. Both the building and the mound upon which it stands are immense.

The *souks* of Aleppo are without equal in the Orient. Their stone vaults and passages reek of history as old as Saladin. Donkeys and heavily laden horses come down the narrow passageways as they have for centuries and at every turn there are marvels of colour and variety of wares. These *souks* give to Aleppo an identity of its own that is neither Turkish or Damascene, and the aggressiveness of the selling has no equal, perhaps mercifully, in all the Mediterranean lands.

The tallest minaret belongs to the Madreseh Othmaniyyeh. It also possesses a legion of cats. The philanthropist who endowed the college must have had British blood in his veins for he left a special legacy to cover the care of the feline strays of the city. Nearby is the Zakariyah Mosque containing the tomb reputed to be that of Zachariyas, father of John the Baptist, and a feature of these wondrous temples is that access is not denied the unshod infidel.

With the exception of the Turk and myself we were a fresh intake in the compartment when the train drew out of the station. I felt like the senior prefect amongst a batch of new boys and my strangeness caused many enquiring glances of the how-far-have-you-come, where-are-you-going variety. The mixture was very much as before, which meant that the barriers of convention were soon down. But we had a lady amongst us – a young and not unattractive one at that – which could have produced problems had she been going further than Adana.

As the sun came up behind Aleppo, we moved north into flat, baked country. I looked out of the window to see a string of camels and guessed they would be the last I would see, for in Turkey the wild, unchanging East has become heavily laced with the West. Within very few hours the train had climbed out of Syria into the mountains of the Turkish Amanus Range.

Where there had been plain was now a bleak land of towering peaks, fir and pine woods and dark valleys full of rushing water. These mountains dividing one country and way of life from another reminded me of Scotland. But when did Fort William sprout mosques? No, this was Fezzipasa, firmly Turkish and a high-flying flag with a white crescent and a star on it was there to show it. A crowd of men hung about the station, wearing cloth

caps and pre-1940 western garments. Many Syrians wear
European suits today but the rural Turk in one looks out of place.
An Arab in rags can achieve a certain dignity where there is but
squalor in a badly-patched suit.

Again the terrain lapsed into inertia. On his many journeys from
Antioch to Asia Minor, St Paul must have seen this country as
I saw it in the late afternoon sunshine: rising and falling and
stretching away to snow-capped mountains. I noticed a shepherd
wearing a square-shouldered cloak, a felt garment of Cilician
goat's hair called a *kapenik*. He might have been St Paul himself.

The train sped downhill in a fervour of free-wheeling to pull up
at Adana in a sweat of steam. On the platform boys were hawking
semit – rings of bread covered with sesame seeds – and my Turk
watched, hawk-eyed, over the ensuing transaction as I purchased a
brace.

Adana is the third largest city in Turkey but you would never
believe it; a typical old Turkish town with some brash 20th-
century concrete structures thrust upon it. I recalled the narrow
streets becoming quagmires when it rained. There was a United
States air base near the town so I was to hear some American
views on the place and they were not complimentary. But
servicemen are inevitably poor judges of other people's towns.

And so for the home-run to Haydarpasha. Just down the line
we crossed the Aksu river, a trickle of water that makes the
heavy, intricate trellis bridge over it a seemingly unnecessary
piece of engineering. More often than not, no rain falls in the
region but when it does there are no half-measures. Dried-up
river beds become raging torrents in a twinkling of an eye, and
I remembered the previous time I had come this way when a
steady downpour had turned the little Aksu into a crazed
cauldron flecked with madness. It had burst its banks and
threatened the bridge.

Being hours late now we were condemned to negotiate the
Taurus Mountains in darkness. A pity this, for they are a fine sight.
In the night you can feel the cruel nature of the tortured landscape
by the panting of the locomotive, its long drawn-out whistle
amplified and distorted by echoes, and the painfully slow progress
of the ascent. There have been times in daylight when I have
walked beside the line on the climb over the Taurus and, with a

co-operative engine-driver, been picked up again by the waiting train at the summit.

Nigde is a province famed for its amazing underground cities and troglodyte villages. These apart, the region is a strange, disturbing territory literally dead to the world. The soil is riddled with blisters from extinct volcanoes and water is in short supply both from heaven and earth. But, without warning, the train comes upon sweet fertility surrounding Nidge town and the transformation is startling. Nor does the place let its saving grace down. The 13th-century Alaeddin Cami proudly bears its three domes and shows off exquisite arabesques on impressive portals. As if to contradict the notion they were always knocking things down, the Mongols built another mosque nearby full of oddly Gothic features.

After a third night of dozing in a semi-upright position, one begins to wonder whether long train journeys have all that attraction after all. Watching others sleeping when you can't, arriving and departing from God-forsaken places at God-forsaken hours, suffering acute discomfort and lack of exercise, being jolted, compressed, questioned by suspicious officials, lied to by ignorant authority, put-upon by merchants of everything, failing to make sense of a score of babbling tongues. These are but a few of the arguments against the conception – but let these gain the upper hand and you'll be ripe for the airlines.

My Turk had left the train and soon we would be clattering into Ankara and on the threshold of the banalities of the West. But it is in such moments of weakness when your mind is soggy, your eyes bleary and your body aches all over that the true test is at hand. Train travel under such conditions is tough and make no mistake about it. Here on the Taurus Express I could, no doubt, have obtained a berth in the *yatakli vagon* – sleeping car – but I would have lost much in the process. In a train compartment you are a member of an exclusive little world. Nationality, religion, creed or colour count for nothing as you become one with a fraternity of travellers. On this journey I had observed many regions and lands. In none of them had I been able to linger for long. Yet most of what I learnt came from that which my eyes had seen and from the wealth of knowledge imparted by those who were my companions. Discomfort and its alleviation by co-operation with one's fellow men sets the final seal on goodwill, of which there is still, thank God, plenty in a crisis-crazed world.

Ankara was a late breakfast stop; its main station a place of ablutions. I am beginning to look upon the Turkish capital as the city I get my back scrubbed but the weather was too chilly this time round.

Ankara to Istanbul is a full day's run, or at least it was for the Taurus Express. Even with Haydarpasha, Istanbul proper is still out of reach across the Bosphorus. We drew importantly into the terminus a full seven hours late, a fact that again appeared to inconvenience nobody at all.

Mirroring the two hills on either side of the Golden Horn, shouldering their roofs and towers, domes and minarets, the sea was clean and cool and versatile with colour. Leander's Tower, poking out of the water, loomed through the dusk as my ferry splashed along a route it had taken a million times. At Galata I set foot once more on European soil with a kind of dread. And yet ... It would be nice to be home.

My small hotel near the Sirkeci Station welcomed me as a long-lost son. Friends of aeons ago still sat at the baize-covered tables.

'Come and play dominoes,' they said, pulling up a chair. A bed, a real bed, was, for me, the wonder of Istanbul that night and my lullaby was the whistle of the trains across the road. For a while I lay awake cogitating upon the further three-day rail journey across Europe that lay in store. 'An aeroplane will take you home in an hour or two,' whispered the still small voice of temptation within me. But the conflict was over before it began. The magic of those train whistles bound me to a firm resolve.

I slept.

Brighton, 1992

Other titles in the Travellers' Tales series:

Journey Along the Andes
From Bolivia, through Peru and Ecuador, to Columbia
Christopher Portway
ISBN 1 874687 12 9 £5.95

The Drive-thru Museum
A journey across the everyday USA
Andy Soutter
ISBN 1 874687 09 9 £4.95

Three Women in a Boat
A journey up the Thames
Kim Taplin
ISBN 1 874687 13 7 £4.95

By Bicycle in Ireland
A personal guide to Irish landscapes
Martin Ryle
ISBN 0 245 54666 9 £4.95

A Gringo's Journey
A bicycle journey from North America to Southern Chile
Cris Osborn
ISBN 0 245 55066 6 £4.95

Kevin and I in India
Travels around the subcontinent
Frank Kusy
ISBN 0 245 54417 8 £4.95

Back to Mandalay
An inside view of Burma
Gerry Abbott
ISBN 0 245 60135 X £5.95

Lemurs of the Lost World
Exploring the forests and Crocodile Caves of Madagascar
Jane Wilson
ISBN 0 245 60045 0 £5.95

The Islands in Between
Travels in Indonesia
Annabel Sutton
ISBN 0 245 54829 7 £5.95

Distant Shores
By traditional canoe from Asia to Madagascar
Sally Crook
ISBN 0 245 60044 2 £5.95

A Winter in Tibet
Letters from Lhasa
Charles and Jill Hadfield
ISBN 0 245 54773 8 £5.95

Other travel titles from Impact Books/Olive Press:

Bicycle Breaks
Between London and the sea
Martin Ryle
ISBN 0 245 06332 8 £5.95

Watching the Dragon
Letters form China
Charles and Jill Hadfield
ISBN 0 245 54390 2 £8.95

Sea and Sardinia
D.H. Lawrence
ISBN 0 946889 20 1 £6.95

Etruscan Places
D.H. Lawrence
ISBN 0 946889 13 9 £6.95

The Other Italy
David Price
ISBN 0 946889 01 5 £3.50

Travels in Japan
David Price
ISBN 0 946889 14 7 £6.95

A Better Class of Blond
A California diary
ISBN 0 946889 04 X £4.50

The Scent of India
Pier Paolo Pasolini
ISBN 0 946889 02 3 £4.95

Assignments in Africa
Per Wästberg
ISBN 0 946889 11 2 £5.95